I0817039

Sins of the Father

Sins of the Father: A Catholic and Biblical Approach to Generational Curses

Dan Schneider, PhD

TAN Books
Gastonia, North Carolina

Cover design by Jordan Avery
Cover image: *Cain Slays Abel*, Gustave Dorè (1832–883) / Public Domain via Wikimedia Commons.

Library of Congress Control Number: 2025951038
ISBN: 978-1-5051-3607-4
ePUB ISBN: 978-1-5051-3895-5

Published in the United States by TAN Books
PO Box 269, Gastonia, NC 28053

Printed in the United States of America

If the battle shall call you out, if the day of your contest shall come, engage bravely, fight with constancy, as knowing that you are fighting under the eyes of a present Lord, that you are attaining by the confession of His name to His own glory; who is not such a one as that He only looks on His servants, but He Himself also wrestles with us, Himself is engaged—Himself also in the struggles of our conflict not only crowns, but is crowned.

—Saint Cyprian of Carthage

Contents

I. Open Wide the Doors for Christ: Theological and Historical Overview 1

II. The Sins of the Fathers and the Jealousy of God 51

III. Their Fathers Ate Green Grapes 95

IV. An Ancient Debate: Saint Augustine Versus Julian of Eclanum 147

V. Vicarious Punishment for Sin in Saint Thomas Aquinas 195

VI. Women and Children First: A Look at the New Testament 231

VII. From Why to How 279

Epilogue: An Interview with Father Chad Ripperger . . . 293

Appendix: Identifying Generational Spirits: The Seven Deadly Sins and "Daughter Vices" 303

Bibliography 309

I.

Open Wide the Doors for Christ: Theological and Historical Overview

Pope Francis declared 2025 a jubilee year, which is a long-standing tradition that involves opening the doors of certain basilicas in Rome that are formerly closed except during one of these unique years.[1] By making a pilgrimage and walking through one of the holy doors, a Catholic can obtain an indulgence.[2] Pope Saint Paul VI defined an indulgence as:

> The remission before God of the temporal punishment due to sins forgiven as far as the guilt is concerned, which the follower of Christ with the proper dispositions, and under certain determined conditions acquires through the interventions of the Church, which, as minister of the redemption, authoritatively dispenses, and applies the treasury of satisfaction, won by Christ and the saints.[3]

This means that under the normal conditions, an indulgence can be attained for oneself or a soul in purgatory.[4] Specifically,

1 On Holy Doors, see Hardon, *Modern Catholic Dictionary*, 252–53.

2 See USCCB, *Jubilee 2025 – Pilgrims of Hope*.

3 Pope Saint Paul VI, *Indulgentiarum doctrina*, Norm 1.

4 "A plenary indulgence can be gained only once a day. In order to obtain it, the faithful must, in addition to being in the state of grace: have the interior disposition of complete detachment from sin, even venial sin;

an indulgence does not forgive one's sins (the person needs to go to confession for that), but it makes "satisfaction" for sins and "the remission before God of the temporal punishment due to sin as far as the guilt is concerned." *Satisfaction* is a legal term meaning *giving security or bail, satisfying a creditor and, therefore, a plea or apology and the making of amends, reparation for injury.*[5] Of significance here are two points. One, a jubilee year, such as this one declared by Pope Francis, highlights the difference between sin and the effects of sin. Namely, the Church, in her mercy, provides an opportunity to make satisfaction for the effects of sin, which is the temporal punishment due to sins already sacramentally forgiven. Secondly, all sin requires satisfaction—that is, making of amends, or reparation for injury. Notably, an indulgence is not the remission of the guilt of sin, as that is reserved for the sacrament of Penance, but of the temporal penalty due to sin. Keep this important distinction in mind as we move along.

The Plague of Modernism

In this book, I hope to contribute to the theological conversation on the topic of what is commonly referred to as "generational sin" and often seen at the parish level in workshops held and Masses offered for "the healing of the family tree." I approach the topic not only as a biblical and patristic scholar but also as one who has worked for many years in the field of exorcism as a lay auxiliary to several exorcists,

---

have sacramentally confessed their sins; receive the Holy Eucharist (it is certainly better to receive it while participating in Holy Mass, but for the indulgence only Holy Communion is required); pray for the intentions of the Supreme Pontiff." Apostolic Penitentiary, *The Gift of Indulgence*, no. 4 (29 January 2000).

[5] Latin lexical information is taken from Lewis and Short, *An Elementary Latin Dictionary*.

including Father Chad Ripperger. On the one hand, anyone who has worked in the field of exorcism or deliverance will have observed *something* at work that seems to interconnect families, patterns, if you will. On the other, those who propose a system of a sin that is "transgenerational" or "intergenerational" (these words appear to be used interchangeably) often fail to give proper theological distinctions when putting forth this novel idea (by novel, I mean not grounded in Tradition). That is, they rightly note that there is *a phenomenon de facto* in the field which suggests a certain connection between parents' sins and their children, but often fail to distinguish between the sin and the effects of sin (something which *is* grounded in Tradition). The collapse of that distinction betrays a Protestant (or at least non-Catholic) influence in asserting that there is an intergenerational transmission of a personal sin of an ancestor that needs to be severed in some way for someone to be healed. Some Catholic theologians, noting that influence, dismiss the concept altogether, but to do so, they have to explain away the words of God Himself at Sinai, when He gave the Ten Commandments to Israel: "For I, the LORD, your God, am a jealous God, inflicting punishment for their fathers' wickedness on the children of those who hate me, down to the third and fourth generation" (Ex 20:5). Others have uncritically accepted this in theory and practice into the charismatic renewal because, at a certain level, they see some fruit. Here, I hope to take the reader on a walk through the relevant biblical texts and key Church Fathers with a view toward a clearer understanding of a Catholic perspective.

A scholar knows to look at the assumptions behind the assertion, so I begin with a brief explanation of modernism. A generation ago, on the heels of the French Revolution and the Enlightenment, Pope Saint Pius X warned against the dangers of modernism, a belief structure which he called "the summation of all heresies."[6] He stated that while the previous generation of Catholics had to contend with the errors of Protestantism, the future generation will be confronted with the problem of modernism.

The danger of this belief system lies in the fact that it identifies truth not by any objective criterion but through some subjective reality. His predecessor, Blessed Pope Pius IX, noted as the crux of the error of modernism: "Human reason, without any reference whatsoever to God, is the sole arbiter of truth and falsehood, and of good and evil; it is law to itself, and suffices, by its natural force, to secure the welfare of men and of nations."[7] That is, truth is whatever I identify it to be because there is no authority over and above the *autonomy* of the individual. I am my own magisterium in determining doctrine, interpreting the Bible, and judging right and wrong. Ultimately, I—the autonomous self—am the standard by which all things may be judged.

The philosophical underpinning of that false autonomy is sometimes referred to as *immanentism,* which reduces truth—even the revealed religious truths, as part of the Deposit of Faith—to human experience.[8] Consequently, not only the truth contained in Scripture but also the nature and reality of the Church and priesthood, doctrine, morality, and even human sexuality and gender are understood by the modernist's own subjective standards.[9] Pope Saint Pius X also

---

6 Pope Saint Pius X, *Pascendi Dominici Gregis,* no. 39.

7 Pope Blessed Pius IX, *Syllabus of Errors,* no. 3.

8 The Latin word *in+manere* means to "remain within" and, therefore, this belief system maintains that exterior reality is inferior to the expression of the interior, subjective, and autonomous self. Pope Saint Pius X addresses the errors of this belief system in *Pascendi Dominici Gregis,* nos. 19–20.

9 Perhaps the most extreme example of this modernist fallacy is that gender is a social construct and, therefore, that one can self-identify in a gender other than one's biological assignment at birth.

referred to "the plague of modernism," which he identified by several marks:[10]

1. Rejection of the dogma of the Fall and the effect of original sin.
2. Rejection of the supernatural.
3. Rejection of the law of the redemptive value of suffering.
4. Rejection of authority structure (ecclesial and civil); and as a result,
5. Rejection for the need of a Redeemer or the mediation of the Church.

I treat this briefly here to highlight a key point—namely, that the concept of inherited guilt and punishment for sin finds subtle overlap with each of these marks, as will be seen. Of significance here as well is a modern tendency to dismiss the effects of sin with a false belief that sinful actions (or curses, for that matter) do not have any effect or punishment, especially if I did not *mean* any harmful effects. The demon always works in the objective, however, while he drives us to react in the subjective, in the emotions.

Where the philosophical underpinning of modernist thought is immanentism, its theological base is called process theology, which is a blend of evolutionary theory and gnostic dualism.[11] Father John Hardon defines this as:

---

[10] Pope Saint Pius X, *Ad Diem Illum Laetissimum*, no. 22.

[11] Gnosticism is theory which purports salvation by secret knowledge and still finds its way into various Christian movements and thought today. As Father Hardon notes, "although Gnosticism is the invariable element in every major Christian heresy, by its denial of an objective revelation that was completed in the apostolic age and its disclaimer that Christ established in the Church, a teaching authority to interpret decisively the meaning of the revealed word of God." Hardon, *Modern Catholic Dictionary*, 232. Dualism is "any view of reality that holds, there are two fundamentally and irreducibly different types of being or operations. Thus, God and the world, spirit and matter, intellect and will, truth and error, virtue and sin are typical expressions of dualism." Hardon, *Modern Catholic Dictionary*, 173.

> A view of reality, including what Christianity calls God, which sees everything still in the process of becoming what it will be, but nothing really is. It is called theology because it is a form of evolutionary pantheism which postulates a finite god who is becoming perfect, but is not (as Christianity believes) infinite and all-perfect from eternity. It is called "process" because it claims that the universe (including God) is moving towards completion, without identifying what this completion is or when or whether it will be reached. On these terms, nothing is stable, nothing certain, because nothing really is. There are no determined moral laws, no absolute norms of conduct, no certain principles of thought, and no means of knowing anything. There is no "thing," since what people call "things" are moving functions that keep changing in their very being. Everything, including the thinking mind, is ever becoming what it was not, and ceasing to be what it was.[12]

Thus, process theology sees both God and doctrinal truths as changing and ever-revealing.

This, however, is decidedly not the same as what the Church teaches as God revealing Himself through stages. As the *Catechism* states:

> The divine plan of Revelation is realized simultaneously "by deeds and words which are intrinsically bound up with each other" and shed light on each another. It involves a specific divine pedagogy: God communicates himself to man gradually. He prepares him to welcome by stages the supernatural Revelation that is to culminate in the person and mission of the incarnate Word, Jesus Christ. (CCC 53)

The *Catechism* here refers to Saint Irenaeus and Saint John Chrysostom in reference to the "divine pedagogy." This second-century Church Doctor spoke of what he called the

---

[12] Hardon, *Modern Catholic Dictionary*, 443.

divine *condescension*.[13] Namely, God lowers Himself to where we are and enters into the human condition and affairs. The ultimate condescension is the Incarnation, and all Revelation points to this event "in the fullness of time" (Gal 4:4).

The movement, however, does not stop with God's condescension. He lowers Himself (in Greek, *synkatabasis*) to where we are to raise us up (*anabasis*) to where He is. The concept of inherited guilt falls within this divine pedagogy, this lowering and stooping of God, whose ultimate goal is to raise, and even divinize, man to share in divine life. While modern man may welcome this *synkatabasis*, however, he often bristles against any suffering required to remove the obstacles to our *anabasis*, our union with God. This raising up of man, however, is found in a threefold continuum of the purifying, illuminating, and transforming effects of grace. God loves us with a passionate love, yet sins and vices are obstacles to our ascent to share in His life. Accordingly, in this divine pedagogy, God uses angels, fallen and glorified, as divine instruments to remove all obstacles to our *anabasis*.

This distinction between a changing God and a God who reveals Himself in stages is relevant to the discussion on generational spirits because many theologians will point to the "green grapes proverb" found in the prophets Jeremiah and Ezekiel as nullifying God's words at Sinai, where He said that He punishes parents' sins "to the third and fourth generation" (Dt 5:9). To the modern mind, moreover, a God who punishes sin seems unloving and unjust. Thus, the assumption behind the assertion is that when what God said in one place of Scripture (the giving of the Law at Sinai) contradicts another (the green grapes proverb in Ezekiel and Jeremiah), then the latter expression is accepted. But is it that simple? In this inquiry, therefore, I attempt to slow down this movement

---

13 Saint John Chrysostom, *Homilies on Genesis*, 17.1. See also CCC 101.

for the reader and explore this concept in depth by first unpacking the relevant Bible passages before looking at the treatment on the topic by two Doctors of the Church, Saint Augustine and Saint Thomas Aquinas.

At the end of each chapter are included three things: an example from the field, a message of hope, and a prayer. The case studies serve a catechetical purpose by grounding the theological discussion in the tangible, through the lived experience of exorcists and those who work with them as lay assistants. In one act, for example, a single Eucharistic miracle substantiates the Real Presence more succinctly than volumes of theological treatises. Accordingly, the stories presented here reveal some aspect of generational curses and illuminate the principles put forth in the chapter. The message of hope is precisely that. While this is a heavy topic that needs precise language to unpack, it can be overwhelming. The Christian, however, should never give in to despair when battling in the spiritual life.

The prayers at the end of each chapter are taken from Saint Alphonsus Liguori, to whom the Church has given the title "The Doctor of Prayer." Pope Saint Pius X offered, as the remedy for the "plague" of modernism, a renewed devotion to Our Lady, recalling her title "the Destroyer of All Heresies." To this end, I have drawn from that great lover of Our Lady, Saint Alphonsus, with the hope that he instills in the reader an increased confidence in her powerful intercession. My hope, as well, is that the reader also learns from him *how* to pray, and the language and attitude of the penitent soul standing in awe before the Lord. Included also is a specific prayer taken from *Deliverance Prayers for Use by the Laity* or *Holy Hour of Reparation*, with the hope that the reader learns the specificity at times required in prayer and also the power of reparation.[14] In the end, is a brief conversation with Father Chad Ripperger on the Catholic approach to identifying and rooting out possible generational spirits.

Healing the Family Tree or Healing Family Members?

The Conference of Catholic Bishops in Spain has recently addressed the issue of the modern notion referred to as "healing of the family tree" and "intergenerational sin," citing Anglican missionary and psychologist Kenneth McCall as having been the first to popularize the phenomenon. The document mentions two Catholic charismatic priests, Fathers John Hampsch and Robert DeGrandis, as introducing the concept of intergenerational sin and healing the family tree (through so-called "healing Masses") into Catholic thought and practice.[15] Both priests, in fact, point to Anglican missionary and psychologist Kenneth McCall as having been the first to popularize the phenomenon, and describe their work as consistent with his.

One problem with this belief system is the implication that the living are helpless victims of the past. McCall, for example, speaks of a person being "a victim of ancestral control," even to the point where, to one such man, "his words are not his own and his actions are not of his own volition."[16] McCall implies that the process is deterministic when he speaks of the "constricting bonds of the dead," as if a "controlling force," which, in

14 The prayers by Saint Alphonsus are cited from their works or compilations. The subsequent prayers are from Ripperger, *Deliverance Prayers for the Laity, Minor Exorcisms, Holy Hour of Reparation*. Used with permission.

15 See Conferencia Episcopal Española, *Su misericordia*, I.

16 McCall, *Healing the Family Tree*, 13.

fact, appears to nullify free will and personal responsibility for sin.[17] Hence, he recommends the family tree be reconstructed and a "Eucharist" be held to help determine where the intergenerational sin lies, so they can break the "controlling force" that is still upon a living person. During such liturgical services, participants often receive alleged visions revealing past events, family secrets, and the like.

While Catholics offer Masses for the individual souls in purgatory, McCall's solution is to "offer Eucharist" or a "Eucharist of deliverance" for a determined number of generations of males or females in a familial line. In McCall's liturgical system, moreover, prayers for the dead are not for the souls in purgatory, in the Catholic sense, but serve as a function to sever the so-called bonds that connect ancestors with the living. The focus is on the sin and the bond so that the living can no longer be under "ancestral control."[18] He describes one such "Eucharist" as offered for "the eldest females of the preceding six generations." Besides McCall and a charismatic woman, this service was presided over by "two clergymen, one doctor [and] two nurses."[19] The purpose was not to pray for the dead per se (in the Catholic sense) but as a means to break the "ancestral control" and spiritual bonds which were the cause of the present suffering of the individual.

---

17 McCall, *Healing the Family Tree*, 11.

18 As the Spanish bishops summarize: "According to this view, sins committed by ancestors in our family tree, which were not forgiven during the lifetime of those who committed them, would be the cause of physical and mental illnesses in their descendants. The way to cure such illnesses consists in identifying the sin in one's own family tree. Then, through intercessory prayer, exorcisms and, especially, the celebration of a Eucharist, the Lord Jesus or the Holy Spirit is prayed to break the bond of sin between the person and his ancestors, thus achieving healing, often total and practically instantaneous." Conferencia Episcopal Española, *Su misericordia*, I (my translation of the Spanish)..

19 McCall, *Healing the Family Tree*, 15.

While McCall himself admits that "I am not a theologian" but "a simple preacher," his theology, reliance on mystical phenomena to look into the past (which can easily be mimicked by the demon or simply false), and his liturgical repurposing seem to have been uncritically brought into Catholic praxis through the Catholic charismatic renewal.[20] Father John Hampsch acknowledges McCall as the one who "pioneered the resurgence of interest in this type of healing program."[21] While Father Hampsch rightly asserts that "although personal sin itself cannot be transmitted, its effects can be," he gives little attention to the role of redemptive suffering or reparation for sins.[22] Rather, he promotes "healing Masses" akin to McCall's "Eucharist of deliverance," which focus on healing the family tree. In these similarly repurposed Masses, attendees are invited to write their ancestral sins and offer them up during Mass so that the chains that bind the past to the present can be broken. Like McCall, his focus is on the use of liturgy (here, Catholic liturgy), not primarily in satisfaction for the sins of the deceased in propitiation (atonement for sins) but as a means for the cessation of suffering through severing intergenerational bonds.

Father Robert DeGrandis also traces his theology back to McCall.[23] While he at times also rightly affirms the Church's teaching that "the effects of sins remain after the actual guilt is removed," he reduces those effects to intergenerational bonds not unlike McCall and Father Hampsch. In addition, he also relies on ecstatic visions to "go back generations" so as to uncover secret familial sins or hidden family history.[24] Like

---

20 McCall, *Healing the Family Tree*, 11.
21 Hampsch, *Healing Your Family Tree*, 11.
22 Hampsch, *Healing Your Family Tree*, 11.
23 DeGrandis and Schubert, *Intergenerational Healing*, 15.
24 DeGrandis and Schubert, *Intergenerational Healing*, 18, 8. Recall immanentism defined above as reducing truth to human experience.

Father Hampsch, Father DeGrandis also advocates using the Mass outside of its liturgical context for healing the family tree. "The Mass," he writes, "is a healing service," and, following McCall's own liturgical practices, he repurposes each part of the Mass with a view toward the healing of the family tree.[25]

The Holy Sacrifice of the Mass, however, is not a "healing service" in this Protestant sense. At its core, the Mass is the unbloody re-presentation of the sacrifice of Calvary, with the same Victim, Jesus Christ, offered in a holy oblation for sins and reconciliation, as affirmed by the Council of Trent (see CCC 1366–1367). As Trent states, "The same Christ, who offered himself once in a bloody manner on the altar of the cross, is present and offered in an unbloody manner." Accordingly, the Mass is a propitiatory sacrifice, the oblation of Jesus Christ on the cross, whereby "the Lord is appeased, He grants grace and the gift of repentance, and He pardons wrongdoings and sins, even the grave ones. For it is one and the same victim. He who now makes the offering through the ministry of priests, and he who then offered himself on the cross. The only difference is the manner of the offering."[26]

This is affirmed in the *Catechism*, which cites Trent, that Mass is a "sacrifice" and "truly propitiatory" (CCC 1367). The Mass is a "visible sacrifice" that re-presents the bloody sacrifice of the cross instituted by Christ at the Last Supper. Every Mass is indeed a "healing Mass" in the sense that Christ's oblation on the cross heals mankind from the effects of sins. To reduce the Mass to a means of obtaining physical healing, apart from its propitiatory nature of the forgiveness of sins (a

---

[25] DeGrandis and Schubert, *Intergenerational Healing,* 72. I agree with Father Alcántara who states that "these Masses divert the charity we should have toward our deceased loved ones. Indeed, instead of offering Masses for them, we are asking for Masses for ourselves, insofar as we want their sins to stop affecting us in this life." Cited in Luis Santamaria, "Can we 'our family tree' and wipe out 'ancestral sin'?"

[26] Council of Trent, Sess. XXII.

spiritual reality), is contrary both to the very essence of the Mass and the Tradition of the Church.

In a theology and praxis similar to McCall, Father Yozefu Ssemanula, for example, seeks to help a phenomenon de facto of *something* afflicting many families, but risks also falling into the same determinism that minimizes free will and personal responsibility. Father Ssemanula speaks of a "generational bondage," "inherited sin patterns," and even "generational predispositions," which are caused by "a family tree issue."[27] Like the abovementioned authors, he emphasizes (albeit well-intendedly) physical over spiritual healing and breaking "bondage" over making satisfaction for sins. Physical healing, not the unbloody re-presentation of the sacrifice of Jesus Christ on Calvary, is the central focus of such "healing Masses." While Mass can be offered for various intentions, Masses said for the healing of, and liberation from, "generational bondage" of the sins of ancestors is counter to the intrinsic nature of the Mass and, therefore, is a distortion.

As the Spanish bishops note, McCall's system finds overlap with modern psychologist Carl Jung.[28] In effect, he builds upon the Jungian concept of a collective consciousness, with focus on dreams and visions, which, for Jung, was to bring about "psychic rebirth" and a "new advent." For McCall, this means physical and spiritual healing by severing the impact of the ancestral patterns on a person (in Jungian terminology, the psyche). When transferred into Christianity, access to that consciousness so as to affect healing relies on charismatic gifts, as well as liturgy (an Anglican Eucharist for McCall and the Mass for charismatic Catholics). The reliance on charismatic seers to identify ancestral burdens from which to be released is quite subjective and certainly problematic. If healing is not

---

27 Ssemanula, *The Healing of Families*, 281–82, 306.

28 Conferencia Episcopal Española, *Su misericordia*, I.

based on a Christian anthropology, it risks becoming gnostic and perhaps even borderline pagan. Our rebirth is not at the level of consciousness but at the level of being, ontologically reborn as children of God through Baptism. Our new advent is the Advent, the coming of Jesus Christ, in the Incarnation and in the fullness of time. Hence, the Spanish bishops note that while this practice is done "with the best intentions and with the desire to alleviate the suffering of people," the concept, in effect, "merg[es] aspects of the Catholic faith with others that are foreign to it." In effect, this "results in a syncretism of Catholic appearance," but a blending of belief systems and a modern psychological understanding of consciousness. In addition, they also rightly caution that such a theology "eliminates personal responsibility for sin and the freedom of the human being."[29] The result, the document states, affects much of theology, to include: "eschatology, particularly the doctrine of purgatory and retribution; of ecclesiology, with regard to the communion of saints, living and dead, in the body of Christ . . . and of the theology of the sacraments, especially the understanding of the Eucharist and baptism."[30] While these practitioners may not directly advocate for this syncretistic theological position (to wit, one that blends various religions with Catholic beliefs and practices), the confusion does point to a general lack of precise language in the Church today, even among theologians.

As the Spanish bishops note, moreover, the subtle (and false) assumption behind the assertion is that if a sin can be transmitted intergenerationally, then a child's soul is created (viz., *generated*) not by God but by the parents. In the Catholic theological tradition, only original sin is generated in this sense, and proponents of this concept reflect an ancient

29 Conferencia Episcopal Española, *Su misericordia*, I.
30 Conferencia Episcopal Española, *Su misericordia*, I.

error called traducianism (from the Latin *traducere*, which means "to hand down, transmit, deliver"; and a *tradux* is a vine branch used to sprout a new vine). Thus, this ancient error maintains that not only the body but also the soul is handed down, like a vine-branch, from parent to child as part of the natural generation of the species. As Father John Hardon notes, however, "the theory [traducianism] is in contradiction with Catholic doctrine that each person's soul is individually and separately created by God at the time of conception."[31] The opposite is called creationism, which is the Catholic belief that every soul is created by God, specifically "that the individual human soul is the immediate effect of God's creative act."[32]

Whether or not modern proponents intentionally adhere to some form of traducianist belief is doubtful and beyond the scope here. That those who put forth this concept appeal more to field experience than theological discourse, however, does highlight the dangers of uncritically accepting Protestant beliefs and practices, and the need to stay grounded in the Tradition of the Church when participating in apostolic works. Accordingly, if by "generational" is meant a personal sin that is committed by an ancestor and then is transmitted down the family line, then this is contrary to Catholic teaching. As a result, this has led some proponents to blame, all too readily, their ancestors for their problems rather than take personal responsibility for their own sinful behavior. As the Spanish bishops note, such a belief tends to "eliminate personal responsibility for sin and the freedom of the human being."[33]

---

31 Hardon, *Modern Catholic Dictionary*, 544.
32 Siegfried, "Creationism," *The Catholic Encyclopedia*.
33 Conferencia Episcopal Española, *Su misericordia*, I.

This, however, has also led some too readily to ignore that sin still has consequences, and to the general modern (and immanentist) idea that falsely thinks that if someone does not intend something to have an effect, then there is no effect. That is, since I did not *mean* for bad things to happen when I committed this or that sin (a father looking at pornography is a good example), then there is no effect such as temporal punishment, especially if I confess the sin sacramentally. Consequently, if I did not *mean* to allow evil into my family line when I joined the Masonic lodge or practiced witchcraft, then there cannot be a negative effect on my children. This is simply inconsistent with the tradition of the Church and the writings of the Fathers. This is to say, while sins themselves are not handed down through a familial line, the effects of sins can be, as will be seen.

Father Gabriele Amorth addressed this phenomenon, specifically asking whether the "consequence of their ancestors' mediumisms and particularly some of their serious sins—such as homicide, abortion, suicide, and magical practices—are passed on to successive generations." He likewise cites McCall as the originator of this concept and defines intergenerational sin as "serious sins and vices" which can be generated and passed down as if "a spiritual pollution that affects children, grandchildren, great-grandchildren, and so on down the genealogical tree." These sins, as Father Amorth explains the McCall theses, are "ascribable to ancestors and propagated from father to son" such that they "repeat the same sinful acts." Assessing the concept after years of his own experience as an exorcist (and, I would add, an accomplished theologian), Father Amorth concludes in the negative to a transgenerational sin. That is, there is no such thing as an intergenerational sin, as McCall and others propose. "In my view," he writes, "there is not enough evidence to support the transgenerational thesis." He cites his mentor, exorcist Father Candido Amantini, for support, specifically that to assert that one has this or that defect in virtue ("sinful tendencies") is the result of a sin one has inherited from an ancestor, allowing a person "to abandon his sense of responsibility for his own life," echoing the conclusion of the Spanish bishops.[34]

What about curses? In that same discussion, Father Amorth does affirm that there is something generational that can afflict families in the overlapping topic of generational curses or spirits. While he denies that this or that sin can carry down a family line, he does affirm that, in his experience, curses can carry down with deleterious effects. "I have ascertained," he writes, "that a curse can be transmitted [from one generation to the next], particularly if it is issued by a father or a mother against a son, his marriage, and his future children."[35] Notice how he contextualizes curses within the familial construct. He also brings in the importance of blessings as a counteraction to curses by stating the following: "Alas! Curses, which are wishes of evil, are extremely powerful, especially if they are made with real treachery by those who are related by varying degrees of kinship to the victim. But they can be conquered with blessings. Jesus said, '[B]less those who curse you, pray for those who abuse you' (Lk 6:28)."[36]

He concludes with the practical. "I always advise the afflicted," he counsels, "to make whatever sacrifices are necessary to break each evil spell."[37] This will provide the backdrop for Jesus's words to the disciples and the father of the possessed boy, "This kind can go out by nothing, but by prayer

34 Amorth, *An Exorcist Explains*, 59.
35 Amorth, *An Exorcist Explains*, 61.
36 Amorth, *An Exorcist Explains*, 60–61.
37 Amorth, *An Exorcist Explains*, 61.

and fasting" (Mk 9:29 DR). This "making sacrifices" will also suggest a remedy for those suffering affliction of this sort.

A further implication, therefore, is that if a sin is intergenerational, then healing can also be intergenerational. This has resulted in Holy Mass being used outside of its proper theological, ecclesial, and liturgical framework, as shown above. To that end, Father Amorth affirms that having Masses for the dead—and not "healing Masses"—is the proper way to help our deceased ancestors.

This seems to be the impetus for the statement by Spanish bishops—that is, to rein in liturgical abuse by addressing a potential theological error.[38] As the *Catechism* states, "There is an organic connection between our spiritual life and the dogmas. Dogmas are lights along the path of faith; they illuminate and make it secure" (CCC 89). That is, orthodoxy (right belief) leads to orthopraxy (right practice). Simply stated, an imprecise theology that is disconnected from Scripture and Tradition can lead to liturgical abuses and misuse of the sacraments.

A "Double Consequence" of Sin and Vicarious Atonement

While in modern parlance we hear such terms *as healing the family tree, generational sin, generational curse,* or *familial sin,* we are speaking broadly within what the Church Fathers referred to as *inherited guilt* or *vicarious punishment*. In Hebrew, this is referred to as *avon avot* (from the Hebrew for "the sins of parents"), from the words of God when He gave the Law at Sinai:

[38] Conferencia Episcopal Española, *Su misericordia*, III D.

> You shall not carve idols for yourselves in the shape of anything in the sky above or on the earth below or in the waters beneath the earth; you shall not bow down before them or worship them. For I, the LORD, your God, am a jealous God, inflicting punishment for their fathers' wickedness on the children (*poked avon avot al banim*) of those who hate me, down to the third and fourth generation; but bestowing mercy down to the thousandth generation, on the children of those who love me and keep my commandments. (Ex 20:4–6)[39]

Poked avon avot al banim is translated as "inflicting punishment for their fathers' sins upon the children." These are the words spoken by God Himself, which affirm that "good deeds as well as evil deeds have consequences not only for a person who performs them, but also for subsequent generations."[40] This may have been true in ancient times that sinful actions have consequences within a family, even extending to future generations, but has this changed? To answer that question, we explore this concept through a biblical, patristic, and theological lens.

While the New American Bible renders the Hebrew of Exodus 20:5 with more of the punitive aspect of sin's punishment ("*inflicting punishment* for the father's wickedness"), the Latin Vulgate translation of Saint Jerome literally reads "visiting the iniquities of the father upon the children." The Latin *visito* means to *go see* or *visit*, but also, specifically in ecclesial Latin, it means *to punish*, a meaning consistent with the Hebrew. Saint Jerome had multiple versions of Hebrew and Greek in front of him when making the Latin translation of the Bible, or the Vulgate. While *visitans* sounds like *visiting*,

---

[39] All translations are taken from the *New American Bible* unless otherwise noted as a variant translation or my own.

[40] Reinhard Neudecker, "Does God visit the Iniquity of Fathers upon their Children?," 5.

we must not too quickly jump to modern English. (Think of what is implied in the English statement, "I am going to have to pay him a little visit," and you hear the nuances of *visitans*.). The word for iniquities is *iniquitas* and also is more nuanced than the modern English "iniquities." The Latin *iniquitas* literally means unequal or uneven, as in unlevel ground, and thus is a legal term meaning injustice or imbalance. Implied here is that sin creates a disorder, an imbalance in the justice of God, which requires restoration of some kind (as seen in the above definition of *satisfaction*). This is what "visiting" the children implies, the effect of the imbalance created by sin.

Instead of visiting or punishing (*visitans*), the Greek biblical text uses *apodidomi*, which has more of the flavor of *rendering what is due, pay back, suffer, allow, deliver,* with the meaning of (significantly) *to make atonement for*, or *to restore, render an account*.[41] Thus, implied in the Greek is more than a divine punishment but the further nuance of a satisfaction owed due to the sins of a father within the familial construct. While the three versions of the text of Exodus 20:5 slightly differ in emphasis, the text in all three sacred languages, however, suggests that sin has a secondary effect of creating an imbalance that has a ripple effect within a familial construct.

Another illuminating contextualization is God's self-revelation as "the Jealous One," which will be explored in the next chapter. In His self-revelation at Sinai, it is discovered that God hates sin, specifically the worship of idols. Implied in that commandment is the need to remedy the imbalance created by grave sin as part of raising man up to participate in divine life. Elsewhere in the Pentateuch, where the divine Law is given, this warning is reiterated by God. In this original biblical context of the giving of the Law at Sinai, those who "hate"

---

41 Greek lexical information is taken from Liddell, Scott and Jones, *A Greek-English Lexicon*.

God are those who apostatize and offer worship to false gods (see Ex 20:2–5; Dt 5:9). This comes into bas-relief in light of the psalmist who reminds Israel that "the gods of the Gentiles are demons" (Ps 96:5, in both the LXX and VUL). Notably, these are God's own words, not mediated by a prophet, and in the context of idolatry, which is the rendering of worship to false gods rather than the one true God.

On this topic of familial curses, moreover, much of the confusion today is largely due to a lack of theological precision and the various ways people use the term "generational sin." The concept of a generational spirit or curse as part of the temporal punishment due to sin within the authority structure consistent with *avon avot*, as is explored here, is decidedly not the same as the modern, charismatic notion and praxis of "healing the family tree" due to an "intergenerational sin" as popularized by McCall and then received into the Catholic charismatic renewal.[42] Most exorcists do report, as did Father Amorth, some familial aspect in relation to some cases, particularly in regard to curses, but few have parsed this out theologically. Here we will examine *avon avot* more in detail, but keep these nuances in mind as we progress.

A distinction first needs to be made from Catholic theology, one that echoes Father Amorth's caution, is that while you cannot heal the family tree, you can heal family members. That is, through your prayers, sacrifices, and voluntary penances, you can help your family members, both living and deceased. When the merits of our suffering are applied in union with the suffering of Christ (cf. Col 1:24) and in reparation for the sins of another, this is referred to theologically as *voluntary vicarious atonement*, or the willful offering of one's suffering in reparation for the sins of another. This happens not only in Jubilee Years but is always available for Catholics

[42] See McCall, *Healing the Haunted*, and *Healing the Family Tree*.

to gain and apply indulgences for themselves and for the souls in purgatory. The basis of this understanding is what the *Catechism* speaks of as the dual nature of sin itself. Every sin, even venial, contains a spiritual and a temporal effect—both of which need to be remedied (see CCC 1471–72).

What is often left unsaid in modern discussions on the familial interconnectedness of sin and curses is that Catholic tradition is clear that, while parents do not hand down a personal sin to their children, the effects of their sins can be inherited as part of the temporal punishment of sin. This is, perhaps, what McCall has obliquely stumbled upon in his field experience on the familial nature of some grave sins. For this reason, the Spanish bishops include in their warning against the transgenerational thesis a particular mention of "the doctrine of purgatory and retribution." According to the *Catechism*, there is "a temporal punishment due to sin *whose guilt has already been forgiven*," which requires that satisfaction be made (CCC 1471). That is, even after the personal, spiritual guilt has been sacramentally removed through confession, there remains a temporal effect for sins.

Thus, the application of the merits of your prayers and sacrifices helps to make satisfaction for personal sins, your own or even those of others. This is because, as the *Catechism* affirms, there are two consequences of sin, a spiritual and a temporal. Therefore, the Church teaches that "it is necessary to understand that sin has a double consequence":

> Grave sin deprives us of communion with God and therefore makes us incapable of eternal life, the privation of which is called the "eternal punishment" of sin. On the other hand, every sin, even venial, entails an unhealthy attachment to creatures, which must be purified either here on earth, or after death in the state called Purgatory. This purification frees one from what is called the "temporal punishment"

> of sin. These two punishments must not be conceived of as a kind of vengeance inflicted by God from without, but as following from the very nature of sin. A conversion which proceeds from a fervent charity can attain the complete purification of the sinner in such a way that no punishment would remain. (CCC 1472)

This "double consequence" of sin, therefore, means that sin affects both the spiritual and temporal realms, with both requiring satisfaction. Accordingly, even when the guilt of a former sin is remitted through sacramental confession (as CCC 1471 states, above), there remains satisfaction to be made as part of the double consequence of every sin.

What will be examined in a later chapter is how, in the developed theological language of the Church, and specifically in the writings of Saint Thomas Aquinas, sin does have a familial component. While personal sins of parents are not inherited, the Church teaches that *the effects of the personal sins* of parents can be inherited—that is, carried down to their children as part of the temporal punishment due to sin. While many may accept that there may be a vicarious *atonement* for sin, which can be remedied by indulgences gained during Jubilee Years, the idea that there may be vicarious *punishment* for sin is admittedly a difficult concept for many to accept. That is, do we take *avon avot* of Exodus 20:5 seriously—namely, does He punish sin in some way (whether "to the third and fourth generation" or some other fashion)—or is that simply hyperbole and anachronistic? Has God changed?

Those who dismiss *avon avot* often claim that to say God punishes sin is anthropomorphic—that is, we are projecting human attributes such as wrath or anger or jealousy upon

God.[43] As the *Catechism* affirms, however, these "two punishments must not be conceived of as a kind of vengeance inflicted by God from without, but as following from the very nature of sin" (CCC 1472). Thus, while the "forgiveness of sin and restoration of communion with God entail the remission of the eternal punishment of sin, *but temporal punishment of sin remains*" (CCC 1473, emphasis mine). Consequently, reconciliation with God means not only confessing our sins sacramentally but also doing penance and making satisfaction for the temporal debt owed.

Original sin, moreover, has created a disorder in the human family and set a pattern that all sin will follow.[44]

Redemptive suffering not only makes satisfaction for sin but also breaks the effects of sin—a volitional act purifies the effects of a volitional act.

As a Jubilee Year implies, just as the effects of sin are objective, so also is the satisfaction. "When someone desires to suffer," wrote Saint Teresa Benedicta of the Cross, "it is not merely a pious reminder of the suffering of the Lord." This from the saint who died at Auschwitz, in her own words, in a self-offering as an oblation for her people. "Voluntary expiatory suffering," she said, "is what truly and really unites one to the Lord intimately"—that is, in a real and objective way. In so doing, she wrote, "Christ the head effects expiation in

---

[43] Father Rogelio Alcántara Mendoza, for example, is correct in his assessment of the error in claiming that sin is transmuted intergenerationally, but he fails to distinguish between the sin itself and the effect of the sin. Nor does he consider the writings of Saint Augustine or Saint Thomas on the matter of inherited guilt in his dismissal of curses as having any familial effect (contra to Father Amorth, above). He rightly cites that there are two types of sin (original and personal) but fails to note that all sin has "double consequence"—namely, upon the spiritual and the temporal. Accordingly, he dismisses *avon avot* as use of the literary device of hyperbole and an anthropomorphism to claim that God punishes sin. Alcántara-Mendoza, "La llamada oración de 'sanación del árbol genealógico.'"

[44] For the consequences of original sin, see CCC 405–9, 418.

these members of His Mystical Body who put themselves, body and soul, at His disposal for carrying out His work of salvation."[45]

Recall the Spanish bishops' warning that the transgenerational thesis also has a poor understanding of "ecclesiology, with regard to the communion of saints, living and dead, in the body of Christ." In an encyclical on the Church as the Mystical Body of Christ, Pope Pius XII wrote on how suffering is efficacious in carrying out the work of the redemption of Christ:

> Moreover, as our Savior does not rule the Church directly in a visible manner, He wills to be helped by the members of His Body in carrying out the work of redemption. That is not because He is indigent and weak, but rather because He has so willed it for the greater glory of His spotless Spouse. Dying on the Cross He left to His Church the immense treasury of the Redemption, towards which she contributed nothing. But when those graces come to be distributed, not only does He share this work of sanctification with His Church, but He wills that in some way it be due to her action. This is a deep mystery, and an inexhaustible subject of meditation, that the salvation of many depends on the prayers and voluntary penances which the members of the Mystical Body of Jesus Christ offer for this intention and on the cooperation of pastors of souls and of the faithful, **especially of fathers and mothers of families, a cooperation which they must offer to our Divine Savior as though they were His associates.**[46]

Whether the offering be great or small, the one who suffers becomes intimately united to Christ and continues His salvific work. Entering the "deep mystery" of reparation for sins

[45] Saint Teresa Benedicta of the Cross, *The Hidden Life*, 92.
[46] Pope Pius XII, *Mystici Corporis*, no. 44. Emphasis mine.

and our participation as co-redeemers in Christ (*co-* means *with*, not *equal*) means wading into the deep waters of the Christian life.[47]

These deep waters of redemptive suffering are part of the spiritual equation often ignored or minimized in the discussion on liberation from evil spirits. As for deceased ancestors, our prayers and sacrifices for their souls, including gaining indulgences such as walking through Holy Doors during a Jubilee Year, help to tap into the treasury of merit and make satisfaction for the debt they owe to God—namely, the "remission before God of the temporal punishment due to sins forgiven as far as the guilt is concerned," as Pope Saint Paul VI explains (above). Specifically, having Masses for our ancestors and the souls in purgatory, not intergenerational healing Masses, is the proper use of the liturgy to help our departed loved ones.

The Familial Construct: Two Ends

Pope Benedict XVI declared 2009–2010 the year for priests and gave three homilies on the *tria munera* of the sacerdotal priesthood. He alluded to the two ends of the authority structure in his third homily on the *munus regendi* (the office/duty to rule) by appealing to the words of Christ to Peter at the Sea of Tiberias, when He thrice asked Peter, "Do you love me?" (Jn 21:15, 16, 17). Pope Benedict XVI highlighted the threefold response of Jesus, who told Peter to "feed my

---

[47] Father Ssemanula, for example, minimizes the redemptive value of suffering when he asserts that "you will discover eventually that your Heavenly Father has absolutely nothing to do with this suffering you are going through—no active part!" On the contrary, just as God has taken an active part in our redemption, He also takes an active part in our restoration, to include purifying, illuminating, and transforming human nature. Ssemanula, *The Healing of Families*, 12.

lambs" (to provide) and to "tend my sheep" (to protect). In this homily, he was speaking of the responsibility of priests to engage their office of priesthood in tending and feeding their flock. As part of his sacred office, Pope Benedict said that the priest has the "mission to govern, to guide with the authority of Christ, not his own portion the People that God has entrusted to him." Governance is based on the authority that flows from one's office and carries with it a duty and responsibility to provide and to protect. "The pastor fulfills his role," he said, "precisely when he guides and protects his flock . . . in truth and holiness." This priestly office, he said, bears "an authority in exercise and responsibility before God, before the Creator . . . an authority whose sole purpose is understood to be to serve the true good of the person." One who holds an office has authority not to wield it over others, but to impart blessing, and in so doing, "to be a glass through which we can see the one and supreme Good, which is God."[48]

What is true of the office of priest is equally true, *mutatis mutandis,* of the office of fathers as head of household and mothers (or any other office in natural law, for that matter). Saint Thomas lists as duties of parents to *provide* for their children's physical needs and safety, as well as moral, physical, and religious education, and to *protect* them from harm.[49] As offspring of the parents, they are part of the bodily goods for which parents are bound to provision and protection as part of their sacred duty. This is echoed in the *Catechism,* which lists the duties of parents as "providing for their physical and spiritual needs" (CCC 2228) to include "their moral education and their spiritual formation" (CCC 2221). Accordingly,

---

[48] Pope Benedict XVI, "Munus Regendi," General Audience (26 May 2010).

[49] For an in-depth analysis on Saint Thomas on the authority structure, ends and duties of parents and children, see Father Robert Slavin, "St. Thomas and His Teaching on the Family."

parents likewise, in regard to their children, are tasked with the same command of Christ to "feed my lambs" (provide) and to "tend my sheep" (protect).

When parents abdicate the responsibility of the provision and protection that comes with blessing and commit evil, however, the "glass" or lens through which the children see God is now obscured. When instead of light they allow darkness into the home, through witchcraft, sexual abuse, or other grave evils, their children no longer enjoy the goods of blessing. A breach in the authority structure through grave sin creates, moreover, a privation of the two ends (recall the above discussion that sin creates a privation of goods). The void created where once was the light of blessing is now filled with the darkness of curse—that is, a deficiency in both protection and provision. God allows this void to be filled, moreover, because He honors our free will and because sin requires satisfaction.

Evil and Curse: Defect of a Good Substance and not a Substance

Some have incorrectly asserted that an unbaptized soul "belongs to the devil" as if the devil and evil are the equal and opposite force to God and goodness. This understanding lacks precision and is subtly close to one of the tenets of the ancient heresy of Manichaeism. Manichaeism was a dualistic and gnostic religion which was a syncretistic blending of the religions of the day at the time of Augustine, not unlike the tenets of Baha'i or Mormonism and even Freemasonry in its theistic claims today. In rejecting matter as evil, the Manichees also rejected the Old Testament and much of the New. Like other early heresies, they wrestled with the concept of a

God who punishes sins and concluded, in part, that the God of the Old Testament is not the Supreme Being as revealed in the New Testament. That Manichean cosmology was dualistic is based in a belief that good and evil oppose each other in equal and opposite forces. They believed in pre-existent and co-equal principles of good and evil, seen as light and darkness. They were also gnostic in that salvation came through secret knowledge, often through private revelation. Mani himself claimed to be the paraclete promised by Jesus, calling himself an "Apostle of Jesus Christ by the providence of God the Father" who regularly spoke and revealed special knowledge to him.[50]

Dualistic and gnostic means not only rejection of the Old Testament but that the material realm is evil. Saint Augustine was once lured into this sect before his conversion to Christianity. As he notes later in his debate with Julian, however:

> The Manichees say that nature was always evil without any beginning, and they maintain that every evil comes from it. But the Catholics—which you refuse to be—claim that our nature was created good, but corrupted by sin, and from the infants to the elderly it needs Christ as a physician, because he has died for all; all have, therefore, died (2 Cor 5:14).[51]

Thus, the Catholic position is that man is created good, but the effect of the Fall means he lacks grace. According to Saint Augustine, "we separate evil from good with our mind and do not believe that what is called evil is a substance." Evil is not its own substance, he says, but a corruption of the good. Going further, he further notes how the "Manichees, after all, say that evil is an evil substance; we say that it [evil] is the defect of a good substance and is not a substance." The remedy, he

---

[50] Arendzen, "Manicheism," *The Catholic Encyclopedia.*
[51] Saint Augustine, *Answer to the Pelagians III*, 302.

says, is we nonetheless "must be healed" of the defects in virtue, or vices.[52] Thus, darkness is not the opposite of light but rather what happens when light is absent. And the "remedy" for this privation of the goods of blessing is growing in virtue.

Darkness, it can be said, is not the opposite of light but its lack, or what remains when there is no light. Similarly, evil is not a substance, but a privation of the good. In the same way, a curse is not the equal and opposite force to a blessing, nor is it substantive in the way goodness and grace are substantive. Rather, a curse, like all evil, is a privation of the provision and protection that comes with blessing. This is what the familial space looks like when there is no blessing, or when parents commit grave sins. Part of the mechanics of these clinging spirits, therefore, is the dereliction of authority, often by the father.

Inherited Guilt: Definition of Terms

While a notion of a "generational sin" can be inaccurate or misleading, the idea itself is not new. The Fathers contextualized the concept of sin and its effects in the debate which produced the dogma of original sin. They looked at the effects of the sin of our first parents as having introduced into the human family an affliction that affects each person. The section of the *Catechism* on original sin concludes with the deleterious effect of the Fall. To wit, we now find ourselves in a cosmic battle:

> The whole of man's history has been the story of dour combat with the powers of evil, stretching, so our Lord tells us, from the very dawn of history until the last day. Finding himself in the midst of the battlefield man has to struggle to do what is right, and it is at great cost to himself, and aided

52 Saint Augustine, *Answer to the Pelagians III*, 302.

> by God's grace, that he succeeds in achieving his own inner integrity. (CCC 409)

Thus, as will be seen, original sin is *generational* in that the sin of Adam and Eve introduced into the human family the twofold effects of sin and death, as Saint Paul writes, "just as through one person sin entered the world, and through sin, death, and thus death came to all, and as much as all sinned" (Rom 5:12). This twofold negative effect—sin and death—means a pathway for diabolic influence. This pathway for evil is a void, or privation, created by original sin. As the *Catechism* states:

> Although it is proper to each individual, original sin does not have the character of a personal fault in any of Adam's descendants. It is a deprivation of original holiness and justice, but human nature has not been totally corrupted: it is wounded in the natural powers proper to it, subject to ignorance, suffering and the dominion of death, and inclined to sin—an inclination to evil that is called "concupiscence." Baptism, by imparting the life of Christ's grace, erases original sin and turns a man back towards God, but the consequences for nature, weakened and inclined to evil, persist in man and summon him to spiritual battle. (CCC 405)

Original sin, therefore, has affected the "inner integrity" of every human being. Elsewhere, and as cited above, the *Catechism* reflects on what the mechanics of the effects of the "deprivation of original holiness and justice" look like. That is, in the section entitled *The Punishments of Sin* (CCC 1472–1473), the *Catechism* makes a key theological distinction for our discussion on generational curses. Specifically, it affirms that all sin is like original sin in that even personal sins have a "double consequence." The first consequence is spiritual. Thus, "[g]rave sin deprives us of communion with God and therefore makes us incapable of eternal life, the privation of which is called the 'eternal punishment' of sin." Thus, the sinner must make satisfaction for sins and reconcile with God through sacramental Penance.

Sin, however, can not only be said to create an alienation from God, but it also creates a negative effect on ourselves, others, and even the environment (familial, social, etc.) in which we live. Thus, the second consequence is temporal. The need for this purification, the *Catechism* states, is to free the sinner from "an unhealthy attachment to creatures." These sinful attachments to creatures draw us away from the Creator and require a "temporal punishment" for sin (CCC 1472). While grave sins deprive us of union with God, "every sin, even venial . . . must be purified either here on earth, or after death in the state called Purgatory." Accordingly, the *Catechism* explains that this "double consequence" means that "forgiveness of sin and restoration of communion with God entail the remission of the eternal punishment of sin, but temporal punishment of sin remains" (CCC 1473). This is not anthropomorphic (projecting human emotions on God): "These two punishments must not be conceived of as a kind of vengeance inflicted by God from without, but as **following from the very nature of sin**" (CCC 1472, emphasis mine). Thus, in the developed theology of the Church, sin results in a privation (of holiness and justice), which is embedded into sin's very nature, and which contains the two-fold effects upon the spiritual and temporal realms.

Accordingly, when we read in the Old Testament that God says He will "curse" the children in punishing the sins of the father, we must also not dismiss it as anthropomorphic. We see a curse as simply the inverse of a blessing and the effects of a curse as the privation of the goods that accompany blessing. As Moses enjoined the people: "I have set before you life and death, the blessing and the curse. Choose life, then, that you and your descendants may live" (Dt 30:19). This language of life and death, blessing and curse, echoes the *Catechism's* assertion that "two punishments" of sinful behaviors follow the same pattern of Adam and Eve: (1) a deprivation of communion with God and (2) a temporal punishment.

The *Catechism* also lists the nature of the satisfaction which assists in that restoration with God, namely, redemptive suffering, that is, "patiently bearing sufferings and trials of all kinds and, when the day comes, serenely facing death." The bearing of trials in this life is, therefore, a means of obtaining the grace of restoration and reconciliation with God. Thus, the sinner "should strive by works of mercy and charity, as well as by prayer and the various practices of penance, to put off completely the "old man" and to put on the "new man" (CCC 1473).

Elsewhere, the *Catechism* states that after the original sin, "all subsequent sin would be disobedience towards God and a lack of trust in his goodness" (CCC 397). This is because "in that sin, man preferred himself to God" (CCC 398). That is, he preferred creature/created thing over the Creator. Accordingly, here are found the weapons for this type of spiritual combat to break from attachment to creature and reconcile with Creator: corporal and spiritual works of mercy, prayer, penance, and conversion of life. Penance and mortification are the preferred weapons in the battle against self-love and disobedience to gain inner integrity and virtue. These preferred weapons also make satisfaction for sins.

As the *Catechism* further states on the connection between original and personal sin, "The human person, created in the image of God, is a being at once corporeal and spiritual." This is seen in the image of creation where man formed from the dust and God "breathes" life into him (Gn 2:7). Rejecting the dualism that places evil and good and spirit and flesh at sword's point, the *Catechism* teaches that man is a body-soul composite, "not two natures united, but rather their union forms a single nature" (CCC 365). Since man is a body-soul composite, a single nature comprised of the spiritual and the material, the things he does with his body have both spiritual and bodily ramifications. This, the *Catechism* elsewhere explains—notably in the context of its teaching on the right understanding of indulgences and making satisfaction for "the temporal punishment due to sins whose guilt has already been forgiven" (CCC 1471). Thus, "sin has a double consequence" (CCC 1472)—spiritual and bodily. That is, because in man the spiritual and the bodily form a single nature, what he does in the body impacts him both spiritually and bodily.

Accordingly, Father Ripperger rightly grounds the discussion on generational spirits in the sin of our first parents. Namely, "Adam and Eve, in their sin, introduced into their entire generational line of humanity, the affliction of spirits as a result of it."[53] This is based upon the *Catechism*'s explanation of how Adam and Eve suffered the same twofold punishment in the primordial garden. Namely, the spiritual/eternal effect is seen in that they lost "the grace of original holiness," while the physical/temporal effects are found in the disordering in relationships—namely, "lust and domination," bodily death and banishment from God (CCC 399). In addition, disorder is introduced into the first human family, as seen in the first offspring—Cain kills his brother Abel.

This is to say, original sin is the *archetypal* sin in that all sin will follow the same pattern in both cause and effect. The Greek word *arche* means *beginning* or *first principle,* and *tupos* means *design or pattern, matrix, mold, cast, replica.* An *archetype,* then, is an original pattern or example of a thing that

[53] Ripperger, *Dominion,* 174.

gets repeated in a patterned, recurring way. Melchizedek, for example, is the archetypal priest (see Ps 110:4; Gn 14:18–20; Heb 7:1–28). Applied here, and following the logic of the *Catechism* on the double consequence of sin, this means that the effect of the Fall upon the human condition is so profound that it sets a pattern which all subsequent sins follow.

Saying the original sin is archetypal, the first principal pattern in which all subsequent models will follow, is notably not the same thing as saying that human parents can commit a personal sin and *that sin itself* (not the effects of the sin) carries down into the family line. In the transgenerational hypothesis, parents can introduce a personal sin into their families in the same way Adam and Eve introduced original sin into the human family. If this were the case, this would mean that the sin of our first parents was not archetypical but *prototypical*. There is a subtle difference between the two terms. The Greek *protos* also means *first*, but not first principle (*arche*); instead, it means *first in sequence, primitive, earliest*. A prototype, therefore, is "a first, typical or preliminary model of something . . . from which other forms are developed or copied."[54] Fans of drag racing, for example, know that the first successful rear-engine dragster was created by a famous racing innovator named "Big Daddy" Don Garlits. He was once injured in a race and decided to improve the earlier, prototypical dragster, which had safety issues. A Florida man, Garlits, called his car the Swamp Rat I-A, but he ended up with over thirty improved models of the Swamp Rat over time. The first dragster, therefore, was *prototypical*, the first of its type, which set a pattern for change, development, and improvement in style, such as moving the engine and transmission to the rear, types of fuel, braking systems, etc.

---

[54] Oxford Dictionary, "Prototype."

Original sin is not prototypical. Consequently, it is false to claim that parents generate or reduplicate their sins in their children. At the same time, however, the Church affirms that the twofold effects of the Fall and primordial sin of Adam and Eve have set an archetypal pattern for all subsequent sin. That is, built into the very nature of sin are two punishments—a *spiritual*, which affects the soul and of the individual sinner, and a *temporal*, which affects the body and temporal things.

What is also clear, moreover, is that "these two punishments (spiritual and bodily) . . . must not be conceived of as a kind of vengeance inflicted by God from without, but as following from the very nature of sin" itself (CCC 1472). Recall that one of the marks of modernism, according to Pope Saint Pius X, is a rejection of the effects of the Fall. The modern mind tends to think that if I do not intend bad things to happen, then God will not allow anything bad to happen to me if I confess my sins. It also thinks that if I do suffer, then it must mean that either God is unjust or vengeful, or that I am not yet forgiven, or God has abandoned me. These are simply false. Sin is offensive to God and requires satisfaction and reconciliation, as seen in the pattern set by the first sin, which resulted in the privation of the goods of man's pre-fallen state.

From *Synkatabasis* to *Anabasis*: Angels as Instruments

The vulnerability created through grave sins of parents falls broadly under the theological concepts of inherited guilt, vicarious punishment, and vicarious atonement. Later, I will look at the writings of Saint Augustine and Saint Thomas for clarity. How do we get to a concept of generational spirits? Are the Manichees correct in asserting that the God of the Old Testament is not the Supreme Being? Is *avon avot* and the visiting of the sins of parents just hyperbole and anthropomorphic?

If not, then there must be some mechanics to this process? Saint Athanasius said that "God became man so that the sons and daughters of men may become sons and daughters of God."[55] This is the *why* of divine condescension and the elevating of man along the threefold continuum of purifying, illuminating, and transforming human nature to share in the life of divine grace. The *how* is found in the angels, who are given by God the duty to assist man in his ascent (*anabasis*) toward a fully actualized divine sonship.

I offer to the reader, moreover, as a starting point, the observation of Saint Bonaventure on why God permits demons to afflict humans.[56] He gives four principal reasons:

1. To reveal God's glory.
2. To punish sin.
3. To rebuke the sinner.
4. To educate us.

While battling with evil spirits can be seen as broadly within any of those four reasons allowed by God, the second—to punish sin—is the point of departure for this discussion on familial spirits in patristic thought. That is, the fallen angels are a source of both correction and punishment, and when we defeat them, we learn how to expel them from our lives (and families). Our victory over sin and death, in turn, brings glory to God. That is, God uses the demons as His instruments of punishment and to remove the obstacles to our ascent to Him.

The affirmation that God uses angels to punish man for sin is found in the writings of Saint Ambrose, who noted that the

---

[55] CCC 460.

[56] Smit, *De Daemoniacis*, 79.

angels, not demons, are the instruments of God's justice. He states that glorified angels, in fact, "grieve" at having to "administer penalties to those who sin." This is because, he says, "they [the angels] who enjoy the life of beatitude would surely prefer to return to that high state of peace rather than be involved in avenging the punishment of our sins."[57] According to these two Doctors of the Church, therefore, God uses both angels and demons to punish man's sin. In fact, the Fathers broadly taught that angels are God's mediators of a threefold mission in the spiritual life of purifying, illuminating, and transforming the human souls entrusted to them as part of man's ascent to God.

This is affirmed by Jean Cardinal Danielou, who gives an overview of patristic thought on the role of guardian angels vis-à-vis sin. Specifically, he cites, as the consensus of the Fathers, that part of the specific duties of guardian angels is to "reprimand and punish the soul that turns aside from the right way." With regard to punishing man's sins with the purpose of purifying the soul of sin's effects, he notes that while the "purifying operations come from God as their one source," nonetheless, "the principal ministers are the Seraphim, who performed the purifications through the lower angels." Notably, the consensus of the Fathers is that the "purifying activity" of the angels is not administered by an angry God. Rather, the purpose of the purification is to remove "the blindness of the flesh that prevents the soul from becoming united with God."[58] This is to say, in the writings of the Fathers, God uses both angels and demons as purifying instruments, both to punish sin and to remove the obstacles to union with God.

---

[57] Cited in Irene Nowell, *101 Questions & Answers on Angels and Devils*, 34.

[58] Danielou, *The Angels and their Mission*, 73.

When we speak of "generational" or "familial" spirits, this is the proper context.

In addition, bear in mind that "generational" can mean "to generate," or it can mean "hereditary," as in familial inheritance. This latter sense of *inheritance* is preferred here, as it is consistent with the Fathers of the Church, who debated the topic of *inherited* guilt and the nuances of *avon avot*. When we speak of a generational (*viz., hereditary*) effect of sin, we refer to the concept within the context of the Church Fathers, primarily here Saint Augustine and Saint Thomas Aquinas, who use the terms in a very specific way. Within this historical and theological context, we can refer to the notion of "generational" as akin to *inherited*—that is, as confined within the familial construct and the effects of sin. When talking about demons being passed on, therefore, we refer to them specifically as generational spirits, who, in actuality, are instruments of purification allowed by God to punish and correct the sinner so as to remove the obstacles to union with God and also make satisfaction for grave sins. This avoids the confusion that the sin itself passes, rather than just the effects. Thus, to be clear, here *generational* is not in the sense of generating something in an active sense, as in parents generating and passing "the sin of adultery" down to their children. Rather, by *generational* is meant familial or heritage (as in the secular phrase "generational wealth"), an inherited guilt which speaks to the effect of the sins of parents as used by the Fathers and found in the developed language of the Church.

I begin, then, with a few assumptions which will help to contextualize the case studies included at the end of each chapter. The correct concept of a generational spirit assumes a right understanding of the authority structure and its twofold ends of provision and protection. Embedded within that structure is also twofold temptation—namely, either dereliction (failure to engage with one's right authority) or usurpation (taking authority where one has none), both of which create a vulnerability to those under one's authority. That is, when one who has been given an office (and concomitant authority) commits a grave sin, a demon can attach himself on account of sinful actions. That attachment is part of the temporal punishment due to sin, as embedded into the very nature and double consequence of sin, as the *Catechism* notes on sin above.

In such instances, the demon, notably, has no objective *right* to attach himself to an individual or those under a person's authority, but he can claim *permission,* to be there. While a demon may claim a right to be present with a person, this is not entirely accurate in the case of the baptized Christian. *By right,* the baptized soul belongs to Jesus Christ. The demon will, however, claim *permission* which allows him to be there as a result of certain sinful actions—by the individual, authority figure, or parent, as will be seen. As a result of that attachment, a vulnerability is presented to those who are under an individual's provision and protection. All of this, notably, is under divine providence for the betterment of the soul. That sin carries a double consequence, or two punishments, is clear. *Avon avot* suggests, however, that punishment is vicarious—that is, the children can suffer for the sins of their parents.

Often, these are first commandment (witchcraft and the occult) and sixth commandment (deviant sexual behavior) violations, although any mortal sin can be regarded as a permission. Thus, Saint John tells us that Satan rebelled and, accompanied by a third of the angels, was cast down from heaven. He now militates as "the accuser of our brothers . . . accus[ing] them before our God day and night" (Rv 12:10). What he accuses us of are those permissions we have granted him through our sinful actions. *Look,* he says, *I have a right to be here—he invited me in! We're old friends, he and I.* The spadework of liberation often involves the severing of these claims and permissions and countering by asserting natural law rights and removing the permissions given through our sinful behavior. This will be explored in depth as we move along.

Sometimes the phrase generational *curse* is used instead of *spirit* to describe the phenomenon. In common language, *cursing* means using profane language. In canon law, it means an *anathema*, or the declaration of excommunication by the Church for some grave offense. To curse can also mean "to call down evil upon God or creatures, rational or irrational, living or dead" as done in witchcraft through various incantations and rituals (in an inversion of the Catholic sacramental system).[59] As used here, however, a *curse* will have a narrow and specific definition. According to the *Catholic Encyclopedia*:

> In its more common Biblical sense, it [to curse] means the opposite of blessing (cf. Numbers 23:27), and is generally either a threat of the Divine wrath, or its actual visitation, or its prophetic announcement, though occasionally it is a mere petition that calamity may be visited by God on persons or things in requital for wrongdoing.[60]

---

59 Fisher. "Cursing." *The Catholic Encyclopedia*. Father Peter Joseph betrays a subtle, philosophical immanency when he dismisses curses altogether in claiming that "curses and superstitions seem to work only on those who believe in them." See Joseph, "False Religion." *In Where Peter Is* (November 21, 2024). Contra, Father Alcántara-Mendoza who rightly affirms that while natural curses have no effect (bad language, cursing at someone who cuts you off in traffic, etc.), "preternatural curses can have an effect, by the will of God, and depending on the person, state of grace, etc." That is, these types of curses where maledictions are invoked, God allows them to have an effect, one's state of grace and virtue are key armaments in resisting their effects. Alcántara-Mendoza, "La llamada oración de 'sanación del árbol genealógico.'"

60 "Thus, among many other instances, we find God cursing the serpent (Gn 3:14), the earth (Gn 3:17), and Cain (Gn 4:11). Similarly, Noah curses Chanaan (Gn 9:25); Josue, him who should build the city of Jericho (Jo 6:26–27); and in various books of the Old Testament there are long lists

Two phrases from the definition are of note here from a biblical perspective. A curse is "the opposite of blessing" and the experience of a "calamity" (of "the visitation of Divine wrath") which "may be visited by God on persons or things in requital for wrongdoing." The use of the word *visit* (twice) in this definition is deliberate and evokes the definition of *visitans* given in the above discussion on Exodus 20:5 ("visiting the iniquities"). In ecclesial Latin, recall, *visitans* means "to punish" (specifically, "wrongdoing") for the purpose of making satisfaction for sins.

The demon's agency in a curse, so defined, is as the instrument of God's punishment, which Saint Bonaventure indicated as one of the reasons why God allows demons to afflict us. According to Father Ripperger, therefore, a generational spirit is "the spirit that is passed from one generation to another as the result of the sin of one of the ancestors or the suffering of grave harm by one of one's ancestors."[61] That is, it follows the familial line because one in authority either committed a grave sin or some grave harm against those he was supposed to provide for and to protect.[62] Accordingly, he notes how demons seek "at all costs" to perpetuate their control and influence. Driven by what he calls the "principle of

---

of curses against transgressors of the Law (cf. Lv 26:14–25; Dt 27:15, etc.). So, too, in the New Testament, Christ curses the barren fig-tree (Mk 11:14), pronounces his denunciation of woe against the incredulous cities (Mt 11:21), against the rich, the worldling, the scribes and the Pharisees, and foretells the awful malediction that is to come upon the damned (Mt 25:41). The word curse is also applied to the victim of expiation for sin (Gal 3:13), to sins temporal and eternal (Gn 2:17; Mt 25:41)." Fisher. "Cursing." *The Catholic Encyclopedia*.

61 Ripperger, *Dominion*, 554.

62 There is some speculation and observation, since other structures also have an authority structure through natural and civil law, that this can also occur in communities and nations (an extreme example would be Nazi Germany), religious orders, cultures, generations (such as the "hippy generation" of the 1960s), and the like.

perpetuity," they desire "to spread that control or influence by working from a platform" within a certain sphere of influence. Notice that the control and influence do not stop at a simple affliction. The demon always seeks a *platform* from which to both manipulate and broadcast. While the demon constantly seeks entry (and an increasingly greater platform) into various human constructs, he gains access more readily when permissions (whether knowingly or unknowingly) are granted to him.[63] For purposes here, however, we limit the examination to familial lines of authority, and from a biblical, patristic, and Thomistic perspective.

In **a general sense**, then, a "generational spirit" means that a spirit can be passed from one person to another. The mechanism of this is not random, as in passing on a cold through sneezing, but, as a general rule, there is some permission granted along the way, while at the same time, some vulnerabilities are present. This works similarly to how we understand guardian angels to work, but in the inverse. A general environment is created where a spirit can cling to a person, place, culture, and work in the inversion of the good angels.

In **a specific sense**, when people speak of a "generational" spirit, they refer to the phenomenon of the passing of a spirit along a family's lineage. Neither the spirit nor the sin is generated in the way we know original sin to pass along a family line, as stated above. However, an evil spirit can be an instrument of satisfaction for sin, as Saint Bonaventure indicated. That is, they are allowed by God to punish sin, and, properly speaking, their activity is the effect of sin. It fills the void created by sin.

Their agency, however, is limited by divine providence and is always for some salvific purpose. In addition, this process, to be clear, is *not deterministic*. That is, everything that the enemy does is allowed by God for the purpose of purifying,

63 Ripperger, *Dominion*, 112.

illuminating, and transforming man, and for the removal of the obstacles to reconciliation (ascent to union) with Him.

Sometimes these spirits skip generations or have little or no effect whatsoever. At other times, however, they are deeply embedded within a familial structure due to the repeated sinful actions (often the same grave sin) by the children and, consequently, quite difficult to get out, as there is now both a personal culpability and a psychological compatibility with the demon. In addition, the old adage, *if you look for the devil, he will find you,* applies here. The devil's power is limited to what God allots him for the betterment of our sanctification and salvation. The demon is causal, not primary, in that process of our ascent toward God through the triad of purification, illumination, and transformation. The demon is, in fact, tertiary in this equation. Our primary focus is upon Jesus Christ. As Hebrews states, we must "[keep] our eyes fixed on Jesus, the leader and perfector of faith" (Heb 12:2). Our secondary focus is upon those obstacles to union with Him and militating against the defects which prevent our *anabasis*. To that end, "Endure your trials as 'discipline'; God treats you as sons. For what 'son' is there whom his father does not discipline?" (Heb 12:7). Satisfaction for sin is part of that spiritual discipline on the path of holiness. For, "at the time, all discipline seems a cause not for joy, but for pain, yet later it brings the peaceful fruit of righteousness to those who are trained by it" (Heb 12:11). This leaves the demon in third place as the instrument God uses to produce that peaceful fruit of righteousness.

Can a Child Be Possessed by an Evil Spirit?

To that end, I note as the problem of this inquiry two passages from Saint Mark's Gospel which are largely ignored by modern scholars who deny *avon avot*—namely, two children possessed by evil spirits: the Syrophoenician woman's "little daughter" (Mk 7:24–30) and a boy possessed "since childhood" (Mk 9:14–21). While the former is arguably near the age of reason, the latter is particularly difficult to explain. While exegetes may accept the biblical text at face value *that* the boy was possessed, rarely do scholars ask *how* he came to be so. The elephant in the room, so to speak, is the biblical evidence of a child possessed (literally) "since childhood" (Mk 9:21). Rather than focus on a full critique of the Protestant and charismatic understanding, here I want to focus specifically on "familial spirits" by looking at specific scriptural references, then how those texts and this theological concept were generally received in tradition, with a view toward understanding how an infant can be possessed by a demon. Although this phenomenon is rare, what is recounted in the Gospels is something which exorcists have experienced in the field. Only after several years of working cases, which included afflicted children and even infants, did these two New Testament stories begin to make more sense.

While the modern mind tends to quickly dismiss that God still punishes sin, the concept of inherited guilt was fleshed out in the early Church by Saint Augustine as part of the theological debate that produced the formulation of the dogma of original sin. Saint Augustine actually used Exodus 20:5 and the punishment due to sin as an inherited guilt in his argument for original sin against Julian of Eclanum, who both rejected original sin and fervently denied that a loving and just God punishes sin. In particular, Julian, the spokesman for the Pelagians, argued against Saint Augustine and fervently held that God does not punish a father's sin in the children but rather asserted two things incorrectly: all sin is imitated, he argued, and no guilt is inherited. This debate is key to our understanding of the mechanics of sin and will be explored in more detail in chapter four. Before we get to that debate, however, we must look at the primary biblical texts involved, first the giving of the Law at Sinai and then the green grapes proverb in the writings of the prophets.

An Example

The Catholic Church has forbidden membership in Freemasonry for centuries. Pope Clement XII first condemned it in 1738 and prohibited as "valid forever," with the penalty of excommunication, which carried into the 1917 Code of Canon Law.[64] Eleven popes have condemned it explicitly. In addition to the condemnation in the current Code of Canon Law, in 1983 the Congregation for the Doctrine of the Faith affirmed:

> The Church's negative judgment in regard to Masonic associations remains unchanged since their principles have always been considered irreconcilable with the doctrine of the Church; and therefore, membership in them remains forbidden. The faithful who enroll in Masonic associations are in a state of grave sin and may not receive Holy Communion.[65]

Father Rumble (of *Radio Replies* fame of a previous generation) wrote clearly on the dangers of Freemasonry at the turn of the century. Rumble reminded Catholics of the longstanding enmity between Freemasonry and Catholicism by stating that the Catholic who joins the Lodge is "guilty in the sight of God and of the Church" and even commits "injury to his own soul." Thus, he concludes that the "duty of

---

64 Pope Clement XII, *In Eminenti*.

65 CDF, *Masonic Associations* (November 26, 1983). See also Canon 1374: "A person who joins an association which plots against the Church is to be punished with a just penalty; one who promotes or takes office in such an association is to be punished with an interdict."

Catholics is clear. Under no circumstances may they become Freemasons."[66]

The demons generally work in patterns, which become more discernible over time and the more cases one works. For example, Freemasonic curses have a distinct pattern: lung disorders, such as asthma, stomach ailments, other bodily maladies, homosexuality, and problems with conception. In cases that involve sexual molestation, Father Ripperger has observed that as much as fifty percent of the time, there is Freemasonry in the family line. We will explore more in the next chapter the mechanics (and the effects) of sacred vows, but I begin here with a recent story from the field.

The wife of a married deacon was doing some research on her family history and discovered that her maternal grandfather was a Freemason. They discussed this with their pastor, who recommended that they do the renunciation prayers as a penance and have Masses regularly said for the deceased grandfather. The woman suffered from terrible rheumatoid arthritis and walked with the assistance of a cane. Each week, the deacon helped her into their quiet church, and she prayed the prayers of renunciation, accompanied by weekly confession and a prayer of consecration of their bodies and their marriage to the Blessed Virgin Mary. She was also very resigned to offering her suffering up for her family members, especially those who have strayed from the Church, but also for the souls in purgatory. Their pastor happened to be the diocesan exorcist and prayed severing prayers over the wife at the end of each week (our protocol has the descendant of Freemasonry pray the renunciation prayers once a week for three weeks).[67]

---

66 Rumble, *Catholics and Freemasonry*, 7.

67 The protocol can be found at https://liberchristo.org/resources/printed-material/ and prayers in Ripperger, *Laity*, 122–35.

After the third week of renunciations, the couple chatted casually with the priest for a short time and then stood up to leave. A smile suddenly came over the woman's face. To everyone's surprise, the deacon's wife handed the priest her cane.

"I don't need this anymore, Father. You can have it."

"What do you mean?"

"I mean, something happened. I don't have any pain anymore. I can walk without it."

Her husband was astonished but left the cane with the priest and walked her to the car. He called the priest a few weeks later and gave him an update:

"Father, you're not going to believe this," the deacon said, "but every night while we lie in bed, I have seen her toes straighten out little by little. And her pain is still gone. I can physically see her fingers and toes straightening out little by little every day."

His wife continued to resign herself to the will of God and continued to offer herself in reparation for her family, whether in pain or not. After a month, the husband took her to a scheduled appointment with her rheumatologist, who checked her joints through a series of tests. "I cannot explain this," the physician told the wife, "but your joints have no evidence whatsoever of any inflammation. It's like a miracle. I just can't explain it."

The Hope

Sometimes God looks down into a family and finds someone who will be a "little Christ," who will offer up prayers and sacrifices and be an instrument of His grace within the familial construct. This is often not the soul most in danger, but one who will intercede on their behalf. Blaise Pascal said that "God instituted prayer to bestow upon man the sublime dignity of being causes."[68] In the case of the woman above, she had conformed herself to the will of God and offered her suffering up for souls. But, in a moment of great grace, they discovered also the presence of a curse, and between her surrender, her husband's prayers for her, and the Church's intercession, she was healed.

A Prayer

My Jesus, I should indeed do great injustice to Your mercy and Your love, if, after You have given me so many proofs of the love You bear me, and the desire You have to save me, I should still distrust Your mercy and Your love. My beloved Redeemer, I am a poor sinner; but You have said that you came to seek sinners: I am not come to call the righteous, but sinners (Mt 9:13). I am a poor infirm creature,—You came to cure the infirm, and You said, They that our whole need not the physician, but they that are sick (Lk 5:31). I was lost through my sins; but You came to save the lost: The son of man is come to save that which was lost (Mt 18:11). What, then, can I fear, if I am willing to amend my life and to become Yours? I have only myself and my own weakness to fear; but my own weakness and poverty ought to increase my confidence in You, who have declared Yourself to be the refuge of the destitute: The Lord is become a refuge for the poor (Ps 9:10). And You have promised to grant their desires: The Lord hath heard the desire of the poor (Ps 9:38). Therefore, I implore this favor of You, O my Jesus! Give me confidence in Your merits, and grant that I may always recommend myself to God through Your merits. Eternal Father, save me from

---

68 Pascal, *Pensées*, 148.

hell, and first from sin, for the love of Jesus Christ; for the merits of this Your Son enlighten my mind to obey Your will; give me strength against temptation; grant me the gift of Your holy love; and, above all, I beseech You to give me the grace to pray to You to help me, for the love of Jesus Christ, who has promised that You will grant to him who prays in His name, whatever he asks of You. If I continue to pray to You in this way, I shall certainly be saved; but if I neglect it, I shall certainly be lost. Most Holy Mary, obtain for me this great gift of prayer, and that I may persevere in recommending myself constantly to God, and also to You, who obtain from God whatever You will.[69]

O Mary, fulfill your office of mediatrix. Whatever cause you take up is never lost. Who has ever called on you and been lost? Therefore, to you I entrust my eternal salvation. I have only one fear—that someday I might lose my confidence in you. O Mary, preserve this confidence, and I will certainly regain the divine friendship.[70]

Simple Prayer of Reparation

My loving Jesus, out of the grateful love I bear Thee, and to make reparation for my unfaithfulness to grace, I give Thee my heart, and I consecrate myself wholly to Thee; and with your help I propose to sin no more.

[69] Saint Alphonsus Liguori, in *The Road to Bethlehem*, 37–8.
[70] Saint Alphonsus Liguori, *Glories of Mary*, 38–9.

II.

The Sins of the Fathers and the Jealousy of God

I begin with two verses from the Pentateuch that are seemingly contradictory. First, God speaks through a theophany, or visible manifestation of His divinity, in the giving of the Law at Sinai: "For I, the LORD, am a jealous God, inflicting punishment for their fathers' wickedness on the children of those who hate me, down to the third and fourth generation" (Ex 20:5; Dt 5:9). Conversely, Moses later tells the newly formed people of God: "Fathers shall not be put to death for their children, nor children for their fathers; only for his own guilt shall a man be put to death" (Dt 24:16). How can both of these statements be true? Many today still cite this contradiction as evidence that individual responsibility has primacy over any national or familial guilt and that God does not punish a father's sins in his children.

This seeming contradiction is only understood, however, when we distinguish between divine law and human law (as do both Saint Thomas and Saint Augustine, which will be seen). In the theophany at Sinai, God is giving the divine Law to His people, with whom He unites Himself through a sacred covenant. There *God says* that He will exact satisfaction for the sins of the father "to the third and fourth generation" in those who "hate me." In this context, those who "hate" God are those who follow false gods, which will have an impact on their children. Thus, God reveals Himself and warns against idol worshippers in the context of the giving of the Law.

This is different from the giving of human/civil law by Moses, as part of the secondary law (the *deuteros nomos*) for the community. The Mosaic statement on individual responsibility is in the later section of Deuteronomy, which contains communal and penal human laws *given by Moses* for the purpose of stable and harmonious communal life. Hence, Moses here gives instructions concerning court testimonies, sexual purity, marriage and divorce, sanitary practices, rules for lending and exacting debt, etc. In human courts, therefore, every individual has personal responsibility for his own violations of the civil statutes. This is decidedly not the same as the Law given directly by God at Sinai. Since God says both of these, however, and God repeats *avon avot* many times throughout the Torah (the first five books of the Old Testament), we must look at the original context for meaning and clarity. In this section, therefore, I will explore the sacred text and flesh out the imagery used in the giving of the Law at Sinai to help contextualize *avon avot*.

The Lord Is a Warrior

For some Christians today, spiritual warfare is considered antithetical to the concept of a loving and merciful God. The earliest of Christian authors, however, consistently saw the victory of Christ on the cross in militaristic language. As early as the second century, Tertullian (155–220 AD) makes direct reference to Jesus Christ as being in battle with cosmic forces, worth here citing at length:

> You suppose that He is predicted as a military and armed warrior, instead of one who in a figurative and allegorical sense was to **wage a spiritual warfare against spiritual enemies, in spiritual campaigns, and with spiritual weapons.** Come now, when in one man alone you discover a multitude of demons calling itself *Legion* (Lk 8:30) of course comprised of spirits, you should learn that **Christ also must be understood to be an exterminator of spiritual foes, who wields spiritual arms and fights in spiritual strife; and that it was none other than He, who now had to contend with even a legion of demons.** Therefore, it is of such a war as this that the Psalm may evidently have spoken: ***The Lord is strong, The Lord is mighty in battle.*** For with the last enemy death did He fight, **and through the trophy of the cross He triumphed.**[71]

Not only does he cite Jesus's battle against Legion, but Tertullian also applies Psalm 24 to Jesus: "The LORD, a mighty warrior, the LORD, mighty in battle" (Ps 24:8). Further, the cross is the war memorial/trophy which recalls the Warrior-King's victory, where the eternal enemy of all (specifically, "the last enemy to be destroyed is death," 1 Cor 15:26) was broken, defeated, and routed in shameful defeat.

The martial imagery as applied to God's intervention in human history is not new to Christianity. What we discover in Scripture as providing the backdrop for the war memorial of the cross of Jesus Christ, moreover, is an ancient image of God as the divine Warrior. As if a conquering King in a triumphal march into Jerusalem, David sees the Lord in glorious enthronement upon the Ark of the Covenant and cries out: "The LORD, a mighty warrior, the Lord, mighty in battle" (Ps 24:8). Therefore, he says, "Lift high your heads, O

[71] Tertullian, *Against Marcion*, 4.20. Emphasis mine.

gates . . . that the king of glory may enter. Who is this king of glory? The LORD of Hosts is the king of glory" (Ps 24:9–10).

The title of God as divine Warrior was first used by Moses. Perhaps no man has known God as intimately as did Moses, through whom God punished Pharaoh of Egypt with ten plagues and liberated His people. After seeing the glory and power of God exacted upon Pharaoh and Egypt, a mighty sight indeed, the people said to Moses, "You speak to us, and we will listen; but let not God speak to us, or we shall die" (Ex 20:19). Moses, however, conversed with God "face to face, as one man speaks to another" (Ex 33:11). God revealed Himself directly to Moses in the burning bush (Ex 3:6), summoned Moses up the mountain with Him for forty days and nights (Ex 34:28), and personally gave him the Ten Commandments (Ex 24:12). Moses, God's friend, even ate and drank with God (Ex 24:11). Suffice to say, Moses had an intimacy with God like no other.

Bear in mind, therefore, the words of Moses who sang a battle song of victory when God delivered His people from Pharaoh's army at the Red Sea. "The LORD as a Warrior," he cried for all to hear, "LORD is his name!" (Ex 15:3). The "LORD" (Greek, *Adonai*) is the divine Name and indicates God's unique entry into human history, to include covenant union and intimacy with His people. The title of "warrior" further describes how the Lord had manifested Himself in visible ways in Egypt to deliver His people from slavery, culminating in the parting of the Red Sea and the destruction of Pharaoh's army (Ex 14:10–30).

The prophets later made frequent use of this image to remind an enslaved people of the Warrior-God who brings salvation and exacts justice against His enemies. As Isaiah writes, "The LORD goes forth like a hero, like a warrior he stirs up his ardor; he shouts out his battle cry, against his enemies he shows his might" (Is 42:13). Jeremiah said that "the LORD is with me as a mighty warrior" (Jer 20:11). Zephaniah proclaims that the people of God should "fear not and be not discouraged" because in their midst is "the LORD, your God . . . a mighty savior" who gives victory (Zep 3:17). Isaiah, prophesying a future return of Israel, described God as "one arrayed in majesty, marching in the greatness of his strength" as the great I AM who delivered Israel: "It is I who am, mighty to save" (Is 63:1–2).

In fact, the divine title "Lord of Hosts"—sometimes rendered in English as the "God of Armies," the "Lord of Soldiers," or the "Lord God Almighty"—occurs two hundred and eighty-five times in the Bible. Divine names have specific meanings that point to deeper divine realities. This ancient title of God, the Lord God Almighty, the Lord of Hosts, "communicates God's role as a warrior who fights both in the cosmic conflict against divine forces and through human historical events for His people, Israel."[72] By *divine* here is meant non-bodily, preternatural beings, commonly referred to as fallen angels or demons. By *cosmic* is meant the unseen, but very real, dimensional space of the created order where disembodied spirits exist, the universe where angels and demons communicate and even do spiritual battle. This is seen in the fact that the Israelites would bring the Ark of the Covenant into battle, which "was understood as YHWH's participation in Israel's war."[73]

Thus, "the royal character of YHWH Seba'ot is combined with the martial character. The cosmic king is surrounded by his heavenly hosts" who defeat the primordial chaos and engage in battle with cosmic forces. Accordingly, this divine

[72] Dempsey Rosales Acosta, "Lord of Hosts," in John D. Barry et al. eds., *The Concise Lexham Bible Dictionary*.
[73] *Anchor Bible Dictionary*, vol. 3, 306.

title evokes images of "the God enthroned as heavenly king, but he is also the brave warrior who defeated the waters and dragons of the sea."[74] The "hosts" of heaven that he commands are the good angels who are symbolized by the stars. As God speaks through Isaiah: "Lift up your eyes on high and see who created these [the stars]: He leads out their army and numbers them, calling them all by name. By his great might and the strength of his power not one of them is missing!" (Is 40:26).

The divine King and Warrior acts in and through His anointed king. The presence of the Lord who empowers and battles for His people is seen in the words of David to Goliath when he reminded the Philistine that he was not alone in this fight. "You come against me with sword and spear and scimitar, but I come against you, in the name of the Lord of hosts, the God of the armies of Israel that you have insulted" (1 Sm 17:45). He reminds the Philistine that after David's victory, "thus the whole land shall learn that Israel has a God" (1 Sm 17:46), which literally reads in the Greek: "all the earth will know/recognize that God is among Israel." He continued His presence among them through David, of whom Samuel remarks, "grew steadily more powerful, for the LORD of Hosts was with him" (2 Sm 5:10).

The psalmist, recall, clarifies the religious context of this battle when he states that "For all the gods of the Gentiles are devils" (Ps 95.5; *daimonia* or demons, Ps 96:5 LXX). In defeating the Philistine through David, the Warrior God was defeating their gods. As Irene Nowell notes:

> Foreign gods were also considered demonic. In both Deuteronomy and Psalm 106 the Israelites are accused of sacrificing their children to demons (Hebrew *shedim*). Deuteronomy

[74] *Anchor Bible Dictionary*, vol. 3, 306.

> observes that these demons are "not God" or "no-gods" (Dt 32:17; see Bar 4:7). Psalm 106 identifies them as "the idols of Canaan" (Ps 106:37–38). The god to whom they are sacrificing is probably Molech, the god who claimed the firstborn. Leviticus forbids sacrificing children to Molech (Lv 18:21; 20:2–5), but the temptation to imitate the Canaanites seems to have persisted through the generations. Solomon built a high place for Molech, along with other foreign gods, in order to please his wives (1 Kgs 11:7); almost three centuries later Manasseh is condemned for the same action (2 Chr 33:6). In the early sixth century one of the reasons God is handing Jerusalem over to the Babylonians, according to Jeremiah, is because they are sacrificing their children to Molech (Jer 32:35). This abomination is happening in spite of Josiah's recent reform in which he destroyed the place where the sacrifices were taking place (2 Kgs 23:10). The Book of Isaiah condemns those who offer sacrifices to the gods called Fortune and Destiny (Is 65:11); in the Septuagint these gods' names are translated simply as *daimon*.[75]

Accordingly, in instituting the Passover, and through the ten plagues of the Exodus, the Lord tells Israel that He is "exacting judgment on the gods of Egypt" (Ex 12:12). As the author of Wisdom states of the tenth plague of Egypt, where the firstborn sons were killed:

> For when peaceful stillness encompassed everything and the night in its swift course was half spent, Your all-powerful word from heaven's royal throne leapt into the doomed land, a fierce warrior bearing the sharp sword of your inexorable decree, And alighted, and filled every place with death, and touched heaven, while standing upon the earth. (Ws 18:14–16 NABRE)

---

[75] Nowell, *101 Questions & Answers on Angels and Devils*, 62.

Moses reminded the people of this in the desert wanderings, in an ancient hymn commemorating God's mighty hand in delivering them from slavery in Egypt:

> They set out from Rameses in the first month, on the fifteenth day of the first month. On the day after the Passover the Israelites went forth in triumph, in view of all Egypt, while the Egyptians buried those whom the LORD had struck down, every firstborn; on their gods, too, the LORD executed judgments. (Nm 33:3–4 NABRE)

God was not just liberating His people from slavery, but also "on their gods, too, the LORD executed judgments" (Nm 33:4 NABRE). Liberation means divine punishment upon the demons who afflict God's children.

This martial imagery is echoed in Job, where the Lord speaks "out of the storm" and tells him to "Gird up your loins now, like a man," that is, prepare for combat (Jb 38:1). God then speaks to Job using imagery of a war horse who stands fearless in the face of battle, "jubilantly paw[ing] the plain" and "frenzied and trembling he devours the ground; he holds not back at the sound of the trumpet, but at each blast cries 'Aha!'" and "rushes in his might against the weapons" (Jb 39:19–25). From the beginning, therefore, the Lord of Hosts refers to the God who plunges into the human condition and wars against the spiritual enemies of His people.

When a Warrior Becomes Jealous

Just after the Warrior-God led Israel out of the slavery of Egypt, destroying their army and exacting judgment on their gods, He revealed Himself at Sinai under another title: "the Jealous One" (Ex 34:14). A Warrior-God maybe, but a *Jealous* God? Some would dismiss these texts that say God is jealous of other gods or vindictive in punishing sins as anthropomorphic—that is, projecting human emotions upon God, changing Him into something more like a creature than the Creator. While we always have to be cautious of remaking God in our image who made us in His (cf. Gn 1:26), to dismiss the names of God in the sacred text in such a way is oversimplistic.[76] The various titles of Jesus, for example, reflect something about His divine identity. He is, among others, called the Son of God (Jn 1:34), Son of Man (Mt 12:40), Immanuel (Mt 1:23 ESV), Bridegroom (Jn 3:29), Son of David (Mt 1:1), Alpha and Omega (Rv 22:13), Bread of Life (Jn 6:35), Holy One of God (Mk 1:24), Beloved Son (Mk 9:7). Like the title Lord of Hosts, each of these titles gives some insight into both who He is and what He does.

There is a difference, moreover, between refashioning God in our image and using metaphor and human analogies to explain the unexplainable mystery of the Triune God. We know this to be true even in our own litanies of various saints. In the Litany of Loreto, for example, we see various titles of the Blessed Mother which reveal both who she is (Mother of God, Mother Inviolate, Tower of David, etc.) and also what she does (Health of the Sick, Refuge of Sinners, Comfort of the Afflicted, etc.). Admittedly, all analogies fall short, but since God uses these words and reveals Himself in human language through the sacred text, we get a glimpse of both who He is and what He does. His titles reveal something about Him. Through the biblical titles of God, we make more visible and comprehensible some aspect of the invisible and incomprehensible God.

---

[76] Also oversimplistic is the idea that God changes, so what He said earlier in the Bible can be erased later by the prophets. He reveals Himself by stages, but He also is unchangeable, eternal.

The concept of generational curses, therefore, flows from this second ancient image of God, "the Jealous One" (Ex 34:14), a self-revealed title which may sound odd to the modern reader: "You shall not worship any other god, for the LORD is 'the Jealous One'; a jealous God is he. Do not make a covenant with the inhabitants of that land . . . [with] their wonton worship" (Ex 34:14–15). What did that wanton worship look like? The worship of the Canaanite gods included sacred poles where ritualistic sex was performed and stone altars where human sacrifices were made. These are abominations to the Lord.

The divine Warrior who led them out of slavery by punishing the gods of Egypt, therefore, now reveals Himself in a new way at the Great Theophany at Sinai as the divine Bridegroom. This self-revelatory title of God gives insight into both the nature of God's love for us as well as the ramifications of infidelity and sin. The concept of generational curses finds its root here, heard in the enigmatic words of God at the giving of the Ten Commandments:[77]

> You shall not carve idols for yourselves in the shape of anything in the sky above or on the earth below or in the waters beneath the earth; you shall not bow down before them or worship them. **For I, the LORD, your God, am a jealous God, inflicting punishment for their fathers' wickedness on the children (*poked avon avot al banim*) of those who hate me,** down to the third and fourth generation; but **bestowing mercy** down to the thousandth generation, on the children of those who love me and keep my commandments. (Ex 20:4–6, emphasis mine)

God repeats it after the Israelites fell into idolatry the first time in the desert:

---

[77] As with the Church Fathers, the concept of the Hebrew *avon avot* ("the sins of the father") was also debated by the early rabbis. See Dov Weiss, "Sins of the Parents."

> The LORD came down in a cloud and stood with him there and proclaimed the name, "LORD." So, the LORD passed before him and proclaimed: The LORD, the LORD, a God gracious and merciful, slow to anger and abounding in love and fidelity, continuing his love for a thousand generations, and forgiving wickedness, rebellion, and sin; yet not declaring the guilty guiltless, but bringing punishment for their parents' wickedness on children and children's children to the third and fourth generation! (Ex 34:5–7 NABRE)

He repeats it in the giving of the Deuteronomic law of Moses:

> You shall not carve idols for yourselves in the shape of anything in the sky above or on the earth below or in the waters beneath the earth; you shall not bow down before them or worship them. **For I, the LORD, your God, am a jealous God, inflicting punishments for their fathers' wickedness on the children of those who hate me, down to the third and fourth generation but bestowing mercy**, down to the thousandth generation, on the children of those who love me and keep my commandments. (Dt. 5:8–10, emphasis mine)

Notice that the context here is the first commandment, and to "hate" God is to "bow down and give worship" to false gods. Not only should they not offer worship to them, but they are also not to offer any sacrifices to the gods of the nations, the Gentiles of the surrounding nations. In the context of warning against such activity, God reveals Himself as "jealous." The Lord later reiterates these same commands as at Sinai: "You shall not worship any other god, for the LORD is 'the Jealous One'; a jealous God is He" (Ex 34:14). These self-revelatory words of the Lord at Sinai ("I am a jealous God," Ex 20:5) do not mean that God is petty or jealous in the way humans are, as if brooding over injury and seeking revenge. Rather, He reveals something of His nature toward us—and what He expects in return. The word used for *jealous* implies a marital fidelity, exclusivity, and holy jealousy, the intense and burning *zeal* of a bridegroom for his bride.

The biblical tradition infers that this nuptial understanding is key to God's loving desire for mankind. As André Villeneuve has shown, the ancient rabbinic tradition suggests Sinai as a place of betrothal where God's mountain is a type of nuptial chamber where God's covenant people have "renewed access to Eden's lost Tree of Life."[78] Thus, Sinai is a place where God restores the fall of our first parents in a redemptive embrace akin to "marriage." Therefore, "betrothal and marriage are symbolic for God's love for his people."[79] The ancient rabbis saw the giving of the Law at Sinai as not merely the execution of a covenant, or sacred contract, between God and Israel, but also where God wed Himself to Israel in spiritual nuptials. Thus, the command to "sanctify/wash themselves" (Ex 19:11) was seen as akin to a pre-nuptial, preparatory bath.[80] This, then, is the context of the warning of *avon avot* that the sins of parents will have an effect upon their children to the third and fourth generation experienced as a lack of blessing that comes with fidelity.

Later in Exodus, God again warns the Israelites not to follow the false gods of the Gentiles in the land of Canaan where He was leading them. Why such repeated warnings? Although Israel had left the idolatry of Egypt, the idolatry of Egypt had not yet left them. Soon after the Exodus and theophany of Sinai, the Israelites evoked God's jealousy by worshipping a golden calf. The people cried out, "This is your God, Israel, who brought you out of the land of Egypt!" (Ex 32:4). The Hebrew and Latin texts of this verse both state the

---

[78] André Villeneuve, *Nuptial Symbolism*, 76.
[79] Schneider, *Eve Was Named an Apostle*, 12.
[80] Schneider, *Eve Was Named an Apostle*, 35.

plural ("These are the gods"), indicating the abandonment of the one, true God for the demon-gods of Egypt. In addition, the graven image made by Aaron was a young bull, suggesting the Apis ritual of the Egyptians and Ba'al of the neighboring Canaanites.[81] The description of their actions before the statue ("they sat down to eat and drink, and rose up to revel," Ex 32:6) suggests the pagan, ritualistic, and sexual practices of this occult.[82]

After this incident in Exodus, He reiterates this title to Moses, adding mention of His steadfast love:

> So Moses cut two tablets of stone like the first. And he rose early in the morning and went up on Mount Sinai, as the Lord had commanded him, and took in his hand two tablets of stone. The Lord descended in the cloud and stood with him there, and proclaimed the name of the Lord. The Lord passed before him and proclaimed, "The Lord, the Lord, a God merciful and gracious, slow to anger, and abounding in steadfast love and faithfulness, keeping steadfast love for thousands, forgiving iniquity and transgression and sin, but who will by no means clear the guilty, visiting the iniquity of the fathers on the children and the children's children, to the third and the fourth generation." (Ex 34:4–7 ESV)

The Hebrew word for "steadfast love" is *hesed*, meaning God's love, fidelity, and mercy toward His covenantal people, the rewards of covenant fidelity. God's covenant faithfulness is a consuming, holy zeal and steadfast love for His bride.

As Moses led the people up to the Promised Land of Canaan before he died, God foretold of the infidelity that still plagued His people, telling him:

---

81 *Catholic Commentary on Sacred Scripture*, 227.

82 "Apis" in Karel van der Toorn, et al., eds, *Dictionary of Deities and Demons in the Bible*, 68–70.

> Soon you will be at rest with your ancestors, and then **this people will prostitute themselves** by following the foreign gods among whom they will live in the land they are about to enter. They will forsake me and break the covenant which I have made with them. At that time my anger will flare up against them; I will forsake them and hide my face from them; they will become a prey to be devoured, and much evil and distress will befall them. At that time, they will indeed say, "Is it not because our God is not in our midst that these evils have befallen us?" Yet I will surely hide my face at that time because of all the evil they have done in turning to other gods. (Dt 31:16–18 NABRE, emphasis mine)

Scott Hahn notes how curses are, in effect, the inverse of blessings: "While the distinguishing mark of oaths is conditional self-malediction, it should be recalled that swearing is primarily motivated by a desire for divine benediction."[83] God's covenant fidelity and mercy are always present, but the one who swears an oath by invoking the divine Name and blessing also invokes a curse upon himself by the very nature of the oath taken. Infidelity to the Law evokes a spousal-like response from God, bearing with it self-inflicted punishments. Thus, God commands Moses to "write out this song, then, for yourselves. Teach it to the Israelites and have them recite it, so that this song may be a witness for me against the Israelites" (Dt 31:19):

> For when I have brought them into the land flowing with milk and honey which I promised on oath to their ancestors, and they have eaten and are satisfied and **have grown fat**, if they **turn to other gods and serve them, despising me and breaking my covenant,** then, when **great evil and distress befall them,** this song will speak to them as a witness, for it will not be forgotten if their descendants recite it. For I know

[83] Hahn, *Kinship by Covenant*, 52.

> what they are inclined to do even at the present time, before I have brought them into the land which I promised on oath. (Dt 31:19–21)

As at Sinai, Moses reminds Israel that to follow false gods is to "despise" or "hate" God, which is repeated in the Mosaic covenant on the plains of Moab in Deuteronomy 29. Moses uses marital imagery to describe covenant infidelity and idolatry. As Hahn notes, therefore, the sworn covenant found here in Deuteronomy involves a conditional self-malediction, whereby a "curse" is the result of the breach of the oaths sworn when making a covenant with God and invoking the divine Name.[84]

Suggestive of the interactive nature of ritual, Hahn further notes that there are "two constituent parts of a covenant oath: a formal declaration (*verba solemnia*) and a ritual enactment ("oath-sign")."[85] Notably, he observes how these two constituent parts are not only applicable to ancient Israel but also to the Christian oaths of the new covenant. The Latin word for oath is *sacramentum* and is defined as a solemn obligation or engagement, or an oath of allegiance. Each time we participate in a sacrament, those two elements are present as well, as the *Catechism* states: every sacrament has "perceptible signs" of "words and actions" (CCC 1084). What occurred in history in ancient Israel we now have in mystery in the Church. We also engage in sacred oaths through those two constituent parts of formal declaration and ritual enactment to invoke blessing, but also, like ancient Israel, there are negative ramifications for breaking those oaths.

This is significant, particularly when looking at witchcraft rituals or the oaths taken in Freemasonry, for example, which also contain those two elements of *verba solemnia* and

---

84 Hahn, *Kinship by Covenant*, 48–49.

85 Hahn, *Kinship by Covenant*, 52.

an oath-sign of some kind. Rather than invoking the blessing of God, however, these oaths invoke some favor (an unholy "blessing" of some kind) from a false god or demon, who takes these oaths very seriously. The same applies when going to a curandera or palm reader. Whether the intention is for something otherwise good (such as love, pregnancy, financial gain, knowledge of future events) or evil (curses upon one's enemies), a self-malediction is also present should the oath swearer break the promises of the oaths sworn.

As the *Catechism* reminds us, all such activities are "a recourse to Satan or demons" (CCC 2116). The paragraph bears repeating for the gravity of white or black magic:

> All forms of divination are to be rejected: recourse to Satan or demons, conjuring up the dead or other practices falsely supposed to "unveil" the future. Consulting horoscopes, astrology, palm reading, interpretation of omens and lots, the phenomena of clairvoyance, and recourse to mediums all conceal a desire for power over time, history, and, in the last analysis, other human beings, as well as a wish to conciliate hidden powers. They contradict the honor, respect, and loving fear that we owe to God alone. (CCC 2116)

The *Catechism* notes as well that "idolatry consists in divinizing what is not God. Man commits idolatry whenever he honors and reveres a creature in the place of God, whether this be gods or demons," and in so doing, "rejects the unique Lordship of God" (CCC 2114). As Father Amorth reminds us, "there are no such things as 'white' or 'black' magic. Every form of magic is practiced with recourse to Satan."[86] The means do not justify the end. Even if one's intentions are good, such as using Reiki or other modalities which invoke "energies" into "chakras" and the like, an invocation is an invitation.

---

86 Amorth, *An Exorcist*, 60.

Accordingly, Moses uses stark imagery for the covenant breach of idol worship as not just a lapse in marital fidelity but as prostitution. He then reminded Israel of the need for faithfulness to God, "the Rock": "The Rock—how faultless are his deeds, how right all his ways! A faithful God, without deceit, just and upright is he!" (Dt 32:4). Yet, despite God's signs and wonders and Moses's warning, they became "degenerate children" and "a twisted and crooked generation" who "scorned their saving Rock" (Dt 32:15, 16). How did they scorn Him? Moses reminds them of their unfaithfulness with nuptial language. The people of God were a once-beautiful bride, God's "darling," but had now "grown fat and frisky" becoming "fat and gross and gorged" because they "spurned the God who made them and scorned their saving Rock" (Dt 32:15). The Canticle of Moses continues to explain what makes a once-darling become unseemly in God's eyes: "With strange gods they incited him, with abominations provoked him to anger. They sacrificed to demons, to "no-gods," to gods they had never known" (Dt 32:16–17).

Moses would later invoke the steadfast love and fidelity (*hesed*) of God during the desert wanderings, and he interceded for the people who repeatedly rebelled against God. He invoked the punishment for rebellion (covenant infidelity) but also called upon God's mercy:

> And now, therefore, let the power of the LORD be great in the way that you promised when you spoke, saying, "The LORD is slow to anger, and abounding in steadfast love, forgiving iniquity and transgression, but by no means clearing the guilty, visiting the iniquity of the parents upon the children to the third and the fourth generation." Forgive the iniquity of this people according to the greatness of your steadfast love, just as you have pardoned this people, from Egypt even until now. (Nm 14:17–18 NRSV)

The story of salvation history henceforth recounts how the Jealous One continually pursues His bride and the negative consequences of infidelity. His promise of mercy always remains.

Spiritual Nuptials in the Song of Songs and the Prophets

The divine Bridegroom is the passionate Lover who demands reciprocal love and fidelity from His bride, His people. The prophets will build upon what God foretold through Moses, that "this people will prostitute themselves by following the foreign gods among whom they will live in the land they are about to enter. They will forsake me and break the covenant which I have made with them" (Dt 31:16). Before we get to the prophets (Hosea here, and Jeremiah and Ezekiel in the next chapter), a brief stopover at the Song of Songs is necessary, as there is found a continuation of this motif of Israel-as-Bride in the symbolic language of the love, but here in its ideal form.

The second-century Rabbi Akiva famously said that "all of Scripture and its texts are holy, but the Song of Songs is the Holy of Holies," and "all the world is not as worthy as the day on which the Song of Songs was given to Israel." Why is the Song so important? So central to understanding righteous living and man's relationship with God, Rabbi Akiva taught also that, had the Torah not been given, we could live our lives by the Song of Songs.[87] One of Rabbi Akiva's contemporaries, Rabbi Joshua ben Levi, saw in the bride's desire for kisses "a petition from the people of Israel for God to speak with them and to give them his commandments so that they might obey

[87] Mishna Yadayim 3:5. Cited in Giszczak, Mark, "The Canonical Status of Song of Songs in *m. Yadayim* 3.5," 205.

them."[88] In the ancient rabbinic midrash, the Song of Songs was broadly seen as a love poem describing the giving of the Law at Sinai and the love of God for His bride, the people of God. The spiritual sense of the Song of Songs is the literal sense; that is, the poem is a metaphor (a word which means "to transfer," and thus to substitute one idea for another) for the love of God for His people. It is a poetic description of the divine Bridegroom and the idealized response of His "bride," expressed in terms of love-as-desire.[89]

Modern scholars, however, often see the Song as God encouraging human love and sexuality.[90] If the Song is meant only to extol human love, the imagery used to describe the female beloved is, in fact, quite grotesque. Here is a list of how Solomon describes the female lover, the one he tells, "How beautiful you are, my beloved!" (Sg 1:15 LXX):

Literalist reading of Song of Songs 4 and 7:

- "your eyes are doves"
- "your hair is like a flock of goats"
- "your teeth are like a flock of newly shorn ewes"
- "your lips are like a scarlet thread"
- "your nose is like the tower of Lebanon facing Damascus"
- "your temples are like a slice of pomegranate"
- "your neck is like the tower of David, strewn with shields"
- "your breasts are like two fawns feeding among the lilies"
- "your lips drip honey and milk"
- "the fragrance of your garment is the fragrance of Lebanon"
- "your naval is like a goblet and your belly, a heap of wheat"

88 Boersma, "Nuptial Reading," 235.
89 See Edmée Kingsmill, *The Song of Songs and the Eros of God.*
90 See Paul J. Tanner, "The History of Interpretation of the Song of Songs."

The male lover also has some interesting features. Where the Hebrew text of Song of Songs 1:4 has the male lover telling his beloved that "your love is better than wine," the Greek and Latin texts are the reverse. They have the female beloved speaking to the male lover: "Bring me, O King, into your chambers . . . *your breasts* are better than wine" (Sg 1:4, LXX and VUL). This highlights, for example, that while the modern mind generally sees breasts in a sexualized manner, the ancients viewed breasts as nurturing and comforting, and as symbolic of the Torah. Isaiah uses the image of breasts in the positive in a prophecy of the future restoration in the messianic age:

> Rejoice with Jerusalem and be glad because of her, all you who love her; Exult, exult with her, all you who were mourning over her! Oh, that you may suck fully of the milk of her comfort, That you may nurse with delight at her abundant breasts! (Is 66:10–11)

The return from exile is described as well: "As a nursling, you shall be carried in her arms and fondled in her lap; as a mother comforts her son, so will I comfort you; in Jerusalem, you shall find your comfort" (Is 66:13). The psalmist uses the same image of breasts: "I have stilled my soul hush it like a weaned child, like a weaned child on its mother's lap, so is my soul within me" (Ps 131:2). In biblical imagery, moreover, "breast" and "milk" are metaphors for the nurturing and comforting aspect of the Law. Thus, the male "breasts" may even evoke the image of Moses carrying the tablets of the Law down the mountain at Sinai.

Of the people who come to the Church for help from diabolic affliction, the majority fail to recognize that God wants more than for someone to be "demon free." He wants all of them, body and soul, in a union of love. Accordingly, I stated elsewhere that "*freedom from* diabolic affliction, and its effects . . . also means freedom for new life in Christ."[91] God was not just liberating Israel *from* something but *for* something, a betrothal-type union with Him as His covenant people. The *freedom for* is a union so deep that the biblical writers described it in nuptial terms. We hear this repeatedly in the writings of the prophets. God says through Jeremiah, for example, "I remember the devotion of your youth, how you loved me as a bride, following me in the wilderness, in a land unsown" (Jer 2:2). Similarly, Isaiah writes: "For your husband is your Maker; the LORD of hosts is his name, your redeemer, the Holy One of Israel, called God of all the earth" (Is 54:5). Note here the connection between "the Lord of Hosts" (the title for the God who directs the angels in battle against cosmic forces) and the nuptial relationship of Israel toward God ("your husband . . . your Maker"). The one leads to the other. Freedom from cosmic forces of evil and their human instruments means freedom for a bridal-type union with God.

In addition, the Song emphasizes wine. For example, "your mouth is like an excellent wine" (Sg 7:10), and "He brings me into his wine cellar and sets charity in order within me" (Sg 2:4 VUL). Wine, specifically, wine in abundance, is a symbol of the joy of the coming of the messianic age. As the prophet Amos writes, "The juice of grapes shall drip down the mountains, and all the hills shall run with it, I will bring about the restoration of my people Israel; they shall rebuild and inhabit their ruined cities, plant vineyards and drink the wine, set out gardens and eat the fruits" (Am 9:13–14). Similarly, the prophet Joel: "On that day, the mountains shall drip new wines, and the hills shall flow with milk; and the channels of Judah shall flow with water" (Jl 3:18). Accordingly, the nuptial imagery of the Song, including "Bring me, O King, into

91 Schneider, *Manual*, 5.

your chambers . . . *your breasts* are better than wine" (Sg 1:4), can be understood symbolically as twofold:

- Breasts → nourishing aspect of Torah
- Wine → symbol of messianic joy

Thus, as the psalmist writes in a psalm extolling the Law, how righteous living of Torah brings delight, consolation, and knowledge of God: "Your decrees are my delight; they are my counselors," and "How I love your teaching, LORD! I study it all the day long" (cf. Ps 119:24, 97).

The ancient rabbis generally saw the Song's engendered imagery as describing three things: (1) God and Israel; (2) God's indwelling presence in the tabernacle; and (3) a future eschatological fulfillment in the messianic age, where humanity will be perfected. The imagery of nuptiality is an allegory ("other speak") for love-as-desire, and a receptive orientation toward God did not end with the Jewish people.

In the move from Old to New, however, we move from shadows to reality (cf. Col 2:17). In the Incarnation, God reveals Himself fully, and the divine Bridegroom continues to call His bride to covenant union and spiritual nuptials. As Saint John the Baptist declared in the fourth Gospel: "The one who has the bride is the bridegroom; the best man, who stands and listens for him, rejoices greatly at the bridegroom's voice" (Jn 3:29). Thus, the Christian writers of the first few centuries made similar interpretations of the Song, what can be described as a "nuptial Christology."[92] The Fathers saw that not only were the events in Israel's history symbolically encrypted in the Song's images, but they found their fullness in Christ, the divine Bridegroom. Thus, in both the Jewish and Christian interpretative traditions, the Song of Songs is

---

[92] Peter J. Tomson, "The Song of Songs in the Teachings of Jesus," 446–47.

a love poem filled with symbolic language to describe God's love for us, as a beloved who seeks his lover in a passionate and chaste embrace.

"Who is this coming up from the desert, leaning upon her lover?" (Sg 8:5). In the ancient Jewish understanding, moreover, when God gave the Law at Sinai in the desert, He took Israel as His chosen people. To describe what it meant to be "chosen" by God at Mt. Sinai, the ancient rabbis used the nuptial language of the Songs. That is, God symbolically chose Israel as His bride and "consummated" His marriage to her at Sinai. While a close examination is beyond the scope here, this movement from Old to New continues in Christian interpretation, where the Song of Songs uses human love as metaphor in *positive* for covenant fidelity, specifically, three things:

1. Sinai as Betrothal between God and Israel →
   Christ and the Church
2. The *Shekinah* Presence of YHWH in Temple →
   Christ and the soul
3. Eschatological fulfillment of humanity in messianic days →
   Christ and Mary

The divine Bridegroom who "betrothed" Israel at Sinai becomes the love, Christ, and His bride, the Church. This is seen in the writings of Saint Augustine, who saw the Song as a spiritual marriage between Christ and the Church. God's indwelling presence in the tabernacle becomes the union of love between Christ and the soul through the indwelling of the Holy Spirit. This is seen in the writings of Saint Teresa of Avila, who used the Song to describe the soul in prayer and the expression of love between Christ and the soul. Saint Bernard of Clairvaux said both of those things but also pointed to the perfections and unique privileges of the Virgin Mary.

Thus, the Song, as descriptive of the future eschatological fulfillment in the messianic age, where humanity is perfected, is found in Jesus's love for Mary, preserved from the stain of sin. What is consistent in the movement from the ancient Rabbis to the Fathers and Doctors of the Church, however, is Christ the divine Bridegroom, the Jealous One, who still passionately calls his bride to fidelity and holiness in a chaste, spiritual embrace.

Nuptial Imagery in the Negative

While the Song presents the positive view of the love of God and His people in a spiritual and chaste embrace, the prophets use the same nuptial metaphor for infidelity, but in the negative. They continued the imagery of Moses, who was the first to describe false worship and idolatry as whoredom. In the Song of Moses, recall from above, God warned of the consequences of "despising" Him through "infidelity," and, specifically, that "this people will prostitute themselves" when among the Gentiles (Dt 31:16–17). A curious choice of words to the modern ear, the Israelites would have recalled the words of God at the giving of the Law at Sinai, specifically the first commandment and *avon avot* for those who "hate" God.

The psalmist would later recount how the people who entered the Promised Land, rather than subdue the nations as they were commanded, "intermingled with the nations and imitated their ways" (Ps 106:34–35). What were their "ways"? As the psalmist recounts:

> But [they] mingled with the nations and imitated their ways. They served their idols and were ensnared by them. They sacrificed to demons their own sons and daughters, shedding innocent blood, the blood of their own sons and daughters,

> whom they sacrificed to the idols of Canaan, desecrating the land with bloodshed. They defiled themselves by their actions, *became adulterers by their conduct.* (Ps 106:35–39)

That *they became adulterers by their conduct* echoes the "Jealous One" and the theophany at Sinai. This spiritual and bodily "defilement" is likened to adultery and the breaking of the marriage bond between God and His people, a metaphor for their infidelity and rejection of God. Thus, the prophets continued also to use the nuptial metaphor in the negative in an attempt to describe the woes that were befalling them. Isaiah, for example, describes how Jerusalem, "the faithful city has become a harlot" (Is 1:21). Through Ezekiel, God states that "you lavished your harlotry on every passer-by, whose own you became" and "you played the harlot" (Ez 16:15–16). She even offered "her sons and daughters . . . as sacrifices . . . slaughtered and immolated them" (Ez 16:20–21).

While the focus in the next chapter will be on two prophets who wrote to the Southern Kingdom of Judah (who both cite the green grapes parable), a prophet who wrote similar warnings to the Northern Kingdom was Hosea. The northern tribes, who had rebelled and were taken captive by the Assyrians nearly a century before the fall of Jerusalem and the southern tribes. Hosea not only evoked the nuptial metaphor in the negative to describe Samaria's break from the Law, but he also lived that reality bodily. He was asked by God to marry an unfaithful woman: "Go, take a harlot wife and harlot's children, for the land gives itself to harlotry, turning away from the LORD" (Hos 1:2). God speaks through him in the language of divorce: "Protest against your mother, protest! For she is not my wife, and I am not her husband. Let her remove her harlotry from before her, her adultery from between her breasts" (Hos 2:4), which is an allusion to the

Song, "my beloved rests between my breasts" (Sg 1:13 LXX and VUL). Israel "played the harlot" (Hos 4:15 DR) when she called Ba'al "my husband" instead of the true God (Hos 2:18 DR). A play on words, *ba'al* means "lord" or "master" but also "husband." God reminds them that He, not the false god of the Gentiles, is their true husband. Mention of "between your breasts" uses imagery of the chaste embrace of the Song of Songs to draw a stark image of the false gods as now interloping as Israel's "lord."

Even amidst the condemnation, the divine Bridegroom continues to call His bride: "I will allure her; I will lead her into the desert and speak to her heart . . . in the days of her youth" (Hos 2:13, 14). "Desert" recalls the Exodus and wanderings of Israel *en route* to the Promised Land and, thus, is a place of both the testing of obedience and also where many signs and wonders take place. Thus, God's enduring love for His people who have strayed is a call to leave the "adultery" of false worship and return to their Beloved: "I will espouse you to me forever: I will espouse you in right and in justice, in love and in mercy; I will espouse you in fidelity, and you shall know the LORD" (Hos 2:1:18–19). Despite God's compassionate pleas to call His bride home, we read: "Yet, though I stooped to feed my child, they did not know that I was their healer" (Hos 11:4). The withdrawal into the desert is the first step in the return to God.

He then moves from the language of divorce to a legal argument against them; the prophet recalls the covenant infidelity of Israel: "Hear the word of the LORD, O people of Israel, for the LORD has a grievance against the inhabitants of the land: There is no fidelity, no mercy, no knowledge of God in the land" (Hos 4:1). His grievances include sins beyond idol worship he decried earlier and include "swearing, lying, murder, stealing and adultery" (Hos 4:2). Because of these sins, he gives a curious indictment: "Therefore the land mourns, and everything that dwells in it languishes: The beasts of the field, the birds of the air, even the fish of the sea perish" (Hos 4:3). Hosea's mention of "languish" would evoke in his listener the punishments for covenant infidelity in the giving of the Law, where "they shall languish because of" their fathers' guilt (Lv 26:39 NRSVCE). Mention of "birds of the air and the beast of the field" reminds them of Moses's warning of "curses" for Israel if they "do not hearken to the voice of the LORD, your God, and are not careful to observe all his commandments which I enjoin on you today, all these curses shall come upon you and overwhelm you" (Dt 28:15). One of which was defeat in battle, where "your carcasses will become food for all the birds of the air and for the beasts of the field, with no one to frighten them off" (Dt 28:26).

God directs His charge against the priests, for they have misled the people: "Let no one complain; with you is my grievance, O priests" (Hos 4:4). God's grievance is due to the wicked deeds of idol worship, which Hosea describes in terms of harlotry (Hos 4:10–15). The priests who led the people into false worship now are under trial: "My people perish for want of knowledge. Since you have rejected knowledge, I will reject you from my priesthood; since you have ignored the law of your God, I will also ignore your sons" (Hos 4:6). Notice how God says He will "repay you [the priests] for your deeds" (Hos 4:9) in a twofold manner that parallels original sin: the priest is expelled from God's presence, while their sons will feel the effects.

What did they do to incur this guilt? Hosea reminds them by evoking the nuptial imagery: "On the mountaintops they offer sacrifice and on the hills they burn incense, Beneath oak and poplar and terebinth, because of their pleasant shade. That is why your daughters play the harlot, and your daughters-in-law are adulteresses" (Hos 4:13). The men are guilty as well: "You yourselves consort with harlots, and with prostitutes to offer sacrifice" (Hos 4:14). This refers to the ritual prostitution performed at Canaanite shrines and even in their sanctuaries.

Samaria was pluralistic and syncretistic, with a religious diversity seen in shrines and places of worship to both YHWH and the gods of the Canaanites. The Canaanite religion was principally a fertility cult, and their cult practices were primarily animal and human sacrifice and acts of sexual perversion. Worshippers of Ba'al offered animal sacrifice to appease him, and, in times of crisis, even through sacrificing their children, often the firstborn (cf. Is 57:5–7).[93] Ba'al was their warrior-god, the storm god/sea deity, and principal deity of fertility cults. Ba'al is a title of lord or husband. His mistress and fertility goddess, Asherah (like Lilith, also has the owl as her symbol), was worshiped with ritualistic sex beneath trees (called "groves") and poles (see 1 Kgs 14:24, 22:46; 2 Kgs 17:29–31; 2 Kgs 17:29–3; Ez 20:27–3; 8:11–12; Jgs 3:7).[94]

Ultimately, God honors man's free will and allows the Samaritans to live with the choice of which "husband" to live under, who she allows the intimacy of "between her breasts"—the merciful and faithful divine Bridegroom, or the cruel "lord/master" Ba'al. They rejected the Jealous One and, as a result—spoken through Hosea, the man who had a harlot wife—God echoes *avon avot* to them: "Since you have ignored the law of your God, I also will ignore your sons" (Hos 4:6). They have rejected the true divine Warrior and their Husband for the Gentile and diabolic version and must live under the effects of their choice.

---

[93] *Dictionary of Deities and Demons in the Bible*, 132–39.

[94] *Dictionary of Deities and Demons in the Bible*, 109–14.

Excursus: A Nuptial Blessing

Interestingly, a reference to "the third and fourth generation" is found in the *Rituale Romanum* and the Nuptial Blessing given at Catholic weddings. In reading the blessing below, keep in mind that curses are an inversion of blessings, a privation of the goods of blessings. As part of a long blessing for the bride, the priest echoes the language of Sinai. Notably, he first blesses the bride who, like Israel at Sinai about to embark for the promised rest in the Promised Land, is on her way to her heavenly home:

> May she be modest and grave, bashful and venerable, and well instructed in heavenly doctrine. May she be fruitful in her offspring, approved and innocent; and may it be at length her happy lot to arrive at the rest of the blessed in the kingdom of God:

He then blesses the couple in language that directly evokes Sinai:

> May they both see their children's children to the third and fourth generation and live to their wished-for old age.[95]

In addition, note that the liturgical context of this blessing is nuptials. Two points to consider. One, the language of "to the third and fourth generation" echoes the ancient understanding of the self-revelation of God at Sinai as spiritual nuptials with His people. Two, significantly, the blessing focuses on the bride and recalls the first couple before the Fall, the great and virtuous women in the Old Testament, before echoing the words of Sinai in blessing. The entire blessing bears repeating in its entirety:

---

[95] Weller, *Roman Ritual*, vol. 1, 469.

> O God, who by so excellent a mystery, hast consecrated this union of the two sexes, and hast been pleased to make it a type of the great sacrament of Christ and his Church. O God, by whom woman is joined to man, and that union, which was instituted in the beginning, is still accompanied with such a blessing, as alone, neither in punishment of original sin, nor by the sentence of the deluge, had been recalled. Mercifully look down upon this thy handmaid, who, being now to be joined in wedlock, earnestly desires to be taken under thy protection. May love and peace constantly remain in her. May she marry in Christ faithful and chaste. May she ever imitate the holy women of former times. May she be pleasing to her husband, like Rachael, discreet, like Rebecca. May she, in her years and fidelity, be like Sarah. And may the first author of all evil at no time have any share in her actions. May she remain attached to the faith and the commandments and, being joined to one man in wedlock, may she fly all unlawful addresses. May a regularity of life and conduct be her strength against the weakness of her sex. May she be modest and grave, bashful and venerable, and well instructed in heavenly doctrine. May she be fruitful in her offspring, approved and innocent. And may it be at length her happy lot to arrive at the rest of the blessed in the kingdom of God. May they both see their children's children to the third and fourth generation, and live to their wished-for old age. Through Our Lord.[96]

The nuptial blessing begins by affirming marriage as *so excellent a mystery* and *as a type of the great sacrament of Christ and his Church*, which points us to the nuptial imagery of the Song of Songs. Mention of *woman is joined to man, and that union, which was instituted in the beginning* as well as *may the first author of all evil, at no time, have any share in her actions* both recall the first marriage in the Garden, before the original

[96] Weller, *Roman Ritual* , vol. 1, 469.

sin and its effects. In fact, the blessing recalls that marriage images something before the curses of the Fall (as the result of original sin). Namely, sacramental marriage *is still accompanied with such a blessing, as alone, neither in punishment of original sin nor by the sentence of the deluge, had been recalled.* This sets the stage for the blessing *to the third and fourth generation,* and the original idea that God not only betrothed Israel in a nuptial embrace at Sinai, but He restored the effects of the Fall through the Law, which Israel was to bring to the world.

Accordingly, Father Ripperger notes the link to the concept of familial curses. "Since demons invert all things Catholic," he says, "just as blessings can be passed on from generation to generation, so can the evil effects of sin be passed from generation to generation." He notes the inner logic found in the *Rituale Romanum.* Namely, if a blessing can pass from generation to generation, it follows that "the inversion of a blessing, namely, a curse, [can] be passed from generation to generation."[97] This is seen in the fact that the nuptial blessing evokes the original union of man and woman, the intimacy of God and His people in covenant union, Christ and the Church, Christ and the soul, and even the perfect love between Christ and His Mother (who uniquely images the Church as both fruitful mother and spotless bride).

The nuptial imagery utilized in the Bible is not only a recurring motif that paints a clearer picture of what union with God looks like, but also why the enemy militates so fiercely against the generative principle. In one sense, we observe that a *generational* curse is often the result of violations of the *generative* principle. Do you think the enemy sees the importance of the generative principle and the sacredness of Holy Matrimony? You bet he does.

[97] Ripperger, *Dominion,* 183.

"Jealousy" Is the Essence of His Holiness

One could argue, however, that Hosea wrote nearly one hundred years before Ezekiel and Jeremiah, and that the green grapes proverb did not apply to the people of Judah and Jerusalem. What is consistent in the writings of the prophets, however, is the use of the nuptial metaphor to describe the "infidelity" of idol worship and the effect of grave sins in light of the holiness of God.

According to biblical scholar and longtime chief rabbi of the United Kingdom J. H. Hertz, the concept of inherited guilt found in Exodus 20:5 (as well as Exodus 34:6–7, Numbers 14:18, Deuteronomy 5:9) reveals both the compassion and the justice of God. In His own self-revelation to Moses, we have an image of God that is amendable to today's Christian: "Thus, the LORD passed before him [Moses] and cried out, 'The LORD, the LORD, a merciful and gracious God, slow to anger, and rich in kindness and fidelity, continuing his kindness for a thousand generations, and forgiving wickedness and crime and sin'" (Ex 34:6). What follows, however, is more difficult and leads many to grasp the green grapes proverb for answers. While abounding in kindness and forgiveness, nonetheless the Lord continues: "yet not declaring the guilty guiltless but punishing children and grandchildren to the third and fourth generations for their fathers' wickedness!" (Ex 34:6–7). That God does not leave the guilty unpunished for sins can be problematic to the modern ear. As Rabbi Hertz explains, however, the "jealousy" of God is "the very essence of His holiness," which means that He "hates cruelty and unrighteousness, and loathes impurity and vice; and, even as a mother is jealous of all evil influences that rule her children, He is jealous when instead of purity and righteousness, it is idolatry and unholiness that command their heart-allegiance."[98] Recall that the root of the word for the "Jealous One" is *zeal*, the holy zeal that demands reciprocal exclusivity and fidelity.

Rabbi Hertz explains, from a rabbi's perspective, the tension between the mercy and justice of God in a manner consistent with what is found in the developed theological tradition of the Catholic Church and expressed in the *Catechism*. According to Rabbi Hertz, in this passage of Exodus where God reveals Himself:

> He distinguishes between the moral responsibility which falls exclusively upon the sinful parents, and the natural consequences and predisposition to sin, inherited by the descendants. He takes into account the evil environment and influence. He therefore tempers justice with mercy, and He does so to the third and fourth generations.[99]

Here, Rabbi Hertz echoes the developed Catholic tradition that sin has a double effect of punishment and effect, the former is proper to the parents and is their "moral responsibility." The latter to the children, experienced as a "natural consequence" and a "predisposition to sin." This is consistent with Saint Augustine and Saint Thomas alike, both of whom distinguish between the sin and the effect of the sin, as well as the notion that a curse is a privation of the protection of blessing.

In the Rabbis and Church Fathers

The ancient rabbis and early Church Fathers alike struggled with the concept of divine justice in light of personal responsibility. The concept of *avon avot* explores these questions,

[98] Hertz, *Pentateuch and Haftorahs*, 295–96.
[99] Hertz, *Pentateuch and Haftorahs*, 296.

specifically how "the sins of the father" can result in an affliction upon one's children. This concept recognizes that inherent within the sinful act—particularly the grave sins committed by parents or those to whom one has obligations—have negative consequences both for the sinner and for those under the protection of their authority. The concept of a vicarious punishment for grave sins along familial lines has long challenged interpreters, and the concept of a loving God who punishes sin in this way, vicariously through the children, even led to a dualistic view of God as different in the Old and the New Testaments. In fact, as Dov Weiss notes, from the second to the fifth centuries, "various Gnostic, Marcionites, Valentinians, Pagans, and Manicheans used this verse to prove—against the emerging orthodox Christian position—that the Old Testament God is not synonymous with the Supreme Deity."[100] This concept led many of these groups to conclude that "the Old Testament God is either morally imperfect, or worse, outright evil."

That emerging orthodox position on Exodus 20:5 took various forms before Saint Augustine and struck a balance between the punitive element of Exodus 20:5 and God's unfailing mercy and kindness. When confronted with difficult passages, many of the early Christian writers, like Origen, used allegory and applied the verse to the life of the soul and to argue against the heretical, dualistic belief.[101] Thus, for Origen, the threat of divine punishment reminds the Christian of the need for constant vigilance. In general, the Fathers sought to explore the deeper meaning of a "curse" as punishment for disobedience to God's commands (consistent with the above definition). While admittedly the phrase "generational curse"

[100] Dov Weiss, "Sins of the Parents in Rabbinic and Early Christian Literature," 1.
[101] Origen, *Homilies on Genesis and Exodus*, 329.

may have been foreign to the Fathers, the concept itself was highly debated and discussed. The debate was also heavily nuanced, as will be seen in Saint Augustine who, as Nathaniel McCallum notes, "consistently uses nuanced language on the topic of inherited guilt in order to avoid the idea of an inherited personal guilt."[102] They debated what sins were punishable and how they would be punished. Was it limited to violations of the first commandment and honoring false gods? Do the children also have to commit the same grave sin for the effects of the sins of their parents to be realized in their own lives? Does the "green grapes" proverb found in Ezekiel and Jeremiah (Ez 18:1–4; Jer 31:29–30) nullify the words of God at Sinai?

This general topic—how children could suffer the effects of the sins of their parents—was certainly a cause of much debate and found its way into the theological percolation that became the doctrinal formulations of the early Church.[103] While a comprehensive historical and theological analysis is beyond the scope here, up until Augustine's debate with Julian of Eclanum, there were three basic lines of thought on what "visiting the iniquities of the father upon the children" meant.

A first group were those who do not separate divine and human justice and who thusly held that the green grapes prophecy of Ezekiel and Jeremiah means that God changes His mind and His words at Sinai are no longer valid. That is, they cite Ezekiel, "Only the one who sins shall die. The son shall not be charged with the guilt of his father, nor the father

---

[102] McCallum, "Inherited guilt in Ss. Augustine and Cyril."

[103] As Saint John Henry Newman notes, doctrine is, as it were, "percolated" in the earlier Christian writers, only to be more precisely formulated by later Fathers and Doctors certainly is found here. One must look, therefore, at the nuances of each writer and within the context of their own work to get a clearer picture of the doctrinal formulation. Newman, *An Essay on the Development of Christian Doctrine* (London: Aeterna Press, 2014), 300.

for the guilt of his son" (Ez 18:20). Among these authors, such as Julian of Eclanum, personal responsibility for sin now means that there is no longer any inherited guilt or vicarious punishment whatsoever.

A second group of authors affirmed that God does indeed punish the children, but only if the children commit the same sins of the father, specifically idolatry.[104] Thus, there is an inherited guilt, but with the limitation to a condition of a "continuous sin" down three generations. That is, children appropriate the sins of the father and are guilty by imitation or learned behavior.[105] The effects of the sins of the parents were limited by either a *ratification* (by willful choice) by subsequent generations for the effect of the sin to continue, or a *righteousness* of a generation to break the effect of the sin.[106] The principal key to the enacting of such a "familial" sin is idol worship among the ante-Nicene fathers, which was the

[104] The shift in patristic thought before Saint Augustine is found in Ambrosiater (a contemporary of Jerome), who states: "Why is it that God, who is declared just, promised that he would assign blame for the fathers' sins to their sons up to the third and fourth generation? It is insane to doubt that the Lord does or says nothing unjust. Thus . . . what is thought to be not just at all [Ex 20:5] will be considered upright . . . God indeed bound himself to assign blame for the fathers' sins to their sons, but to those who hate him, that is to those who serve idols, having remained in their fathers' evils, just as their fathers did." Cited in Weiss, "Sins of Parents," 9.

[105] Not only did the early Christian writers wrestle with this concept, but the ancient rabbis as well. For some of the early rabbinic midrash, for example, "a child of a third generation would only be punished for the sins of his grandparent if there were a continuous line of evildoers from the grandparent to the grandchild. If the grandparent, parent or child were righteous, then the child would not be punished for any of his or her ancestors' sins." Weiss, "Sins of the Parents in Rabbinic and Early Christian Literature," 3.

[106] In citing Exodus 20:5, Saint John Chrysostom states: "Not as though one were to suffer punishment for the crimes committed by others, but in as much as they who, after many sins and have been punished, yet have not grown better, but have committed the same offenses, are justly worthy to suffer their punishments also." Saint John Chrysostom, *Homily on Matthew*, 446.

context of the Deuteronomic text (to wit, "those who hate me . . .").[107]

A third group were those who affirmed that the effect of a father's sin, not the sin itself, is passed down to the children in the form of a vicarious punishment. Among that group, however, there was debate as to what "to those who hate me" means. Some asserted that idolatry is what triggered *avon avot,* while others included sexual sins or other gravely sinful acts. In the early centuries leading up to the time of Saint Augustine, among the Christian authors, the punishment of the sins of the parents upon their children was broadly limited to (1) the children who continued the sin and (2) when that sin was grave (primarily idolatry).

The continual sin argument boils down to ratification or righteousness. Thus, there was a limitation to the sins of the parents when there was a *ratification* by subsequent generations for the effect of the sin to continue and *righteousness* of a generation to break the effect of the sin. The principal key to the enactment of such a "familial" curse is idol worship, among the ante-Nicene Fathers, which was the context of the Deuteronomic text. In his earlier writings, Saint Augustine affirmed the continuous sin theory:

---

[107] Similarly, Saint Jerome comments on Jeremiah 2:4–5 ("What fault did your fathers find in me that withdrew from me, went after empty idols and became empty themselves?"): "He reckons the offense as deriving from the parents, not because the sins of the parents are imputed to the children, but because the children are being similar to their parents, **and because they will be punished both for their own wickedness, and for the wickedness of their parents.** We often read that God has compassion on children on account of their holy parents, yet, the ancestors of this sinful people have forsaken God—and not just for a moment, but for a long time. In place of God, they have followed worthlessness, namely, idols, which are of no benefit to those who worship them, and which have been made in the likeness of their worshipers, as is written: 'those who make them are like them; so are all who trust in them.'" Saint Jerome, *Commentary on Jeremiah*, 9.

> It was correct to say that God punished children who hated him for the sins of the parents. For from the addition, "who hated me [*qui oderunt me*]," it is understood that he punishes for the sins of their parents those who have chosen to continue in the same wickedness. Such people, after all, are punished not because of God's cruelty but because of His justice and their sinfulness . . . it is quite clear that God is not brutal but that each person is brutal to himself when he sins.[108]

He will further develop the concept in his later writings to include a vicarious punishment as an effect of original sin.

Up to this point, nonetheless, a certain unanimity among the Fathers did emerge in asserting that God does punish sin, but they distinguished between the sin itself and the effects of the sin. Hence, the concept of *avon avot* is, properly speaking, one of inherited guilt or the effects of sin. This important distinction is the key to unlocking the phenomenon of generational spirits.

As the debate over the effects of original sin and its effects reached its peak in Saint Augustine (who gave us the term and formulated our initial theology of an "original sin"), we discover how the authority structure is also central to inherited guilt. To get to that conclusion, however, the first step is to make a clear distinction between divine justice and human justice. God's justice is expressed in ways that may seem unjust in a human court. This understanding will be fleshed out over time with more precision in the developing theological language of the Church, but for our purposes, the general concept of inherited guilt brings into bas-relief the tension between the justice and the mercy of God, the authority structure and the effects of sin upon both families and communities, the interplay between nature and grace, the effects of baptism and a lingering concupiscence, and the

[108] Saint Augustine, *Against Adimantus*, 7.1, 184.

need for satisfaction for sin. It also may offer a backdrop for Christ's mission to the Gentiles, where He encounters children afflicted by demons.

At issue here, therefore, is the interplay between divine justice and divine mercy. The contrast between the effects of disobedience to "the third and fourth generation" and the abundance of blessings to "one thousandth" gives insight into the depth of divine mercy while not denying divine punishment for sin. In the end, as Saint James tells us, "mercy triumphs over justice" (Jas 2:13). Even when we are sinful and incur the justice of God in the form of punishment, His mercy and covenant faithfulness (*ḥesed*) is always available. In the end, the divine Lover continually invites us to enjoy the blessings that come from fidelity, which we read in the prophets as a message of hope amidst suffering.

An Example

A modernist theology dismisses the effects of the Fall because it challenges our very concept of God and even reveals the impact of sin within the authority structure. The reality of the effects of sins of parents, however, is found in the common, prudential experience of exorcists, which echoes Father Amorth's observations on the effects of familial curses. Freemasonic rituals closely follow the two constituent parts of oath-making (a formal declaration, or *verba solemnia,* and a ritual enactment, or "oath-sign"). Their highly symbolic rituals involve ritualistic curses, the invoking of pagan deities, and ceremonies which symbolically reject the Catholic Church and the papacy. The Church has had a three-hundred-year, unchanging and unwavering prohibition against Freemasonry and secret societies.

A particular case shows how these curses work and the power to break them. A successful businessman had a son in the seminary. He was a well-educated and a lifelong Catholic, but, by his own admission, marginal in his faith. The man went to visit his aged mother who lived some hundred miles away. His father being long dead, he now has a very difficult conversation with her about moving into an assisted living facility. The man goes to confession with a newly assigned local priest, a hundred miles from home, in his mother's town. Within the confessional, he brings up some things which prompt the priest to encourage him to remain after the confessions are over to discuss these things in the external forum. Unbeknownst to the man, the priest was an experienced exorcist.

What the man told the priest was that his son was within a few weeks of being ordained to the transitional diaconate, but has had difficulty in seminary. His son developed undiagnosed allergies and other issues but had actually had no health problems, no allergies, no problems at all until he entered seminary. As he approached ordination to transitional diaconate, he was struck dumb, as if he had had a stroke. His larynx was paralyzed, and one side of his face drooped with facial paralysis. Neither a medical examination nor an MRI could give a medical explanation for what the seminarian was experiencing. The young man's interpretation of his illness, however, according to his father, was: "Obviously God does not want me to be a priest."

With his mother's health declining and his son stricken, the father was beside himself. And so, the priest said to the father:

"Do you have any history of Freemasonry in your family?"

"Yes, my grandfather (who would be this boy's great-grandfather and four generations back) was a worshipful master, 33rd degree Mason."

The priest explained the problems with Freemasonry and that his son's issues were the effect of a generational curse that follows the family bloodline. In addition, the priest explained that there were renunciation prayers that are effective in negating or nullifying the effects of the curse. Since the father was going to visit his mother each weekend for several weekends, the priest suggested that the renunciations be done three times, over the next three Sundays.

The man returned home and informed his wife and son what the exorcist priest had said. The son, however, wrote down in response:

"We got none of this in seminary. I do not believe it."

"But it's worth a shot. Why not do it with me?"

"Dad, this is superstition. It's clear that God does not want me to be a priest. He has taken the power of speech from me. So obviously I'm not supposed to be a priest."

The businessman nonetheless returned the next Sunday and went through the first round of prayers. The boy, however, was more adamant. He told his father, via text:

"God has taken my powers of speech. I'm not to be a priest." The father returned for the second round of renunciations the following Sunday, but was pretty discouraged. The priest told him, "Well, just do it one more time. You got one more week and that's it."

The third Sunday came, and the father went through the renunciations. Although he was experiencing nothing, he went all the way through the prayers. On the way to his car, he called his wife, but his son answered the phone. His son was speaking.

"Your speech has been returned!"

The son says, "—and my facial paralysis has gone." The son went on to say, however, "Obviously, this is a mysterious thing, it went as mysteriously as it came. And it correlated with my decision not to be a priest. God was happy with this decision, and he returned my power of speech."

"I don't think so," the father said. "What really happened was I went through the Freemasonic renunciation prayer for the third time. And if your speech was returned at 3:45 this afternoon, that was right when I finished."

The son was quiet, but finally said, "Well, we've got to talk." That the son's speech was returned at the precise moment when renunciations were completed by his father is rare but extraordinary. The young man ended up being ordained a Catholic priest and continues to serve to this day.

The Hope

Here we see the interplay between faith and family and vocation, particularly how the enemy militates against the priesthood. A father's prayers for his family are very powerful and should not be underestimated. As Sirach writes:

> Children, listen to me, your father; act accordingly, that you may be safe. For the LORD sets a father in honor over his children and confirms a mother's authority over her sons. Those who honor their father atone for sins; they store up riches who respect their mother. Those who honor their father will have joy in their own children, and when they pray, they are heard. Those who respect their father will live a long life; those who obey the LORD honor their mother. (Sir 3:1–6 NABRE)

And: "A father's blessing gives a person firm roots, but a mother's curse uproots the growing plant" (Sir 3:9 NABRE).

A Prayer

O my God! Many years of my life are already past, already death is near at hand, and what good have I hitherto done for Thee? Give me light, and strength, to devote the remainder of my days to Thy service. Too much, alas! have I offended Thee; I desire henceforth to love Thee.[109]

Give me, O Lord! time to lament the offences I have committed against Thee before Thou summonest me to judgment. I will no longer resist Thy calls: who knows but that this meditation may be the last call I may receive? I confess that I have deserved hell, and as many hells as I have committed mortal sins; but Thou wilt not despise poor penitent sinners. I am sincerely sorry with my whole soul for having abused Thy infinite goodness by sensual gratifications. Forgive me and grant me grace to obey Thee and to love Thee till the end of my life. O Mary! I place myself under thy protection and confide in thy holy intercession.[110]

O Mary, because you are so merciful, I have recourse to you. Only two things will keep me from receiving mercy: my failure to ask you or little confidence in your intercession. Therefore, help me always to ask and to seek with confidence.[111]

Prayer for Protection Against Curses, Harm, Accidents

Lord Jesus, I ask Thee to protect my family from sickness, from all harm and from accidents. If any of us has been

[109] Saint Alphonsus Liguori, *The Way of Salvation and of Perfection*, 24.
[110] Saint Alphonsus Liguori, *The Way of Salvation and of Perfection*, 124.
[111] Saint Alphonsus Liguori, *Glories of Mary*, 49.

subjected to any curses, hexes, or spells, I beg Thee to declare these curses, hexes, or spells null and void. If any evil spirits have been sent against us, I ask Christ to decommission you and I ask that you be sent to the foot of His Cross to deal with as He will. Then, Lord, I ask Thee to send Thy holy Angels to guard and protect all of us.

III.

Their Fathers Ate Green Grapes

I begin by way of preface the understanding of what the *Catechism* teaches that "God communicated himself to man gradually as part of 'divine pedagogy' where He reveals Himself 'by stages' which 'culminate in the person and mission of the Incarnate Word, Jesus Christ'" (CCC 53).[112] Jesus Christ is the fullness of all revelation. As Saint Paul writes, "but when the fullness of time had come, God sent his son, born of a woman, born under the law, to ransom those under the law, so that we might receive adoption" (Gal 4:4–5). God reveals Himself by both natural and supernatural means in "stages" through Noah, Abraham, Moses, and later, "through the prophets," where "God forms his people in the hope of salvation, and the expectation of a new and everlasting covenant intended for all" (CCC 64).

Thus, as the *Catechism* states, the writings of the prophets find the ultimate fulfillment in Christ:

[112] As *Dei Verbum* states, God "from the start manifested Himself to our first parents," then through the patriarchs, Moses and later the prophets. His pedagogy: "He taught this people to acknowledge Himself, the one living in true God, provident father and just judge, and to wait for the Savior promised by Him, and in this manner prepared the way for the Gospel down through the centuries." DV, no. 4.

> The economy of the Old Testament was deliberately so oriented that it should prepare for and declare in prophecy the coming of Christ, redeemer of all men. Even though they contain matters imperfect and provisional, the books of the Old Testament bear witness to the whole divine pedagogy of God's saving love . . . the mystery of our salvation is present in a hidden way. (CCC 122)

We refer to this as *salvation history*, God's gradual self-revelation. As Hebrews states, "In times past, God spoke in partial and various ways to our ancestors through the prophets; in these last days, he spoke to us through a son, whom he made heir of all things and through whom he created the universe" (Heb 1:1–2). The Fathers spoke of the divine economy (*oikonomia*), which is seeing the mystery of Christ through the lens of the history of the people of Israel, with the incarnation, death, and resurrection of Jesus Christ as both the ordering principle and climax. Thus, the *Catechism* states that "the Holy Spirit has spoken through the prophets" (CCC 243).

That God reveals Himself "in stages," however, does not mean God changes, as in the modernist Process Theology (see above). As the author of Hebrews states, "Jesus Christ is the same yesterday, today, and forever" (Heb 13:8). Those who object to the concept of generational spirits or inherited guilt often cite Ezekiel and Jeremiah and the green grapes proverb regarding fathers who ate "green grapes and the children's teeth are on edge" (Ez 31:2; Jer 18:31) as indicating that God has further revealed that *avon avot* no longer applies. A cursory reading of the texts in question does seem to suggest that the warnings given at Sinai have been softened or outright nullified. Compounding the matter is Ezekiel's personal responsibility ("Only the one who sins shall die. The son shall be charged with the guilt of his father, nor the father for the guilt of his son," Ez 18:20) seems to affirm Moses's ("Fathers shall not be put to death for their children, nor children for their fathers; only for his own guilt shall a man be put to death," Dt 24:16). So, has God changed His mind?

The prophets fleshed out the interplay between a national/familial guilt and an individual/personal responsibility, writing to a people seeking meaning in their suffering. Their writings reveal the complexity of inherited guilt and the consequences of sin. Here is the proverb as used by each:

Ezekiel 18:2–4	**Jeremiah 31:29–30**
What is the meaning of this proverb that you recite in the land of Israel: "Fathers have eaten green grapes, thus their children's teeth are on edge"? As I live, says the LORD God: I swear that there shall no longer be anyone among you who will repeat this proverb in Israel. For all lives are mine: the life of the father is like the life of the son, both are mine; only the one who sins shall die.	In those days they shall no longer say, "Their fathers ate unripe grapes, and the children's teeth are set on edge," but through his own fault, only shall anyone die: the teeth of him who eats the unripe grapes shall be set on edge.

The key to understanding this proverb is first to understand the context within which the two prophets were writing, which would give the plain, or literal, sense of the passage. This means first contextualizing within the immediate section of the book the life situation of the people of God at the time, the other prophets, and then within the broader Old Testament canon. Thus, Saint Augustine's famous dictum: "The New Testament is hidden in the Old and the Old is made manifest in the New."[113] An ancient rabbinic phrase similarly states, "Scripture is the best interpreter of scripture,"

[113] Cited in CCC 129.

which means that to better understand a passage of the sacred text, search for verbal clues in other parts of the Bible. This approach keeps the exegete grounded in the literal and historical yet opens vistas into a wider landscape of spiritual and theological meaning.

The dual nature of prophetic literature means that the literal meaning gives way to a penultimate fulfillment in the life of Israel, and then in its ultimate fulfillment in Jesus Christ. According to the *Catechism*, the writings of the prophets were not only for the present generation but pointed to the future hope of the New Covenant:

> Through the prophets, God forms his people in the hope of salvation, in the expectation of a new and everlasting Covenant intended for all, to be written on their hearts. The prophets proclaim a radical redemption of the People of God, purification from all their infidelities, a salvation which will include all the nations. Above all, the poor and humble of the Lord will bear this hope. (CCC 64)

When interpreting Scripture, moreover, all meaning (whether spiritual or theological) is based upon the literal, historical sense, while at the same time recognizing an inner dynamic that drives to higher levels of meaning (see CCC 115–19).

For example, Christians recognize the prophecy of Isaiah, "the virgin shall be with child and bear a son and shall name him Immanuel" (Is 7:14) as pointing to Christ as its ultimate fulfillment. This was not spoken, however, without its own historical context. Isaiah wrote in the time of national crisis, with Jerusalem under siege by Syria allied with the Northern Kingdom of Israel. The Davidic monarchy, facing annihilation with the fall of Jerusalem, the prophet gives the people a "sign" of hope: "a young maiden/virgin shall conceive and bear a son" and the David kingship will be preserved through her son.[114] This prophecy would have a partial fulfillment in the life of Israel. Isaiah speaks of the hope for a future, righteous king. Christians, however, have also read this verse as a messianic prophecy, finding its ultimate fulfillment in the virgin birth of Jesus Christ (Mt 1:23). The angel Gabriel likewise alludes to this verse at the Annunciation: "Behold, you will conceive in your womb and bear a son, and you shall name him Jesus. He will be great and will be called Son of the Most High, and the Lord God will give him the throne of David his father, and he will rule over the house of Jacob forever, and of his kingdom there will be no end" (Lk 1:31–33). Prophecy, then, is read at two levels and two fulfillments—one partial in the time and life of the people of God and another in the fullness of time at the coming of Christ.

With regards to the purpose of prophetic literature, the *Catechism* further states, "The people needed education and faith and conversion of heart; this was the mission of the prophets, before and after the Exile" (CCC 2581). How Ezekiel and Jeremiah use the green grapes proverb is no exception, as they both were writing to a people facing exile and, notably, blaming their fathers for the dire predicament in which they found themselves. The dual nature of prophetic writings, moreover, means that there is often a penultimate fulfillment in the life of Israel, but the ultimate fulfillment in Christ. That is, the prophets were masters of stating the obvious, albeit poetically, in their condemnation of the sins of their generation. Nonetheless, they always reminded the people of God's covenant fidelity and mercy, the need for penance and conversion, and a hope-imbued message for a temporal and spiritual renewal.

---

114 See Mary Mills, "Isaiah" in *The Jerome Biblical Commentary for the Twenty-First Century*, 824–25.

Prophetic Writing and Historical Backdrop

Below is a chart and timeline of kings and events leading up to the fall of Jerusalem and the Babylonian deportation, as this helps to contextualize the events surrounding the use of the proverb. The kingdom split into two after the death of King Solomon, King David's son, in 930 BC. While most of the prophets were writing to the ten northern tribes of Israel who fell to the Assyrians in 722 BC, Jeremiah and Ezekiel wrote much later to the southern tribes (of Judah and Benjamin) and the inhabitants of Jerusalem. The following is a list of the kings of Judah in the roughly four generations leading up to the fall of Jerusalem and the Southern Kingdom of Judah to the Babylonians in 586 BC:[115]

Name	Dates	Notes
Manasseh	696–642	Perhaps the most wicked kings of Judah; sacrificed his own sons to pagan idols (1 Kgs 21:1–9; 2 Chr 33:1–10)
Amon	642–640	Continued the idolatry of his father; assassinated by conspirators (2 Kgs 21:20–22; 2 Chr 33:22)

[115] Adapted from Hahn, ed., *Catholic Bible Dictionary*, 983.

<table>
<tr><td rowspan="3">Josiah</td><td>640–609</td><td rowspan="3">One of Judah's noblest of kings; reformer, repairing and purging the temple of idolatry, rediscovered the book of the Law which had been lost (2 Kgs 22:3–7); renewed covenant and feasts</td></tr>
<tr><td>627
Jeremiah called to be a prophet (Jer 1:2, 4)</td></tr>
<tr><td></td></tr>
<tr><td>Jehoahaz</td><td>609</td><td>Ruled for only three months, deposed by Pharaoh Neco; died in captivity (2 Kgs 23:30–35)</td></tr>
<tr><td rowspan="3">Jehoiakim</td><td>609–598</td><td rowspan="3">Mutual dislike with Jeremiah who foretold of Jerusalem's fall (Jer 22:13–19); ripped Baruch's letters containing Jeremiah's prophesies from the scroll (Jer 26:1–27, 23–24)</td></tr>
<tr><td>593
Ezekiel called to be a prophet, receives first vision (Ez 1:4; 3:15)</td></tr>
<tr><td></td></tr>
<tr><td>Jehoiakin</td><td>598–597</td><td>Deported along with his family by Nebuchadnezzar (2 Kgs 24:6–16; Jer 22:24–30)</td></tr>
<tr><td>Zedekiah</td><td>597–586</td><td>Led a rebellion against Babylon, against the advice of Jeremiah; blinded and taken into exile (2 Kgs 25:4–7; Jer 39:4–6, 52:2–30)</td></tr>
</table>

A brief timeline of the kings of the Southern Kingdom Judah is as follows. I begin with the wicked king Manasseh, who reigned in Judah after the rule of the reformer King Hezekiah because this frames the green grapes proverb within the "to the third and fourth generation" of *avon avot* with the generation of Jerusalem inhabitants who were taken into exile. Manasseh was perhaps the most wicked king of Judah, committing full apostasy of idol worship, even sacrificing his own sons to pagan idols (1 Kgs 21:1–9; 2 Chr 33:1–10). His rule began in 696 BC and lasted until approximately 642 BC, and was followed by another wicked king, Amon (642–640 BC), who continued in his father's pagan footsteps. Then came Josiah, a righteous king who ruled from 640–609 BC. He rediscovered the Law (probably the book of Deuteronomy), which had been lost, and instituted many liturgical and social reforms, to include destroying the idols that had been set up in the temple and leading the people in renewing the Covenant (reminding them of the curses for infidelity as recounted in Leviticus). His reforms did not last long, however, and the leader and people fell into idolatry again. The remaining period of approximately twenty years before the fall of Jerusalem in 586 BC was one of socio-political upheaval until the inevitable arrived in the form of a Babylonian army. Jeremiah received his call during the reign of Josiah and watched the good reforms be undone by Josiah's sons. Ezekiel received his call nearly twenty years after the death of the good king Josiah. Scripture is silent on when he was born, but he likely only heard the final death rattle of the Southern Kingdom as they lapsed from Josiah's restoration and renewed adherence to the Law.

The people of Judah and the inhabitants of Jerusalem faced a decade-long threat and attack and pillaging from 597–586 BC until a long siege (historians say it lasted from one to three years) where over four thousand inhabitants died before the city, and kingdom, fell. As Isaiah recounts, the last king of Judah (Zedekiah) was taken away into Babylonian captivity and the line of Davidic kings was cut off. The people of Jerusalem watched as their king was blinded and led off in chains, knowing they would soon follow him into slavery and exile. The last thing Zedekiah physically saw before being blinded was his sons being killed to ensure no successor to the kingdom. Accordingly, the green grapes proverb was a claim of innocence by those living at the time under such woes.

What brought this about? Elsewhere God promises to punish the sins of Manasseh, who "did evil in the sight of the LORD" (2 Kgs 21:16). God speaks through Jeremiah that, "I will make them an object of horror to all the kingdoms of the earth, because of what Manasseh, son of Hezekiah, king of Judah, did in Jerusalem" (Jer 15:4). What did Manasseh do? In the historical texts of Second Kings (which a tradition holds was written by Jeremiah), we read:

> The king defiled the high places east of Jerusalem, south of the Mount of Misconduct, which Solomon, king of Israel, had built in honor of Astarte, the Sedonian horror of Chemosh, the Moabite horror, and of Milcom [Molech], the idol of the Ammonites. (2 Kgs 23:13)

Those three characters—Astarte, Chemosh, and Molech—were pagan deities of the surrounding Gentile nations who were worshipped through ritual prostitution in groves, lustful orgies, and child sacrifice, respectively. Broadly speaking, one was invoked for fertility, one for military success, and one to appease through human sacrifice. These three deities (among others) kept resurfacing in the life of Israel, invoking God's wrath. Jeremiah makes earlier mention of the familial nature of these things. Namely, it was King Solomon, King David's heir, who first introduced the cultic worship to these same three demons brought in by his foreign wives. There, the reader is told that his wives had "turned his heart to strange gods" and named these as "Astarte, the goddess of Sidonians, Milcom, the idol of the Ammonites . . . [and] Chemosh, the idol of Moab" (1 Kgs 11:4–8). Jeremiah continues:

> Yet, because of all the provocations that Manasseh had given, the LORD did not desist from his fiercely burning anger against Judah. The LORD said: "Even Judah will I put out of my sight as I did Israel. I will reject the city, Jerusalem, which I chose, and the temple of which I said, "There shall my name be." (2 Kgs 23:26–27)

One hundred years elapsed before this happened.

The prophet Jeremiah, whose name means "the Lord will restore," was born near Jerusalem around 650 BC, and for a brief period, the prophet enthusiastically witnessed the abolition of idol worship as part of the temple reforms under the pious king Josiah (who reigned from 640–609 BC).[116] He wrote while Jerusalem was under siege. Ezekiel, whose name means "God makes strong," was a contemporary of Jeremiah and was born around 623 BC.[117] He wrote from exile in Babylon to a people in exile who were searching for meaning as to why God had seemingly abandoned them. They both witnessed the last four kings of Judah, each of whom who did evil in God's sight, just like Manasseh.

Elsewhere (2 Kgs 22–23), Jeremiah gives a detailed account of the depth of idolatry at the time of Manasseh, Josiah's apostate predecessor, as well as the latter's discovery of the Law and subsequent reforms. As to King Josiah's brief, but righteous, rule amidst a line of wicked rulers, Jeremiah

[116] Hahn, ed., *Catholic Bible Dictionary*, 422.
[117] Hahn, *Catholic Bible Dictionary*, 271.

states: "Before him there had been no king who turned to the LORD as he did, with his whole heart, his whole soul, and his whole strength, in accord with the entire law of Moses; nor could any after him, compare with him" (2 Kgs 23:25). This affirmation of Josiah's righteousness echoes the great commandment heard in the Shema Yishrael ("Hear, O Israel") given by Moses after the giving of the Law in Deuteronomy: "Therefore, you shall love the LORD, your God, with all your heart, and with all your soul, and with all your strength" (Dt 6:5). When Josiah died in battle in 609 BC, however, the seduction of idolatry brought a quick return to false worship. As the king goes, so the people.

Jehoahaz was then made king but reigned for only three months before being deposed and taken to Egypt (2 Kgs 23:31–34). Jehoiakim then ruled until his death in 597 BC. The last king of Judah, Zedekiah, reigned until the fall of Judah and the Babylonian deportation in 597–586 BC. Roughly eighty years passed from the time that Manasseh committed idol worship in Jerusalem and the current generation and over one hundred years from the beginning of his rule to the destruction of Jerusalem. The elapse of one hundred and ten years between the beginning of Manasseh and the fall of Judah under Zedekiah, moreover, is significant. With a generation generally considered to be twenty-five to thirty years, the two prophets now find themselves in the fourth generation since the great apostasy of Manasseh.

Jeremiah wrote while their city was under attack and facing exile and slavery, while Ezekiel wrote to a people already in exile. Struggling to understand their calamity, the people claimed not only innocence but also that God is either disinterested in their fate or unjust in His punishment. Thus, the people inhabiting Judah at the time of the prophets pointed to the sins of Manasseh (and his successors) as the green grapes which are putting the teeth of the children of this generation on edge.

Ezekiel and Green Grapes

Ezekiel is writing not just prophecy but also a prophetic judgment against Israel. The proverb of green grapes is likely an allusion to Exodus 20:5 and Deuteronomy 5:9 and *avon avot* as an explanation of their current woes. According to Paul Joyce, "the book of Ezekiel wrestles with the trauma of defeat and exile by the Babylonians, articulating the meaning of the disaster and announcing also a new beginning."[118] Seeking to explain their defeat and exile, therefore, is "the essential key to understanding Ezekiel and his tradition."[119] Accordingly, to read this section as solely a treatise on personal responsibility, moreover, is oversimplistic and misses the point. "Ezekiel's overriding concern," asserts Joyce, "is consistently to explain a disaster that is national."[120] As they struggled with grasping why God could allow Jerusalem to be captured and His covenant people fall into the enemy's cruel hands, they directed the blame at their fathers. To that end, Ezekiel echoes the words of his fellow exiles: "Yet the house of Israel says, 'The LORD's way is not fair!' Is it my way that is not fair, house of Israel, or rather, is it not your ways are not fair . . . ?" (Ez 18:29). The green grapes proverb, moreover, addresses the fairness of God. That is, Ezekiel's treatment of it is a prophetic deep dive into the interplay between human and divine justice.

---

[118] Joyce, "Ezekiel," in *The Jerome Biblical Commentary for the Twenty-First Century*, 972.

[119] Joyce, "Ezekiel," in *The Jerome Biblical Commentary for the Twenty-First Century*, 973.

[120] Joyce, "Ezekiel," in *The Jerome Biblical Commentary for the Twenty-First Century*, 973.

In effect, the popular proverb was not only a claim by the people in exile that God's ways are unjust but that the people are, in fact, innocent of any guilt. Father Michael Leahy asserts that "this teaching on personal responsibility and divine mercy was particularly necessary when overemphasis on national responsibility and divine justice led to despair." Thus, the proverb itself "attributes injustice to Yahweh and claims innocence for the speakers."[121] According to Joyce, however, the opposite is true: "Chapter 18 is devoted to making it clear that the present generation is punished for its own sins and not for those of previous generations."[122] The same could be said today, moreover, of those who overemphasize the sins of ancestors over their own sinful behavior and hope in the mercy of God. Accordingly, Ezekiel unpacks the proverb to show the interplay between individual and national responsibility. He also sees within it a call for repentance and a promise of return from exile.

Is this generation of Judahites as innocent as they claim to be? That is, are they in exile because of the sins of their fathers since they themselves are righteous? If so, then perhaps their appeal to personal responsibility would be valid and God is being either unjust or indifferent in the face of their suffering. Leading up to this treatment of the green grapes proverb, however, Ezekiel details the hidden idol worship, notably of *this* generation, which he calls the "abominable evils" of idol worship of "all kinds of creeping things and loathsome beasts" which had been taking place (Ez 8:8–10). God sees the wicked things they do in secret and is deeply offended: "Do you see the great abominations that the house of Israel is practicing here, so that I must depart from my sanctuary? But you

---

[121] Leahy, *Catholic Commentary on Holy Scripture*, 610.

[122] Joyce, "Ezekiel," in *The Jerome Biblical Commentary for the Twenty-First Century*, 974.

shall see greater abominations!" (Ez 8:6). He then describes the increasingly graver acts of false worship in the temple, secret offerings of incense to idols (Ez 8:11–12), a fertility ritual to the Babylonian god Tammuz where women ceremonially weep and wail (Ez 8:14), and finally the inner court of the sanctuary itself "where about twenty-five men with their backs to the LORD's temple and their faces towards the east . . . were bowing down to the sun" (Ez 8:16). Mention of an Egyptian god (Re was their god of creation) recalls the idolatry of the first generation in the desert.[123] That they "turned their backs to the LORD's temple" and "put a branch to my nose" (Ez 8:17) evokes a sure punishment: "Therefore, I will act furiously: I will not look upon them with pity nor will I show mercy" (Ez 8:18). Idol worship has its own built-in punishment, and Ezekiel witnesses God's presence departing from the temple in Jerusalem (Ez 8:18). That a "curse" is the privation of the provision and protection of blessing is seen in the result: God will "inflict punishments upon you" to included being despoiled, handed over "to foreigners" and to the gods they worshipped (Ez 11:9).

The purpose of the section of Ezekiel where he cites the green grapes proverb, moreover, is not to argue for individual responsibility and thereby acquit the present generation from culpability. On the contrary, as Joyce notes, "the purpose . . . is to demonstrate the collective responsibility of the contemporary house of Israel for the national disaster of defeat and deportation." That is to say, Ezekiel is seeking "to convey the true meaning of historical events that inevitably affected the nation as a whole."[124] The prophet affirms that in His perfect

---

[123] "Re" in Karel van der Toorn, et al., eds, *Dictionary of Deities and Demons in the Bible*, 689.

[124] Joyce, "Ezekiel," in *The Jerome Biblical Commentary for the Twenty-First Century*, 988.

justice, God does, in fact, "inflict punishment" for sins. To this end, as Joyce also notes:

> There has been a long tradition of interpretation that has insisted that Ezekiel emphasizes individual responsibility, that is, the moral independence of contemporary individuals. However, this must be contested, particularly on the grounds that Ezekiel's overriding concern is consistently to explain a disaster that is national. It is important to distinguish the issue of individual responsibility from the question of the moral independence of generations. Consideration of the nature of Israel's responsibility as presented in Ezekiel has focused, especially, on chapters 9, 14, and 18. The expression of this responsibility is throughout a good deal less individualistic than has often been suggested. Moreover, the overwhelmingly corporate nature of these chapters dealing with judgment, is echoed in the hopeful material in the book, where renewal is consistently presented as the experience of the people of God.[125]

I agree with Joyce, who concludes that, admittedly, "this may seem a problematic message to many modern readers" who are uncomfortable with the idea that "Israel's God manipulates world events and uses war as an instrument to punish sin."[126] He concludes that the prophet takes up the proverb, therefore, "for precisely the purpose of making it known that this generation is being punished for its own sins, not only their fathers."[127] That is, neither they nor their fathers are innocent, as they have continued their fathers' sin.

When you drive Yahweh-Shalom ("the Lord is Peace," another title of God found in Judges 6:24) from the temple and replace Him with the demon-god of war, should you

---

[125] Joyce, "Ezekiel," in *The Jerome Biblical Commentary for the Twenty-First Century*, 975.

[126] Joyce, "Ezekiel," in *The Jerome Biblical Commentary for the Twenty-First Century*, 974. Father Ripperger explains from the writings of the saints on why demons are allowed to attack. See Ripperger, *Dominion*, 212–17.

[127] Joyce, "Ezekiel," in *The Jerome Biblical Commentary for the Twenty-First Century*, 988.

expect anything but peace's absence, which is war? When you perform ritual prostitution to the demon-god of fertility, do you not think the Jealous One, the divine Bridegroom, will take note and let you live in the barrenness of His absence? Ezekiel is not exonerating the people—he is pronouncing divine judgment upon them.

To do this, the prophet invokes the priestly language of legal courts and uses the analogy of three generations (Ez 17:5–17), paralleling the three-generation prescription of *avon avot*. The three examples are presented as if in a legal proceeding, filled with legal language, and with a judgment of either guilty or not guilty pending. Each of the three are test cases which he will examine by the objective standard of righteous living of the Law, and righteousness as the measuring rod. The prophet begins with: "If a man is righteous and does what is lawful and right . . ." (Ez 18:5). He then lists the righteous deeds to include religious/cultic purity, sexual purity, and communal purity—justice towards one's neighbor, acts of charity, and love of neighbor as evidence of righteousness. Thus, he fulfills his obligations towards the first commandment with social law given by Moses. "Such a one," the prophet declares, "is righteous; he shall surely live, says the LORD God" (Ez 18:9).[128] The unrighteous man, however, who "practiced all these abominations . . . will surely die; his death will be his own fault" (Ez 18:13). That Ezekiel repeats the Hebrew word for "person" or "life" four times in 18:4 in combination with "only the one who sins shall die!"

[128] This verse continues: "If he does not eat upon the mountains or lift up his eyes to the idols of the house of Israel, does not defile his neighbor's wife or approach a woman during her menstrual period, does not oppress anyone, but restores to the debtor his pledge, commits no robbery, gives his bread to the hungry and covers the naked with a garment, does not take advance or accrued interest, withholds his hand from iniquity, executes true justice between contending parties, follows my statutes, and is careful to observe my ordinances, acting faithfully."

means, for Joyce, that the prophet is citing "the legal principle." Namely, "that it is the person who is guilty, and not another, who should be punished (cf. Dt 24:16)" which is "the working basis of criminal law in Israel from early times." Therefore,

> in what follows, this legal principal (properly described as that of "individual responsibility") is reapplied to discussion of the national crisis of exile. In verses 5–18, three cases are presented, those of a righteous man, his wicked son, and his righteous grandson. Behaviors define three combinations of positive and negative statements, covering both cultic and ethical conduct. Each test case concludes with a verdict, reached on the basis of the principle annunciated in verse four: "that man is just—he shall surely live (v.9) . . . [or] Because he practiced all these abominations he shall surely be put to death (v. 13)."[129]

While alluding to the civil/criminal law given by Moses, Ezekiel also echoes the words of Moses as prophetic judgment: "I have set before you, life and death, the blessing, and the curse. Choose life, then, that you and your descendants may live" (Dt 30:19).

The three test cases represent three generations of inhabitants of Jerusalem. Each "man" on trial is symbolic of a generation of the inhabitants of Jerusalem. That generation's deeds are judged as emblematic of fidelity or infidelity to the Law (cultic and criminal), which will determine life (blessing) or death (curse). To show that, Ezekiel rejects the claim that this generation is innocent, and therefore God is unjust, and draws an analogy with three generations of a family, showing that each generation is judged independently.

---

[129] Joyce, "Ezekiel," in *The Jerome Biblical Commentary for the Twenty-First Century*, 988.

Early on, he also uses familial imagery—namely, mothers and fathers. For Ezekiel, the nation's past reveals the present generation's inclination to repeat the sins of both their mothers and their fathers, whom this generation now blames for their plight. The prophet first evokes Sinai and the nuptial imagery of Israel as bride. In a chapter previous to the green grapes proverb, Ezekiel cites another proverb: "See, everyone who is fond of proverbs will say of you, 'Like mother, like daughter'" (Ez 16:44). Jerusalem is the mother, and the current generation is the daughter, while both Sodom and Samaria are their "sisters" (Ez 16:46–47)—the former was destroyed and the latter conquered and exiled by the Assyrians.[130] This generation of Jerusalem's inhabitants is the "daughter" who will suffer the same fate as her "sisters." In fact, Ezekiel tells them, not only are they not innocent, but their hated evil "sister" to the north, Samaria, "did not commit half your sins!" (Ez 16:51).

To show how wicked this people are, Ezekiel evokes the language of harlotry for covenant infidelity and the image of the "Jealous One" of Sinai and the divine Bridegroom motif. The measuring stick of righteous living of the Law becomes the rule by which they are judged. This section before the green grapes proverb also contains the parable of the faithless spouse, and the "harlotry" of immolating children and ritualistic sex (Ez 16:20–25; 35–40). They are like their mothers in their harlotry, who "poured out your lust and revealed your nakedness and harlotry with your lovers and abominable idols" (Ez 16:35). Here Ezekiel makes the connection between the nuptial imagery, Israel as bride, and the Jealous One quite clear:

[130] Psalm 87:4–6 shows how Jerusalem was as if a mother to the nations, and the Law as nurturing and maternal.

> Therefore, harlot, hear the word of the LORD! Thus says the LORD God: Because you poured out your lust and revealed your nakedness in your harlotry with your lovers and abominable idols, and because you sacrificed the life-blood of your children to them, I will now gather together all your lovers whom you tried to please, whether you loved them or loved them not; I will gather them against you from all sides and expose you naked for them to see. I will inflict on you the sentence of adulteresses and murderesses; I will wreak fury and jealousy upon you. I will hand you over to them to tear down your platform and demolish your dais; they shall strip you of your garments and take away your splendid ornaments, leaving you stark naked. They shall lead an assembly against you to stone you and hack you with their swords. They shall burn your apartments with fire and inflict punishments on you while many women look on. Thus I will put an end to your harlotry, and you shall never again give payment. When I have wreaked my fury upon you I will cease to be jealous of you, I will be quiet and no longer vexed. (Ez 16: 35–42)

At the end of the scathing verdict, however, God leaves them with a message of hope not because of them but because of His faithfulness and mercy (*hesed*):

> For thus speaks the LORD God: I will deal with you according to what you have done, you who despised your oath, breaking a covenant. Yet I will remember the covenant I made with you when you were a girl, and I will set up an everlasting covenant with you. Then you shall remember your conduct and be ashamed . . . that you may be utterly silenced for shame when I pardon you for all you have done, says the LORD God. (Ez 16:59–61, 63)

Here we see, in the wildly poetic imagery of prophetic and crisis literature, what it looks like when a Warrior becomes Jealous.

For Ezekiel, the use of gender and nuptial imagery in the negative, however, goes both ways. In the section after the green grapes proverb, Ezekiel reminds them that it is not just their mothers that they emulate but also their fathers, who likewise "defiled" themselves with idols. This generation of inhabitants imitates their fathers who had also committed the "lust" of idolatry. "Therefore, say to the house of Israel," God speaks through the prophet, "will you defile yourselves like your fathers? Will you lust after their detestable idols? (Ez 20:30). What did this "lust" look like? He reminds this generation—namely, his listeners and fellow exiles—that "by offering your gifts, by making your children pass through the fire, you defile yourselves with all your idols even to this day" (Ez 20:31). This generation of fathers is like their ancestor Manasseh. Rather than seeking the Lord and providing for and protecting their children, they instead offered them in human sacrifice to appease the gods of the nations. Should they not expect to now live under the cruel dominion of the gods with whom they defiled themselves? Should they not expect the fires they burned for the purpose of immolation of human sacrifice (of their own children, no less) not now burn in their streets as Jerusalem is under siege? The punishment fits the crime. Curse fills the void of blessing.

The nuptial imagery and covenant infidelity frames and contextualizes the green grapes proverb. Consequently, as Joyce explains, "the prophet here addresses an audience that is blaming the sins of previous generations for the disaster of exile. Ezekiel rejects the proverb, and with it, his audience's denial of responsibility for their fate (vv.1–4)." According to Joyce:

> The first two cases established a precedent for the third case, that of the righteous son of a wicked man (vv. 14–17), which

> is crucial, because Ezekiel listeners imagine themselves to be the righteous descendants of wicked ancestors. Although a single person is considered in each of the three cases, the proverb blames the sins of previous generations for the sufferings of the present, and accordingly the individuals of the test case each represent a generation.[131]

While they see themselves as the victims of wicked ancestors and claim to be the righteous grandson deserving to live, they are, in fact, the wicked son of wicked parents. The righteous grandson will be the generation borne in exile who will repent and return to true worship.

To that generation—their children who will be born in exile—is the promise of restoration, penultimately realized in the life of Israel when the pagan King Cyrus will free them from slavery (cf. Is 44:28), whom God called "my anointed/ messiah" (Is 45:1). Ultimately, however, God will liberate all humanity, likewise sinful and adulterous in conduct, in the messianic age when Christ, the true Messiah, comes (cf. Is 54:5–8). On the interconnectedness of family and personal guilt, Joyce's explanation bears repeating at length:

> When the legal principal of verse 4 is applied to the case of the righteous son of a wicked man, it is clear that the verdict must be: "He shall surely live!" (v. 17). Ezekiel is asserting that if members of the present generation were righteous, they would not be suffering; since they are suffering, this must be because of their own sins. Ezekiel's audience is even pictured (v. 19) as demanding that "the son" (with whom they identify themselves) *should* suffer for the iniquity of "his father." This is because they have a vested interest in the "sour grapes" proverbs; unless it can be established that one generation suffers for the sins of previous generations,

[131] Joyce, "Ezekiel," in *The Jerome Biblical Commentary for the Twenty-First Century,* 988–89.

> they will have to admit that they are to blame for the current situation. Ezekiel takes for granted the legal principle of "individual responsibility," but the possibility of the Lord judging individuals in isolation from their contemporaries is nowhere in view.[132]

In their search for understanding their current situation of woe, therefore, the people failed to distinguish between the promises of the Law which goes back to Sinai whereby evil is passed down hereditarily (the effect of the sin, not the punishment itself) and the law of personal responsibility. This means, moreover, that while their actions can appropriate the sins of their fathers, they cannot blame their fathers. This is echoed in the final section of the chapter in Ezekiel, which explores the theme of repentance. The prophet argues, again by analogy with particular cases, that God always wants people to repent (18:21–32).

Ezekiel concludes the trial with a case summary: "Only the one who sins shall die. The son shall not be destroyed with the guilt of his father, nor shall the father be charged with the guilt of his son. The virtuous man's virtue shall be his own, and the wicked man's wickedness shall be his own" (Ez 18:20). Personal responsibility for sins remains, and yet the next generation (the righteous "grandson") will bear the cross of exile and their penance and righteous return to the Law will restore peace and freedom. The people in exile were searching for meaning as to why God's promises had seemingly failed, and they were being taken into exile. "It is our fathers' fault," they in effect claimed, "and we suffer because of them." To wit, "the house of Israel says, The LORD's ways are not fair!" (Ez 18:29). No, God says through the prophet, you are going into exile because you also sinned, just like your

[132] Joyce, "Ezekiel," in *The Jerome Biblical Commentary for the Twenty-First Century*, 989.

fathers. The prophets, however, always leave a message of hope in God who always calls His wayward bride to return, just as He always calls us to repentance: "Turn and be converted from all your crimes, that they may be no cause of guilt for you. Cast away from you all the crimes you have committed and make for yourselves a new heart and a new spirit . . . Return and live!" (Ez 18:30–32).

Jeremiah and Green Grapes

Ezekiel's older contemporary, Jeremiah, similarly contextualizes the proverb by reminding the people of their covenant and the blessings which come with fidelity and woes (curses) which follow infidelity:

> Thus says the LORD, the God of Israel: Cursed be the man who does not observe the terms of this covenant, which I enjoined upon your fathers the day I brought them up out of the land of Egypt, that iron foundry, saying: Listen to my voice and do all that I command you. Then you shall be my people, and I will be your God. Thus, I will fulfill the oath which I swore to your fathers, to give them a land flowing with milk and honey; the one you have today. (Jer 11:3–5)

Jeremiah then denounces, as did Ezekiel, the generation "who did not listen or give ear" and failed to observe the precepts of the covenant (Jer 11:8). Was it only Manasseh and the generations after him who also ate the green grapes of disobedience and showed that they "hated" God by their idolatry? Jeremiah tells the people that this present people, that is,

> the men of Judah and the citizens of Jerusalem . . . have returned to the crimes of their forefathers, who refused to obey my words. They also have followed and served strange gods; the covenant which I had made with their fathers, the

> house of Israel and the house of Judah have broken. (Jer 11:10)

This is the reason for their "misfortune" which "they cannot escape" (Jer 11:11). Only then, in their distress and living under the effects of the lack of covenant blessing will they seek His help, but "though they will cry to me, I will not listen" (Jer 11:11). God has allowed them to live with their decision to follow strange gods and invites them to "cry out to the gods to which they have been offering incense." These false gods, however, "will give them no help whatever when misfortune strikes" (Jer 11:12). Where Ezekiel uses the "like mother like daughter" to condemn this generation, Jeremiah calls out guilt of the Queen Mother and her son, King Jehoiacin/Jeconiah (see also Jer 29:2). Thus, "Say to the king and to the queen mother: come down from your throne; from your heads fall your magnificent crowns" (Jer 13:18). Jeremiah voices a confession of guilt of this generation as well as their fathers: "We recognize, O LORD, our wickedness, the guilt of our fathers; that we have sinned against you" (Jer 14:20). He then appeals for mercy by recalling God's promise of *hesed:* "For your name's sake, spurn us not . . . remember your covenant with us, and break it not" (Jer 14:21). Accordingly, if the children's teeth are set on edge, it is because they and their fathers alike have eaten the sour grapes.

Jeremiah then cites a version of the same proverb as Ezekiel. Of significance is that Jeremiah briefly states the proverbs within what is often referred to as "the book of consolation" because of its hope-filled language of restoration: "At that time, says the LORD, I will be the God of all the tribes of Israel, and they shall be my people" (Jer 31:1). He evokes the language of the Exodus and the nuptial language of the giving of the Law at Sinai, they "have found favor in the desert"

(Jer 31:2:). The divine Lover is faithful and reminds "O virgin Israel" (Jer 31:4) that "with an age-old love, I have loved you; so I have kept my mercy (*hesed*) toward you" (Jer 31:3), for they will "make merry" (Jer 31:4) as when He led them from Egypt. In that nuptial context of the Old Covenant, Jeremiah gives promise of a New: "The days are coming, says the LORD, when I will make a new covenant with the house of Israel and the house of Judah" (Jer 31:31). In between these two promises, Jeremiah cites the green grapes proverb. His version:

> In those days they shall no longer say, "The fathers ate unripe grapes, and the children's teeth are set on edge," but through his own fault only shall anyone die: the teeth of him who eats unripe grapes shall be set on edge. (Jer 31:29–30)

With regard to the proverb, Father C. Lattey asserts that, like Ezekiel, Jeremiah affirms that "the present generation of the Hebrews" was not "free from guilt." Rather, the responsibility of the individual will be the ultimate measure of God's treatment of him."[133] Jeremiah asserts as much as the Lord says to the fathers of this generation:

> Why should I pardon you these things? Your sons have forsaken me, they swear by gods that are not. I fed them, but they committed adultery; to the harlot's house they throng. Lustful stallions they are, each after another's wife. Shall I not punish them for these things? says the LORD. On a nation such as this shall I not take vengeance? (Jer 5:7–9)

In this condemnation, notably, the Lord evokes His ancient title, "the LORD, the God of Hosts" (Jer 5:14). We see here not only a condemnation of this generation who ratified the sins of their fathers through imitation but two sins which

[133] Lattey, "Jeremias" in *Catholic Commentary on Holy Scripture*, 584.

particularly provoke the anger of the Warrior God—idolatry and fornication. That a curse is a privation of the provision and protection of blessing is heard in God's words here through the prophet: "Your crimes have prevented these things [fruitful harvests and peace on their borders], your sins have turned back these blessings from you" (Jer 5:25). This generation, therefore, is not as innocent as they claim in invoking the green grapes proverb. In addition, their sins have evoked the withdrawal of blessing's effects.

Nonetheless, prophetic echoes of a universal blessing are heard in Jeremiah's promises. According to Benedetta Rossi, moreover, "this [the green grapes proverb] is the prelude for the new covenant," which is more evident in Jeremiah than Ezekiel.[134] Accordingly, Jeremiah cites the proverb within context of the promise of a future restoration of Jerusalem (penultimate) and suggesting a New Covenant (ultimate). This will be more clearly seen in Augustine below.

Immediately after his brief treatment of the green grapes proverb (Jer 31:29–30), Jeremiah echoes a promise of "a new heart and a new spirit" similar to Ezekiel, also in the same context of the green grapes proverb. He consoles the people with the hope and promise of a New Covenant (Jer 31:31–34):

> The days are coming, says the LORD, when I will make a new covenant with the house of Israel and the house of Judah. It will not be like the covenant I made with their fathers the day I took them by the hand to lead them forth from in the land of Egypt; for they broke my covenant and I had to show myself their master, says the LORD. But this is the covenant which I will make with the house of Israel after those days, says the LORD. I will place my law within them,

[134] Rossi, "Jeremiah" in *The Jerome Biblical Commentary for the Twenty-First Century*, 921.

> and write it upon their hearts; I will be their God, and they shall be my people. (Jer 31:31–33)

Where Ezekiel uses the nuptial metaphor in the negative, evoking the "harlotry" to explain their infidelity, Jeremiah also uses the betrothal language of Sinai. The Vulgate version includes the language of the harlotry motif of Ezekiel. Jeremiah's phrase "I had to show myself their master" in the Latin text reads "though I was her husband"—perhaps showing the double meaning of Lord as both master and husband. Thus, like Ezekiel, Jeremiah evokes the bridal imagery of the divine Bridegroom of Sinai the context of the proverb echoes the betrothal language of "the Jealous One" giving the Law (and *avon avot*) at Sinai. Immediately following this, and while the army of Babylon "was besieging Jerusalem" (Jer 32:2), King Zedekiah threw the prophet in prison, where he is told by God to buy a field (Jer 32:7) as a sign of hope for return.

Written at roughly the same time during exile as Ezekiel, moreover, the author of Lamentations (which is often attributed to Jeremiah, or within his tradition) confesses the communal guilt of the people: "Our fathers, who sinned, are no more; but we bear their guilt" (Lam 5:7). The sacred author then shows the interplay between the sins of the father and the appropriation of the sin, as the people confess: "The garland has fallen from our heads: woe to us, *for we have sinned!*" (Lam 5:16, emphasis mine). Thus, their fathers sinned, resulting in guilt, but they did not break the punishment by righteous living.

A similar statement is found in Baruch, who has traditionally been regarded as Jeremiah's secretary and is mentioned in Jeremiah 32:12–16 as having recorded the deed of purchase of a field. In that same chapter where Jeremiah mentions Baruch, Jeremiah makes another reference to *avon avot*.

While some modern interpreters quote the previous chapter in the green grapes proverb as nullifying the words of the Lord in Exodus 20:5, Jeremiah himself affirms the validity of *avon avot* as well as individual responsivity when he prays:

> Ah, LORD God, you have made heaven and earth by your great might, with your outstretched arm; nothing is impossible to you. You continue your kindness through a thousand generations; and you repay for the fathers' guilt, even into the lap of their sons who follow them. O God, great and mighty, whose name is LORD of hosts, great in council, mighty in deed, whose eyes are open to all the ways of men, giving to each according to his ways, according to the fruit of his deeds. (Jer 32:17–19)

Like the "wicked son" of Ezekiel's court case as indicating this generation, Jeremiah does not let his listeners blame their fathers, nor does he deny an inherited guilt. Here, he begins with the promise of God's mercy and covenant blessing to "the thousandth generation," but he limits the punishment for the fathers' sins from "the third and fourth generation" to the immediate generation—namely, "into the lap of their sons who follow them."

Like Ezekiel, Jeremiah is not nullifying the words of God at Sinai and using the green grapes proverb as a universal statement on individual responsibility. Rather, and significantly, he recalls the title of God as Lord of Hosts, the God of Armies, the God who battles with cosmic forces of evil on behalf of His people. He reminds the Lord of Hosts that He is also merciful; Jeremiah also calls upon the "loving kindness" of God, or the Hebrew *hesed*.

His approach differs from Ezekiel, who used poetic language and invoked the image of a legal court proceeding to describe this generation as the second of three case studies, to declare them guilty: "Because he [the wicked son = this generation] practiced all these abominations, he shall surely die; his death shall be his own fault" (Ez 18:10–13). Perhaps because Jerusalem was under siege at the time of his writing—"See, the siegeworks have arrived at this city to breach it; the city will be handed over to the Chaldeans who are attacking it" (Jer 32:24)—Jeremiah's treatment is less poetic and more direct than Ezekiel's. God will always honor His covenant, but it does not mean that there are no consequences when His people do not. They and their fathers have deeply offended God by their sinful actions and deserve punishment. Jeremiah, however, reminds us that God is just, even when He allows us to suffer the consequences for our sins. Accordingly, the prophet recalls the wondrous deeds God has done and continues to do for Israel, beginning with delivering them from slavery in Egypt: "You have wrought signs and wonders in the land of Egypt and to this day" (Jer 32:20). His wonders and mercy are present to each generation.

Therefore, Jeremiah reminds them, God has not abandoned Jerusalem. On the contrary, Jeremiah is saying that Jerusalem has abandoned God, and they now suffer the effects. He recounts for them why this is happening, stating that "the men of Judah and the citizens of Jerusalem"—all the inhabitants to include kings, princes, priests, and prophets—have "turned their backs to me, not their faces; though I kept teaching them, they would not listen to my correction" (Jer 32:33). Jeremiah reminds them, as did Ezekiel, that they are the unrighteous sons of unrighteous parents who committed the same evils as their ancestor Manasseh: "They defiled the house named after me by the hoard idols they set up in it. They built high places to Ba'al . . . and immolated their sons and daughters to Molech, bringing sin upon Judah" (Jer

32:35). They could have atoned for their fathers' sins by righteous living of the Law, like Josiah and that generation, but they did not.

As in times past, Jeremiah is saying this generation is no different than their ancient fathers who rebelled even when God had led them into the Promised Land. He shows that the rebellion of their fathers is their own rebellion, and He prayed: "They [the generation who were led by God into the Promised Land] entered into possession of it, but they did not listen to your voice; by your law they did not live, and what you commanded they failed to do. You let all these evils befall them" (Jer 32:23). *You let all these evils befall them.* As stated above, a curse is the inversion of a blessing, the deprivation of the protection that comes with blessing. God allows us to bear the consequences of our decisions and honors our free will.

One can imagine the intensity of this prayer as Jeremiah hears the enemy erecting siegeworks and has begun to take Jerusalem, months on end, recalling for them what God had promised would happen to this equally rebellious generation. They, not their fathers, burned incense to the gods of the Chaldeans, set up idols in the sanctuary, and committed the horror of human sacrifice of their own children (Jer 32:35–35). Jeremiah reminds this generation—who is claiming to have their "teeth set on edge" because of their fathers' and not their own wrongdoing—that the evil is again befalling them as a consequence for their own sins.

This is a good reminder for each of us that when evil besieges us, we must not look for causality outside of ourselves. In accepting no culpability for our "teeth on edge" is claiming ourselves innocent and God guilty when in reality we are no better than our fathers and show that by our own sins. We refer to this as "ratifying a curse." God is just in His punishment and always gives the next generation the chance to break the curse through righteous living and fidelity to His commandments. Thus, God tells Jeremiah that the attackers who besiege the city will capture it, "and set fire to it, burning it and its houses, on the roofs of which incense was burned to Baal and libations were poured out to strange gods as a provocation to me" (Jer 32:29). No, this generation cannot blame their fathers, for they are no better than them. The Jealous One has allowed His adulterous Bride to live with the effects of her sinfulness. The irony of the invader's burning Jerusalem is not lost on the astute reader: they immolated their children in human sacrifice to false gods; now it is their children who suffer the fires of war and invasion.

A Prayer of Supplication and Hope

Writing later from exile, Baruch holds the letter that Jeremiah wrote to those soon to be led away. In it, he pronounces the guilty verdict: "For the sins you committed before God, you are being led captive to Babylon by Nebuchadnezzar, king of the Babylonians" (Bar 6:1; Jer 19:10ff). Certainly, if God meant to nullify His words at Sinai on the effects of sins as visited upon their children, Baruch, who sat at the feet of the great prophet, would have echoed Jeremiah's green grapes proverb and declared them innocent. He would have reinforced personal responsibility, echoing the modernist claim that God has further revealed Himself, that any punishment for sin is anthropomorphic, and that *avon avot* and the penalty for sin was the literary device of hyperbole. But he does not. Instead, Baruch reads a prayer of a penitent people who do not blame their ancestors, but rather at long last acknowledge both the sins of their fathers as well as their own evils, echoing the words of his master Jeremiah:

Justice is with the LORD, our God; and we today are flushed with shame, we men of Judah and citizens of Jerusalem that we, with our kings and rulers and priests and prophets, and with our fathers, have sinned in the LORD'S sight and disobeyed him. We have neither heeded the voice of the LORD, our God, nor followed the precepts which the LORD set before us. From the time the LORD led our fathers out of the land of Egypt until the present day, we have been disobedient to the LORD, our God, and only too ready to disregard his voice. And the evils and the curse which the LORD enjoined upon Moses, his servant, at the time he led our fathers forth from the land of Egypt to give us the land flowing with milk and honey, cling to us even today.For we did not heed the voice of the LORD, our God, in all the words of the prophets whom he sent us, but each one of us went off after the devices of our own wicked hearts, served other gods, and did evil in the sight of the LORD, our God.

And the LORD fulfilled the warning he had uttered against us: against our judges, who governed Israel, against our kings and princes, and against the men of Israel and Judah. He brought down upon us evils so great that there has not been done anywhere under heaven what has been done in Jerusalem, as was written in the law of Moses that one after another of us should eat the flesh of his son or of his daughter. He has made us subject to all the kingdoms round about us, a reproach and a horror among all the nations round about to which the LORD has scattered us. We are brought low, not raised up, because we sinned against the LORD, our God, not heeding his voice. (Bar 1:15–2:4)

What is Baruch referring to with *Even today evils cling to us, the curse the Lord pronounced to Moses?* As they received the Law at Sinai and prepared to enter the Promised Land, God again spoke to them through Moses:

> I set before you here, this day, a blessing and a curse: a blessing for obeying the commandments of the LORD, your God, which I enjoined on you today; a curse, if you do not obey the commandments of the LORD, your God, but turn aside from the way I ordain for you today, to follow other gods, whom you have not known. (Dt 11:26–28)

Baruch then acknowledges before God in his prayer that, like those who rebelled in the desert at the time of Moses, "we did not heed your voice" (Bar 2:24). He does not blame their fathers or accuse God of being unjust; rather, he affirms that God is just in His actions, that even God's justice is merciful: "but with us, O LORD, our God, you have dealt in all your clemency, and in all your great mercy. This was your warning through your servant Moses, the day you ordered him to write down your law in the presence of the Israelites" (Bar 2:27–28). What was that warning? The words of *avon avot* and that "their children will suffer for the sins of their parents who hate me" (Ex 20:4; Dt 5:9) and follow false gods. When the children imitate their parents' sins, the situation is even more dire.

Interestingly, here, moreover, Baruch also recalls Leviticus 26 and the promises of blessing for covenant obedience and woes for disobedience. Specifically, Baruch recalls the final woe and "languishing" as part of the "sevenfold" punishment for sin that God gives through Moses, should Israel fall into hardness of heart:

> If, despite all this, you still persist in disobeying and defying me, I, also, will meet you with fiery defiance, and will chastise you with sevenfold fiercer punishment for your sins, till you begin to eat the flesh of your own sons and daughters. I will demolish your high places, overthrow your incense stands, and cast your corpses on those of your idols. In my abhorrence of you, I will lay waste your cities and devastate

> your sanctuaries, refusing to accept your sweet-smelling offerings. So devastated will I leave the land that your very enemies who come to live there will stand aghast at the side of it. You yourselves I will scatter among the nations at the point of my drawn sword, leaving your countryside desolate and your cities deserted. (Lv 26:27–33)

Baruch seems to affirm that the fiery siege of Jerusalem is a divine judgment against them.[135]

The Leviticus text referred to states that "those of you who survive in the lands of their enemies, will waste away [languish] *for their own and their father's guilt*" (Lv 26:39, emphasis mine), affirming *avon avot* and that future generation's complicity in their own demise. In this sense, then, we see how personal sins ratify, or appropriate, a curse which is experienced in the form of woes. That is, the privation of blessing that comes as the result of rejecting God means *avon avot* but also the selfsame hope for return.

There awaits a righteous generation to make reparation through penance so as to unlock the abundance of blessing. This can only be undone, however, through satisfaction for sin. Leviticus states a promise that the pathway to liberation is penance on our part and mercy (*hesed*) on His:

> Thus, they [that generation in exile] will have to confess that they and their fathers were guilty of having rebelled against me and of having defied me, so that I, too, had to defy them, and bring them into their enemy's land. Then, when their uncircumcised hearts are humbled and they make amends for their guilt, I will remember my covenant with Jacob, my covenant with Isaac, and my covenant with Abraham; and of the land, too, I will be mindful. But the land must first be rid

[135] Their fate is the same as the Mosaic law of punishment for the daughter of a high priest who commits adultery: capital punishment by fire (see Lv 21:9).

> of them, that, in its desolation it may make up its lost sabbaths, and that they, too, may make good the debt of their guilt for having spurned my precepts, and abhorred my statutes. (Lv 26:40–43)

"Making good the debt of their guilt" is echoed by the *Catechism* reminder that sin has a "double consequence" and temporal satisfaction even after the guilt of sin is removed (CCC 1472). While God's covenant fidelity will always remain, justice demands satisfaction for sin. Thus:

> Yet even so, even when they are in their enemies' land, I will not reject or spurn them, lest, by wiping them out, I make void my covenant with them; for I, the LORD, am their God. I will remember them because of the covenant I made with their forefathers, whom I brought out of the land of Egypt under the very eyes of the Gentiles, that I, the LORD, might be their God. (Lv 26:44–45)

With this backdrop, Baruch invokes the mercy and covenant fidelity (*hesed*) of God:

> LORD Almighty, God of Israel, afflicted souls and dismayed spirits call to you. Hear, O LORD, for you are a God of mercy; and have mercy on us, who have sinned against you: for you are enthroned forever, while we are perishing forever. LORD Almighty, God of Israel, hear the prayer of Israel's few, the sons of those who sinned against you; they did not heed the voice of the LORD, their God, and the evils cling to us. Remember at this time not the misdeeds of our fathers, but your own hand and name: for you are the LORD our God; and you, O LORD, we will praise. For this, you put into our hearts the fear of you: that we may call upon your name, and praise you in our captivity, when we have removed from our hearts all the wickedness of our fathers who sinned against you. Behold us today in our captivity, where you scattered us, a reproach, a curse, and a requital

> for all the misdeeds of our fathers, who withdrew from the LORD, our God. (Bar 3:1–8)

Certainly, if God were nullifying the punishment of the sins of the father in his children, then Jeremiah's scribe Baruch would have echoed that. Instead, he prays prayers of reparation for their fathers' sins and invokes the merciful kindness and covenant fidelity of God.

In addition, a psalm likely composed at this time also appeals to God's mercy and acknowledges that Jerusalem's present evils are the result of iniquities of previous generations: "Do not hold against us the sins of past generations; may your mercy come quickly to meet us, for we are in desperate need" (Ps 79:8 NIV). This verse has a variety of translations: sins of past generations (NIV), guilty deeds of our forefathers (NASB); iniquities of our forefathers (NAB); iniquities of our ancestors (NRSV); our lawless deeds of long ago (NETS). The Greek (Ps 78:8 LXX) uses the word *archaios* ("old, ancient, former"), which Saint Jerome translates literally in the Latin with *antiquus*. Both are vague in whether it is our iniquities or the iniquities of the ones before us. The meaning is open-ended: ours, mine, our ancestors/fathers. The root meaning of *antiquus* is "of old times, our antiquities/ancients" and, therefore "our ancestors," implying those who are centuries older. That is, the psalmist here evokes Israel in desert wanderings in antiquity. At the same time, however, he also recalls the sins of the fathers that led to the invasion of Babylon. That the psalmist uses the "our" also implies that we are no better than our ancestors, so now "we" suffer as well.

Significantly, this particular psalm is a communal lament probably written to describe the destruction of Jerusalem by Babylon in 586 BC, the time period that Jeremiah and Ezekiel were writing, evidenced by the opening verse: "O God, the nations have invaded your heritage; they have defiled your holy temple, have laid Jerusalem in ruin" (Ps 79:1).[136] The second verse is equally telling: "They have left the corpses of your servants as food for the birds of the heavens, the flesh of your faithful for the beast of the earth" (Ps 79:2). Of all the images the psalmist could have used to describe the aftermath of the fall of the great city—and there certainly would have been a variety of shocking images in the violent aftermath of such an invasion—he notes "birds of heaven" and "beasts of the earth" as devouring corpses.

The astute reader would hear the promises of the giving of the Law in Deuteronomy, specifically the blessings that come with covenant fidelity (Dt 28:1–14) and the curses of covenant infidelity (Dt 28:15–69). The latter would include sickness and defeat (Dt 28:20–29), despoilment (Dt 28:29–35), exile (Dt 28:36–37), fruitless labors (Dt 28:38–47), invasion and siege (Dt 28:49–56), plagues (Dt 28:58–62) and, ultimately, exile (Dt 28:63–69). Remember, a curse is the privation of the provision and protection that comes with blessing. This is not an anthropomorphic projection of human emotions or justice upon God, but rather stark language to describe the withdrawal of God's blessing.

God has endowed human beings with free will and He allows His people to suffer the consequences of their unfaithfulness and sinful behavior. God Himself uses language to describe what this privation of blessing looks like: "But if you do not harken to the voice of the LORD, your God, and are not careful to observe all his commandments, which I enjoy on you today, all these curses shall come upon you and overwhelm you" (Dt 28:15). One image He uses to describe the effect of the rejection of the Law and following false gods is stark (and is echoed in Psalm 79:2 lamenting Jerusalem's fall):

[136] T. E. Bird, "Psalms," in *Catholic Commentary on Holy Scripture*, 463.

"Your carcasses will become food for the birds of the air and for the beast of the field, with no one to frighten them off" (Dt 28:15, 26). This imagery connects the woes of this generation to the consequences of sin and rebellion and forsaking the covenant.

Jeremiah evokes this same image when he decries *this generation* of Jerusalem's inhabitants should they be unfaithful to the covenant and continue in their wickedness: "The corpses of this people will be food for the birds of the sky, and for the beast of the field, which no one will drive away" (Jer 7:33). This is the same generation who cited the green grapes to blame their fathers. What had these people done? "The children gather wood, their father's light the fire, and the women need dough to make cakes for the queen of heaven" (Jer 7:18), who is none other than the Babylonian fertility goddess, the demon Ishtar (Ashterah), the worship of which King Josiah had banished but his successors restored. They "defiled the house which bears my name by setting up in it their abominable idols" and also built altars "to immolate in fire their sons and their daughters" (Jer 7:30, 31). They abandoned the true God and followed false gods, their ritualistic and deviant sexual practices and their child sacrifices, which God Himself warned them of in the giving of the Law. He then reminds the people that their covenant infidelity is an act of defiance by invoking the nuptial language of the Jealous One, the divine Bridegroom who took Israel as if His bride at Sinai. As a result of their worship of false gods and these horrible practices, there will no longer be "the cry of gladness, the voice of the bridegroom and the voice of the bride; for the land will be turned to rubble" (Jer 7:34).

Here is reinforced that the poetic language of nuptiality best describes God's love for His people, and to offer worship to false gods means shedding off the blessing of covenant protection. Also, this reinforces that a curse is a privation, the lack of protection and provision that comes with blessing, something which carries its own temporal punishment, one which does affect subsequent generations, particularly those who commit the same sins of their fathers, but—notably—is staved off by righteous living (as seen in the righteous king Josiah in 2 Kings 23:4–1). True worship displaces false, as light displaces darkness.

Thus, by using the language of "birds of the air and beasts of the field" as devouring the slain corpses of Jerusalem, the psalmist is evoking the giving of the Law at Sinai to explain the reason for their demise—namely, infidelity to the covenant. The Gentiles have invaded Jerusalem and defiled the temple with their false gods. The people offer a communal lament, asking why, yet also appeal to God's mercy and forgiveness. The psalmist merely echoes here what Jeremiah and his scribe Baruch also said: our fathers—and we—have sinned. This is far from hyperbole; rather, this is a people repenting of their sins, casting off the yoke of idolatry, enduring the effects of both their own sins and those of their fathers, and appealing to the mercy of God. In shaking off the patina of blessing, what remains is a vulnerability to its privation. Once that patina is removed, God uses the demon as an instrument of punishment, as seen in the invasion by their enemies, whose gods they had come to worship.

By no means is this examination claiming that there is no personal responsibility for sins. That is, when a man dies, he is judged for his own sins and not those of his father. What the fall of Jerusalem shows, however, is the tendency to blame others for our own faults and the failure to take personal responsibility for our own sins. It also shows that when children imitate their father's sins, the situation is often worse (as Saint Thomas also notes). In a sense, a child who imitates his father's sins accelerates the woes. At the same time, the fall of Jerusalem also shows how the effects of one's father's sins can be felt in the next generation. The "righteous grandchildren" will be the ones to make satisfaction for the sins of their fathers. Their fathers were wicked, as were their grandfathers before them. While the present generation used the green grapes proverb to divert the blame to others, they themselves were being punished for their idolatry. The punishment fits the crime, so to speak, and they fall at the hands of the Babylonians, whose gods they worshiped. From God's perspective, He allows them to live by the free will choices: because you want to worship the gods of the Chaldeans, you can now live under their cruelty. You reject the God of freedom, then I will give you what you want—you will now live under the cruel slavery of the gods you have erstwhile appealed to in your apostasy.

Recall, moreover, the above discussion on how the *Catechism* asserts that original sin had both a familial and a communal effect. The punishment for the father's grave sins is penal to him, but the result of the lack of the protection of blessing, meaning the effects and not the sins themselves, can remain and have a medicinal effect. As Father Leahy writes concerning the green grapes parable, "God's mercy to the repentant sinner and the need of perseverance in the practice of justice complete the teaching. God is more pleased to pardon than to punish, but repentance is necessary for pardon, and no sinner is safe from chastisement."[137] Whether one lives a righteous life that breaks the curse or a sinful life that appropriates it is up to that person.

What is meant to be highlighted here is that sin does have a communal effect, which is often experienced as a temporal oppression by those under one's authority (whether familial

[137] Leahy, "Ezechiel" in *Catholic Commentary on Holy Scripture*, 610.

or communal). The abnegation of the green grapes proverb by the two prophets was not meant to nullify the reality of God's warning at Sinai but rather to declare guilty the current generation who claimed innocence. The threefold case study of Ezekiel should be a warning to all of us who blame others for our own problems. Curses are generally ratified by sinful behavior of the next generation and await the "righteous son" to live a life of purity to break the effects. This, in turn, brings in the promise of the blessings of God to those formerly hardened hearts who now turn to Him with all sincerity. Jeremiah speaks of the hope for the one who chooses to live righteously and atone for sins.

Summary: A Formula for Reparation and a Message of Hope

In the midst of darkness, there is hope. Writing to those in Babylonian exile, the prophet Isaiah gives a message of hope for return. A righteous king would come, "a shoot shall sprout from the stump of Jesse, and from his roots, a bud shall blossom. The spirit of the LORD shall rest upon him" (Is 11:1–2). The "shoot" shall rise up from the Davidic line (1 Chr 3:17) and be crowned king and restore Israel. The Persian King Cyrus conquered the Babylonians and in 538 BC, allowed for the repatriation of the deported exiles, even providing funding for the rebuilding of the Jerusalem temple.[138] The people were released from exile and soon began the arduous task of rebuilding the walls of Jerusalem and restoring the temple (Ezr 1:1–11; Hg 1:1–15). Included among the exiles was Zerubbabel, the grandson of King Jehoiakim, (Ezr 2:2; Zec 4:9; Hg 1:1), exciting the hopes of a return of the Davidic

[138] Hahn, ed., *Catholic Bible Dictionary*, 184–85.

monarchy and the fulfillment of Isaian prophecy of a "shoot" (see Zec 3:2).

Perhaps there is irony in the names of the two prophets. Ezekiel—"God makes strong"—reminds the people to be strong, courageous, and longsuffering in the face of trials and suffering. For in that, they will make satisfaction for their sins and the sins of their fathers. Jeremiah—"the Lord will restore"—reminds them of the promises of their divine Bridegroom and His covenant faithfulness. While using different styles, both point to the future hope of the New Covenant.

God's unfailing covenant fidelity (*hesed*) and mercy always leave hope for those who suffer, even when under the consequences of sins. Jeremiah dictates a letter to Baruch with a message from the Lord who offers a pathway out of their despair: "perhaps, when the house of Judah hears all the evil I have in mind to do to them, they will turn back from their evil way, so that I may forgive their wickedness and their sin" (Jer 36:3). This is not negating the very words of God in the Law regarding punishment for covenant infidelity; rather, it is addressing the situation in which Israel finds themselves. Namely, the previous generation (for Ezekiel, the "wicked father") whose infidelity had brought about slavery, has now passed and the present generation (the "wicked son") is lamenting as to why they are in slavery (that is, claiming as due to the sins of their parents). Embedded into the consoling promise of liberation is a reminder that each person is accountable for his own sin, something which should give hope to the next generation (the "righteous grandson"). *The Lord will restore*. That is, as God plans to liberate Israel from slavery and return them to their land, he reminds the next generation of the need for covenant fidelity and holiness. *God makes strong*. Satisfaction can be made by righteous descendants through penance and loving trust.

In the context of inherited guilt and *avon avot,* moreover, Father Ripperger points to a principle in canon law called *immemorial custom,* which teaches that "a custom becomes immemorial by virtue of the fact that it existed for a hundred years or more." That is, it becomes immemorial due to "the fact that the normal lifespan of a human being is about eighty years, and so one hundred years is outside the memory of any human being currently living." This principle gives insight into *avon avot.* As Father Ripperger writes:

> The reason God will allow the evil of the parents to affect the children for up to the third and fourth generations is because that is roughly the time of human memory, and so far as human beings can, generally speaking, find someone who is alive, who can remember back eighty years ago, but not a hundred years ago. In order to stop an evil or have knowledge about the source or cause of some type of evil, it is necessary to have someone alive, who can recount it, or have it transcribed into some type of monument. That being the case, God will allow the evil extended in the family lines for up to a hundred years, and then He normally brings to the surface, something which will force the remedy of it by the family.[139]

This is consistent with his years of experience as an exorcist and difficult cases where some investigation into family ancestry is required. "Normally," he states, "when one discovers possession in a case such as this, it will often be done around the eighty-to-hundred-year mark of the sin of the ancestor."[140] This parallels the same time frame from Manasseh to Zedekiah, the time frame in which the green grapes proverb was popularized.

---

[139] Ripperger, *Dominion,* 175–76.
[140] Ripperger, *Dominion,* 176.

While these prophecies evoke harsh language and even challenge the modern mind, let us recall also the words of the *Catechism* concerning the power of Satan as being limited. That is, while very powerful, the devil is yet "only a creature." In fact, all the devil's actions are "permitted by divine providence," and it is God who "with strength and gentleness, guides human, and cosmic history." Thus, "it is a great mystery that Providence should permit diabolical activity, but 'we know that and everything God works for good with those who love him'" (CCC 395). Thus, God allows the privation of blessing and honors our free will which, in turn, allows the devil to be His instrument of justice so that we can make satisfaction for sin. The enemy besieging Jerusalem at the time of Jeremiah is a type of evil that afflicts a soul.

Accordingly, Baruch offers hope to those who suffer: "My children, bear patiently the anger that has come from God upon you; your enemies have persecuted you, and you will soon see their destruction and trample upon their necks" (Bar 4:25). He calls those who suffer to have hope. His words then apply today to the "generation" called to make satisfaction to God. "Fear, not, my children; call out to God! He who brought this upon you will remember you. As your hearts have been disposed to stray from God, turn now ten times the more to seek him. For he who has brought disaster upon you will, in saving you, bring you back enduring joy" (Bar 4:27–29). The call to arms is the call to conversion. Satisfaction for sin brings the joy of reconciliation.

Nuria Calduch-Benages summarizes the theological message of Baruch: "remembrance of past sins; recognition of guilt; recalling of the punishments inflicted by God's justice; plea for, and hope in, the divine promises; the search for wisdom; and Jerusalem personified, which becomes the city of peace, joy, and justice."[141] The message of the prophet is still valid today, for we are Jerusalem. What applied to them is applicable today. The peace and joy that comes with justice (reconciliation with God) is the fruit of confession of sins, surrender to God's providence, enduring under suffering, and hope in His mercy.

Herein lies the solution to the generation that suffers for their own sins and the effects of the sins of their parents. Several key points emerge from the first two chapters of Baruch that have enduring value. The breaking of curses involves:

- liturgical prayers → "he read from the scrolls" (Bar 1:3)
- the entire household engages → the entire people are present, "the whole people, from the small to the great" (Bar 1:4)
- penance, repentance which include bodily mortification (not just a single prayer) → "they wept, fasted and prayed before the LORD," including alms (Bar 1:5, 6)
- confession of sins → "each of us went off after the devices of our own wicked hearts, served other gods, and did evil on the side of the LORD, our God" (Bar 1:22)
- the admission of guilt not just for ancestors and the need for satisfaction → "justice is with the LORD our God; and we today are flushed with shame" (Bar 1:15); "we have sinned against the LORD, our God, and the wrath and anger of the LORD have not yet been withdrawn from us to the present day" (Bar 1:13)
- prayers for deliverance → "Hear, O LORD, our prayer of supplication, and deliver us for your own sake; grant us favor in the presence of our captors, that the whole earth may know that you are the LORD, our God, and that Israel and his descendants bear your name." (Bar 2:17)

[141] Nuria Calduch-Benages, "Baruch," in *Catholic Commentary on Holy Scripture*, 954.

- the embracing of suffering in satisfaction for sin → "we call upon your name, and praise you in our captivity" (Bar 2:7)

Baruch's continuation of the message of Jeremiah (cf. Jer 29:1; Bar 1:1) and message of hope for those in exile offers insights into the pathway out of generational curses and offers a blueprint for breaking the effects of personal and familial sin.

God makes me strong. The Lord will restore.

An Example

A story from the field highlights how the two sins of idolatry and adultery/fornication still evoke divine judgment of the Lord of Hosts—as well as the power of blessing and the tropaion of the cross. A young man had continually shown up at the rectory of a country priest seeking help for diabolic affliction. Living in a hotel with his girlfriend, he would come almost daily to this particular parish, not knowing the country priest was also the diocesan exorcist. The exorcist arranged for the lay team members to do an intake and start the man on the protocol.

His parents accompanied him to the intake, during which time the man was fidgety and elusive. Before the meeting, he had gone into the parish bookstore and purchased a wooden cross with an image of Jesus carved on the front. The man was visibly nervous and elusive, at one moment demanding to be prayed over and at another saying he did not know why he was there. His father and mother were also nervous but sat silently praying. Noticing a large, ornate tribal tattoo on the man's left shoulder, the team leader asked him:

"What's that?"

"That's the symbol of the Aztec god of war. That's my Mexican heritage."

"I thought you were Catholic."

"I am. But I thought I was cool. But now when the demon manifests it starts burning, and the left side of my body paralyzes."

He then asked the man if there was ever a time when things changed and became different with regard to the demon that was afflicting him.

"No."

"It has nothing to do with the tattoo?"

"Nope. It's my heritage."

"So what did you do after you got the tattoo?"

The man changed his demeanor and admitted that not long after getting the tattoo, he went down to Mexico and hired a prostitute. After that, he said, things were different. He could no longer control what the demon was doing to him. Extending his left arm, revealing a long scar in the crook of his arm, and he says, "So, right after that, I tried to commit suicide."

"But there's no relation between the tat, the prostitute, and the demon?"

"Nope. I don't even know why I am here."

The man then took the unblessed wooden cross he had just purchased and placed it on the scar. "Look," he said, "if I were possessed, then I wouldn't be able to put this on my arm, and look, nothing."

"Is that cross blessed?

"No. Does that matter?"

"Yes, it makes a difference." The team leader then handed him a Saint Benedict crucifix blessed by the exorcist with the old ritual in Latin.

"Put this on there," he told the young man.

The man took the crucifix in his hand and said, "See, nothing." When he placed it on the spot where he had tried to commit suicide, however, the man's demeanor changed as the crucifix weighed heavily on his arm and began to burn.

"Get it off! Get it off! It's burning! It's burning me!" the man screamed.

The team leader grabbed the blessed crucifix and pulled it away. As if it had been heated up by a blowtorch, the crucifix left a fiery red burn mark in the perfect shape of a cross atop the spot of the scar of the suicide. At that, however, the demon immediately manifested, and the left side of the man's body became completely rigid. His entire body froze and began to shake. Tears slowly flowed down his cheeks.

The mother continued to silently pray the Rosary. The father, meanwhile, became visibly afraid. The team leader asked the father to pray for his son. Not knowing if he was in a state of grace, he told the father:

"Do not lay hands on him or bind the demon but repeat after me."

"Uh, ok."

"In the name of Jesus Christ . . ."

He prayed, "In the name of Jesus Christ . . ."

"And by the authority given to me by the promulgation of the natural law by God the Father, and as his father . . ."

The father repeated, "And by the authority given to me by the promulgation of the natural law by God the Father."

"And as his father . . ."

"And as his father . . ." he repeated, his hands shaking.

"I bless my son, in the name of the Father, and of the Son, and of the Holy Spirit."

Meanwhile, the young man was still frozen but shaking, his left side completely locked up. At those words, however, the father's fear left him, and his love for his son emerged as he gave his son a genuine, heartfelt blessing. At the exact moment when the father blessed his son with the words, "I bless my son, in the name of the Father, and of the Son, and of the Holy Spirit," and to the father's surprise, the manifestation immediately stopped.

The father and son both indicated that he would be going back to Mass, as they both had been away from the Church for many years.

The Hope

Here we see how the demon lures us into sin and drives us to self-destructive behaviors when we drift from friendship with God, live a life of rebellion, and cast off the protection of the state of grace. When a father does not bless his children, and even worse, when a father falls away from the faith, he places his family in a vulnerable position. Where the light is lacking, darkness sets in. Are we any different than the Israelites when we offer homage to the gods of this world and use our bodies in most impure ways? Do we see ourselves through a cultural lens or as Catholics first? While the *condescensio* of God has its goal of our ascent and transformation, the devil militates in the opposite: he raises himself so as to lower us. God raises up, he pulls down; God purifies, he contaminates. The things we do with our bodies have spiritual ramifications. Body-soul composite means we use our bodies either for our salvation or our damnation, our moving toward God or our withdrawal away from Him.

Here also, we see the power of a father's blessing and a mother's fervent prayer. The demon wanted to keep the father out of the picture, but God waited for the father to shed his fears and bless his son in faith and paternal love. Perhaps he allowed the father to see the son in his sufferings to incite some compunction for his own sins and commitment to return to the faith. By allowing him to witness the demon respond to his paternal blessing, God showed him how he needed to engage as head of household. God wants the whole family to be healed and reconciled, and it begins with the father. The father needs to echo the words of Joshua as he addressed the Israelites before they entered the Promised Land:

> Now, therefore, fear the LORD and serve him completely and sincerely. Cast out the gods your fathers served beyond the River and in Egypt, and serve the LORD. If it does not please you to serve the LORD, decide today whom you will serve, the gods your fathers served beyond the River or the gods of the Amorites in whose country you are dwelling. As for me and my household, we will serve the LORD. (Jo 24:14–15)

A Prayer

O my God, enlighten me and do not forsake me. How often have I sold my soul to the devil, and exchanged Thy grace and favor for a wretched transitory indulgence of sense! I am sorry, O God! for having thus dishonored Thy infinite majesty. My God, I love Thee: suffer me not to lose Thee anymore. O Mary, Mother of God! deliver me from hell, and from the guilt of sin by thy holy intercession.

O Lamb of God! who didst come into the world to take away our sins, have pity on me. I am sorry for having offended Thee, and will love Thee above all things; suffer me not to offend Thee anymore. I seek not worldly goods; give me only Thy grace and Thy love, and I ask for nothing more. O Mary, thou art my refuge and my hope.[142]

---

[142] Saint Alphonsus Liguori, *The Way of Salvation and of Perfection,* 127, 126.

O Mary, if your hand had not delivered me, I would be in an abyss of evils. I would have been in hell. My sins drove me there. God's justice condemned me and the devils wanted to fulfill the sentence. Then, you saved me without being asked. Please, never allow me the misfortune of cursing you from hell. What return can I make you? Can I forget the love that lifted me up? O most amiable Mother, I hope to love you in time and in eternity.[143]

Prayer Against Every Evil

Almighty God, Father, Son, and Holy Spirit, Most Holy Trinity, Immaculate Virgin Mary, Angels, Archangels, and Saints of heaven, descend upon me. Please purify me, Lord, mold me, fill me with Thyself, and use me. Banish all the forces of evil from me, destroy them, vanquish them, so that I may do Thy Holy Will. Banish from me all spells, witchcraft, black magic, malefice, ties, maledictions, and the evil eye; diabolic infestations, oppressions, possessions; all that is evil and sinful; jealousy, perfidy, envy; physical, psychological, moral, spiritual, diabolical ailments. Cast into hell all demons working these evils, that they may never again touch me or any other creature in the entire world. I command and bid all the powers who molest me by the power of God Almighty, in the Name of Jesus Christ our Savior, through the intercession of the Immaculate Virgin Mary to leave me forever, and to be consigned into the everlasting hell.

[143] Saint Alphonsus Liguori, *Glories of Mary*, 43.

IV.

An Ancient Debate: St. Augustine Versus Julian of Eclanum

In this chapter, I explore the reception of our primary biblical passages of *avon avot* (Ex 20:5, et al.) and the green grapes proverb (Ez 18:2–3; Jer 31:29–30) in the writings of Saint Augustine, specifically in his debate with the Pelagian spokesman Julian of Eclanum. Here is found Saint Augustine's mature thought on the effects of sin, the need for grace, and a clear articulation of his teachings on original sin. Saint Augustine specifically argues for an original sin of Adam as having a twofold effect upon later generations by appealing to the words of God at Sinai as punishment for covenant infidelity. He argues, in effect, that original sin is true because we know *avon avot* is true, with the caveat that an inherited *personal* guilt does not pass down generationally, setting the stage for Saint Thomas to flesh out centuries later.

For the Fathers, all of the events in the life of Israel take on new meaning in light of Jesus Christ. As Saint Paul wrote, "These things happened as examples [Greek: *typos,* or types] for us (1 Cor 10:6). And elsewhere, he states: "These are shadows of the things to come; the real reality belongs to Christ" (Col 2:17). With a vision sanctified through the lens of the

Incarnation and pascal mystery, the Christian sees the images of the Old as "shadows" of the realities to come in Jesus Christ (cf. Heb 10:1). The Church Fathers also used Scripture to hammer out various key doctrines in antiquity, particularly in the third and fourth centuries. One of these was the doctrine of original sin.[144] While in modern parlance we hear such terms as *generational sin, generational curse,* or *familial sin,* we are speaking of what the Church Fathers referred to as *inherited guilt* and *vicarious punishment for sin.* In the theological percolation of this key doctrine pertaining to man's origins and the effects of sin, the initial context for the concept of an inherited guilt was the fall of Adam and Eve. Do the effects of the original sin of our first parents carry to us in some way? The debate turned to Saint Paul's letter to the Romans: "Therefore, just as through one person, sin entered the world, and through sin, death, and thus death came to all, inasmuch as all sinned" (Rom 5:12).[145] The sin of Adam, he said, is a "pattern," and Adam "is the type of the one to come," that is Jesus (Rom 12:14). Thus, in Romans we see a twofold effect or inheritance of the first sin—namely, sin and the corruption of bodily death. Saint Augustine was central in showing that the effects of the sin of Adam do carry down to subsequent generations in that same twofold pattern.

---

[144] I limit my patristic examination to Saint Augustine and his debate with Julian of Eclanum. Not only does this debate represent Saint Augustine's mature thought on grace, but his nuanced arguments also represent a significant contribution in the theological development of the development of doctrine, particularly the doctrine of original sin as the archetypal sin in which all sin is patterned. Due to space limitations, I do not examine here the differences expressed in the East and West, and in various centuries, by various Fathers. Even less do I wish here to discuss the Protestant arguments, often made by a selective reading of the writings of Saint Augustine, against the ontological effects of baptism and the debate of free will and errors of *sole fide* or predestinationism.

[145] On the Catholic understanding of original sin and its effects, see Ludwig Ott, *Fundamentals of Catholic Dogma,* 106–14.

Nowhere is this seen more clearly than in the debate between Saint Augustine and the Pelagians. Pelagianism is a fifth-century heresy named after its originator, Pelagius. This belief system,

> stressed the essential goodness of human nature and the freedom of the human will. Pelagius was concerned about the slack moral standards among Christians, and he hoped to improve their conduct by his teachings. Rejecting the arguments of those who claimed that they sinned because of human weakness, he insisted that God made human beings free to choose between good and evil and that sin is a voluntary act committed by a person against God's law. Celestius, a disciple of Pelagius, denied the church's doctrine of original sin and the necessity of infant baptism.
>
> Pelagianism was opposed by St. Augustine, bishop of Hippo, who asserted that human beings cannot attain righteousness by their own efforts and are totally dependent upon the grace of God. Condemned by two councils of African bishops in 416 and again at Carthage in 418, Pelagius and Celestius were finally excommunicated in 418; Pelagius's later fate is unknown.
>
> The controversy, however, was not over. Julian of Eclanum continued to assert the Pelagian view and engaged Augustine in literary polemic until the latter's death in 430. Julian himself was finally condemned, with the rest of the Pelagian party, at the Second Council of Ephesus in 431.[146]

While a full examination of Pelagianism is beyond the scope here, the debate between Saint Augustine and Julian marks a key stage in patristic thought on sin and its effects. Namely, the argument centered around how a just and loving God would punish the sins of one person (Adam) in another (us). Julian of Eclanum, a bishop and primary theologian for the Pelagian

---

[146] "Pelagianism," in *Britannica Encyclopedia.*

movement, held the position that it is only through imitation of the same sin of a father that a child can be punished and, therefore, there is no such thing as an inherited guilt (either spiritual or temporal) or an original sin, as we understand the terms today. Citing the green grapes proverb, Julian argued that each individual is solely responsible for his own behavior and can attain salvation, as the Pelagians claimed, without the help of God's grace. That is, they argued that the effect of the Fall is minimal and, consequently, man can make it to heaven unaided by divine grace. Their position was, in effect, a denial of the effects of original sin, and notably, this denial is one of the marks of "the plague of modernism" cited above.

The Debate with Julian of Eclanum

In his debate with Julian of Eclanum, Saint Augustine uses the concept of inherited guilt as one of his main arguments for the doctrine of original sin. Julian, however, argued that man did not inherit the guilt of original sin, but rather the sin of Adam and Eve is only imitated in personal sins. That God would punish children for the sins of their parents, Julian argued, goes against divine justice and our understanding of God as merciful and loving. Saint Augustine counters by making a key differentiation between human and divine justice. Divine justice is a higher form of justice, he argues, and therefore what may be unjust in a human court may not be so in God's justice. He appeals to both Scripture and the teaching authority of the Church in his defense of the general concept, reminding Julian that these are not isolated words, but rather repeatedly spoken by God. The Pelagians, meanwhile, asserted that all sin is imitated and that a loving God would never punish a child for his father's sins.

We find in Julian's writing an early articulation of a modernist struggle with the image of God who is both perfectly merciful and perfectly just. For Julian, there was no such thing as a guilt inherited by the children of Adam and Eve which must be remedied by graces contained in the sacramental waters of Baptism. For him, personal responsibility means that God "repays to each one what is owed without injustice and without grace, that is, without partiality."[147] This means that the "essence of that virtue, however, is preserved if he does not punish any of his subjects except for those sins which it is clear were committed by free will."[148]

Julian thus directly denies all inherited guilt, to include original sin, by limiting sin and punishment only to those willfully committed. He further denies that sin has any effect outside of, or generates a guilt beyond, the self. This, he says, goes against the justice of God:

> Nor would he attribute to anyone the sins of another, and for this reason he would not on account of the sins of their parents condemn innocent children to eternal punishments. For by themselves they did nothing either good or bad by which, as we are taught, they imitated the sins of their parents. From these premises it was established that God both exists and is just, and it has been shown that, if he did something unjust, he would have undergone as great a loss in divinity as he suffered a loss in justice.[149]

Saint Augustine, Julian argued, had a corrupt view of God in thinking that God would punish children for the sins of their parents. Julian focused on the justice of God and free will, and not man's need for grace. Specifically, he argued that the fall of our first parents had no real effect on humanity. Each

---

[147] Saint Augustine, *Answer to the Pelagians III*, 285.
[148] Saint Augustine, *Answer to the Pelagians III*, 286.
[149] Saint Augustine, *Answer to the Pelagians III*, 286.

of us is capable, through human effort alone, to attain virtue and shun vice. He maintained, moreover, that man is capable of "earning the favor of God" through strenuous human effort.[150] Julian held that the "essence of that virtue, however, is preserved only if God does not punish any of his subjects except for those sins which it is clear were committed by free will."[151] To hold otherwise, he argued, would give more credit to the devil than to God. Personal responsibility for sin, he asserts, preserves the justice and mercy of God.

Since Julian argued against original sin by denying that the sins of parents can have an effect on their children, Saint Augustine uses *avon avot* and God's warning at Sinai to prove that guilt can, in fact, be inherited. He counters Julian's argument against an inherited guilt of original sin by maintaining what Nathaniel McCallum calls a "parallel distinction of original versus personal sin."[152] This is to say, Saint Augustine argues that the words of God in the giving of the Law at Sinai reveal how personal sin not only parallels the original sin, but it also proves it. He first points out that the enigmatic words of God "cursing" generations should be taken at face value because they are spoken not by a prophet or even Moses but God Himself. "It was not a human being," Saint Augustine emphasizes, "but God who said, 'I will punish the children for the sins of their parents' (Ex 20:5), and God did not in this passage command that a human being should do this. Rather, he indicated what He Himself does."[153] He warns Julian to "not be deaf toward God" when He says that "I shall punish the children for the sins of their parents (Ex 20:5)."[154] For Saint Augustine, the sheer number of times that

[150] Saint Augustine, *Answer to the Pelagians III*, 285.
[151] Saint Augustine, *Answer to the Pelagians III*, 286.
[152] McCallum, "Inherited guilt in Ss. Augustine and Cyril."
[153] Saint Augustine, *Answer to the Pelagians III*, 291–92.
[154] Saint Augustine, *Answer to the Pelagians III*, 293.

God Himself repeats the warning is significant. "Not once," he recalls, "but many times God said that he punishes children for the sins of their parents."[155] Thus, for Augustine, this is not an isolated verse open to debate or to gloss over, but one which God speaks "repeatedly" in the Torah.[156] As such, it is significant both to our understanding of God and the effects of sin.

Julian then argued more pointedly how the concept of inherited guilt goes against the justice of God. He states that it is both "a hateful opinion . . . and a perversion of judgment" to claim (as did Saint Augustine) that "children are declared guilty for sins of their parents."[157] Innocent children "by themselves . . . did nothing either good or bad by which, as we are taught, they imitated the sins of their parents."[158] Only when a child imitates the sins of his parents, Julian argued, does he suffer the consequences of sin—not as a consequence of the sins of the parents. By limiting sin only to those willfully committed, he directly denies any inherited guilt. This is because, he argued, God is just and "the innocence of the newborn can by no means be condemned on account of the sinfulness of their parents." Therefore, Julian continued, "it is unjust for the sins of parents to be attributed to the children," here failing

---

[155] Saint Augustine, *Answer to the Pelagians III*, 296.

[156] Saint Augustine, *Answer to the Pelagians III*, 293. As further proof, Saint Augustine points to the commands of God to destroy certain cultures in the OT due to their grave evil. The flood is an example, "**when he destroyed all the rest except for Noah and his family, he did not separate out the infants** who had not yet imitated their parents, **nor did that fire wipe out the people of Sodom without their children.** If he had wanted to do this, the almighty certainly could have." He asks, for example: "What evil, then, did the little ones do? Was it not on account of the sins of their parents, sins which they could neither know nor imitate, that they suffered the common punishment by divine judgment? God, then, judges in one way and commands human beings to judge in another, though God is undoubtedly more just than any human being." Saint Augustine, *Answer to the Pelagians III*, 292–93.

[157] Saint Augustine, *Answer to the Pelagians III*, 293.

[158] Saint Augustine, *Answer to the Pelagians III*, 293.

to distinguish the sin with the effect of the sin. In denying any original sin with a double consequence (a deprivation of communion with God and also the effects of a temporal punishment), Julian wrongly concluded that all sin is imitated, not inherited or based upon natural generation. What is left is the need to "earning the favor of God" through "strenuous human effort," but no need for vicarious atonement, penance, or for reparation by children for the sins of their parents.[159]

In response, Saint Augustine emphasized first that the commandments of the old Law remain. Certainly, he admits, "parents could also imitate their evil children." He brings the debate back to the familial authority structure:

> God still never said, "I will punish parents for the sins of their children." But whenever he spoke in this vein, for he did so often, he said that he would punish the children for the sins of their parents, and by this he showed that he punishes the sins contracted by birth, not by imitation.[160]

And elsewhere:

> You cannot, nonetheless, deny . . . that God never said, "I shall punish parents for the sins of their children." When, therefore, he says, *I shall punish children for the sins of their parents* (Ex 20:5), he does not lay the blame on imitation, but on generation—not on generation from that one in whom nature itself was changed for the worse so that on its account human beings even had to die.[161]

Saint Augustine then counters by contextualizing the concept of vicarious guilt within the larger discussion of the authority structure. He reminds Julian that God "did not say that he punishes parents for the sins of their children or punishes one

[159] Saint Augustine, *Answer to the Pelagians III*, 288.
[160] Saint Augustine, *Answer to the Pelagians III*, 291.
[161] Saint Augustine, *Answer to the Pelagians III*, 292.

child for the sins of another or friends for the sins of their friends or citizens for sins of fellow citizens or something of the sort." On the contrary, he notes that "He wanted us to know that, when this is said, it is generation, not imitation that is blamed."[162]

He then makes a key distinction between human and divine justice. He further tells Julian, "You go in circles and say nothing" and that Julian collapses human and divine justice to protect an image of God that would not be "unjust" by some human standard:

> Distinguish divine justice from human justice, and you will see that God justly punishes children for the sins of their parents, but that, if human beings claim that for themselves in their judgment, they are unjust. Do not wander off from the just path so that, when you hear that the sins of parents are punished in their children, you either do not want God to act that way or you want human beings to act that way, because you resist God's testimonies or commandments.[163]

Here is exposed the argument of Julian against any form of inherited guilt seen in generational spirits that is still common today. Namely, Saint Augustine tells Julian that to recoil against divine punishment for sin often implies that "you do not want God to act in that way." For him, punishing sin at its source falls solely upon the divine, not human, prerogative. He recalls again for Julian that "God says that he punishes children for the sins of their parents." He emphasizes, moreover, with respect to *avon avot*, that "God says." Repeat: God says. With brutal honesty, Saint Augustine states:

> It annoys me to state the truth so many times, even though it does not embarrass you to utter nonsense so many times.

[162] Saint Augustine, *Answer to the Pelagians III*, 296.
[163] Saint Augustine, *Answer to the Pelagians III*, 295.

> God says that he punishes children for the sins of their parents; God says—but says to human beings—that they should not punish children for the sins of their parents. We should approve of both statements since God says both of them.[164]

Here he addresses Julian's appeal to the contradictory statements given by Ezekiel ("Only the one who sins shall die. The son shall be charged with the guilt of his father, nor the father for the guilt of his son," Ez 18:20); and by Moses ("Fathers shall not be put to death for their children, nor children for their fathers; only for his own guilt shall a man be put to death," Dt 24:16).

He first makes two key distinctions. First, he notes the difference between personal sin and guilt. The former exists in the will (seen often in imitation of sins), and the latter (guilt) comes specifically through an active generation in the case of original sin and a passive inheritance of the effect of sin in personal sin. Second, he draws a distinction between divine justice and human courts. Saint Augustine vehemently opposed the error of giving a power to human courts that which is reserved solely to God. Recall the words spoken through the prophet Isaiah: "For my thoughts are not your thoughts, nor are your ways my ways, says the Lord. As high as the heavens are above the earth, so high are my ways above your ways, and my thoughts above your thoughts" (Is 55:8–9).

Not only did Julian accuse Saint Augustine of making God unjust, but he also accused the Scriptures of being contradictory, noting Deuteronomy 5:6 as saying one thing ("I will punish to the third and fourth generation") and Deuteronomy 24:16 another ("Fathers shall not to be put to death for their children, nor children for their father; only for his own guilt shall a man be put to

---

[164] Saint Augustine, *Answer to the Pelagians III*, 301.

death"). Julian, moreover, argued that Deuteronomy 24:17–18 effectively nullifies *avon avot* because the Mosaic law meant that, as he said, "blood relationship would not weigh down the innocent and so that the hatred which a particular person deserved would not carry over to the family."[165] For Julian, these seemingly contradictory texts are proof that it is not valid to say guilt can be inherited. "By that lightning bolt," he claimed, "the whole structure of inherited sin collapses."[166]

Accordingly, Julian repeatedly denied that a God would allow an infant to be afflicted, because all sin is imitated and guilt is not inherited and, therefore, there is even no need for infant baptism. Saint Augustine, however, reminds him that infants do suffer the effects of sin due to the human condition after the Fall:

> If you were not deaf to the words of God where it says, "He will judge the world in justice" (Ps 9:9), you would also recognize God's justice in the punishments of infants. For by reason of their nature they are good because God creates them, but they are evil by reason of the defect on account of which God heals them.[167]

By "defect" here he emphasizes the state of original sin that man is born into, a state which needs the remedy of Baptism. Physical sickness, like moral sickness, he argues, is a privation of the good, a defect in nature as the result of the first sin. Saint Augustine continues:

> Therefore, when we say: Human beings are born with a defect, you think that we are saying that the devil is their creator. You are so blind or stubborn that you cannot or will not notice even the bodily defects with which some are born.

[165] Saint Augustine, *Answer to the Pelagians III*, 289.
[166] Saint Augustine, *Answer to the Pelagians III*, 293.
[167] Saint Augustine, *Answer to the Pelagians III*, 344.

> If we ask you how they merited such defects, you will find nowhere to flee except over the cliff, as long as you do not want to return to the solid rock of the Catholic Church.

Saint Augustine alludes to the bodily defects as an effect of original sin. This does not mean that "the devil is their creator," he says, but that "sin does have an effect on both the bodily as well as the spiritual."[168]

He further distinguishes between divine and human justice: "By divine, not human, justice children are also punished for the sins of other parents." This is because, he says, "God, after all, knows when and how to do this with perfect justice, but human beings do not know this and must pass judgment in accord with their knowledge."[169] Here he affirms the reality of a temporal punishment as generational (in the sense of *inheritance*, as per the above discussion) but, notably, the effects are weighed and measured, tempered by God's mercy.

Julian then again pointed out where God seems to contradict Himself in Scripture, at one place saying He punishes the sins of the fathers in their children and other places where each person is responsible for his own sin. Saint Augustine counters again with frankness and reminds him that God gave both commands:

> For you want it to seem that these two ideas are contradictory to each other: that children are punished for the sins of their parents and that children ought not to be punished for the sins of their parents, as if I say one of them and God says the other. Are you deaf? God said them both! Therefore, both of them are just because it is the Just One who said them. But in order that you may understand that God did not say things that are mutually contradictory, distinguish the persons of God and of the human judge in accord with the different cases. Then you will not make God out to be

---

[168] Saint Augustine, *Answer to the Pelagians III*, 318.
[169] Saint Augustine, *Answer to the Pelagians III*, 317.

> guilty, even though he punishes children for the sins of their parents, nor will you force a human judge to act that way. But you raise the objection against me that these two statements are mutually contradictory with such great wordiness and complication for no other reason than that you talk much and think too little.[170]

Here are the two texts Julian refers to as contradictory and, therefore, he dismisses the words of God when giving the Law:

God Giving the Law at Sinai	Moses Giving Communal Laws
For I, the LORD, your God, am a jealous God, inflicting punishment for their fathers' wickedness on the children of those who hate me down to the third and fourth generation. (Ex 20:5; Dt 5:9)	Fathers shall not be put to death for their children, nor children for their fathers; only for his own guilt shall a man be put to death. (Dt 24:16)

As noted in a previous chapter, the context of each is different. The former is God Himself speaking at Sinai, and the latter is Moses giving precepts for human courts which govern community life. Saint Augustine tells Julian that there are two systems of justice, divine and human. While "human beings also punish sinful actions," he explains, God punishes sin itself, "from our origin." For this reason, God commands human beings that they should not also condemn the children for the sins of their parents, though he affirms that God punishes the children for the sins of their parents: "Distinguish [between] divine and human judgments," Saint Augustine explains, "and you will find that these two are not self-contradictory."[171]

Lest we think that this an irrelevant and antiquated debate, we find examples even today where divine justice is collapsed

[170] Saint Augustine, *Answer to the Pelagians III*, 300.
[171] Saint Augustine, *Answer to the Pelagians III*, 302.

into human justice. Abortion and gay marriage are two areas where human courts grasp a power reserved only to God. Perhaps more clear evidence of a usurpation of divine justice by human hands is the punitive system of "collective punishment" in North Korea. In that authoritarian system, for example, as human rights activist Han Man-su reports, "if your relative is accused of 'anti-state' or 'anti-socialist' crimes, then you and three generations of your family can be punished for it." That is, "If a family member commits a crime against the regime, the entire family, including children who are not even born yet, can be punished and ostracized for life."[172] Note the subtle mockery of the decree of God at Sinai seen in the familial punishment of "you and three generations" (so, to the third and fourth generation) as well as the principle of immemorial custom, described above. This is a clear example of an oppressive human justice system where human law assumes an authority it does not possess. That is, authoritarian dictatorships collapse divine justice into human justice and, in so doing, exact unjust punishments.

Saint Augustine, therefore, clearly distinguishes between human and divine law as the key to understanding Scripture's seeming contradiction. Simply stated, God's ways are not our ways, and God's justice is not our justice. As God says through Isaiah, "As high as the heavens are above the earth, so high are my ways above your ways and my thoughts above your thoughts" (Is 55:9). And Moses: "The Rock—how faultless are his deeds, how right all his ways! A faithful God, without deceit, how just end upright he is" (Dt 32:4). And the psalmist: "God's ways are unerring" (Ps 18:31). Human courts punish sinful actions. God, however, punishes sin itself.

[172] George W. Bush Presidential Center: Freedom Collection. "Interviews with Han Nam-su."

Thus, Saint Augustine warns Julian to "not be deaf toward God" when He says that "I shall punish the children for the sins of their parents (Ex 20:5)." The full response bears repeating at length:

> After all, who says to you that it is false that God wanted this to be observed in human courts when parents and children have their own personal cases pertaining to the life which each of them individually leads so that children are not punished for their parents or parents for their children? No one is opposed to the law or to you when you say this. But do not be deaf toward God. He says, *I shall punish the children for the sins of their parents* (Ex 20:5), and, though he says this repeatedly, he never says that he punishes the parents for the sins of the children. Hence, you should know that he looks not to who of them imitates whom, but to who are begotten by whom.[173]

Thus, he notes that the concept of inherited guilt is generational and familial—that is, something that passes from parents to children and not the other way around. "He never says that he punishes the parents for the sins of the children," Saint Augustine says. This indicates that we "should know that [God] looks not to who of them imitates whom, but to who are begotten by whom."[174] Using Augustinian logic, therefore, the North Korean courts are a diabolic inversion of justice where punishment is to prevent imitation of something opposing the state and generations as a pretext for causing fear and control. This totalitarian system of (in)justice, in fact, proves Saint Augustine's point against Julian.

The key point here is that human beings punish sinful actions, but God punishes sin at its origins, and the effect

[173] Saint Augustine, *Answer to the Pelagians III*, 302.
[174] Saint Augustine, *Answer to the Pelagians III*, 293.

of the pattern can be passed on through generations. Saint Augustine states:

> What are you saying, you, a human being with such foolish ideas? To the extent that it is higher, divine justice is more inscrutable than human justice, and further removed from it. After all, does any just human being permit that a crime be committed which that person has the power to prevent? And yet God permits this, though he is incomparably more just than all just human beings, and his power is incomparably greater than all other powers. Bear these ideas in mind, and do not compare God as judge to human judges, for we must not doubt that he is just, even when he does what seems unjust to human beings and does what would be unjust if human beings did it.[175]

God permits, in His perfect justice, the effects of sin so as to bring about a greater good. God, he says, "is incomparably more just than all just human beings, and his power is incomparably greater than all other powers." He permits certain evil according to His own prerogative, not as man but as God. He is incomparably more just than all human beings, and His power is incomparably greater than all other powers. "Bear these ideas in mind," Saint Augustine says, and do not compare God as judge to human judges, "for we must not doubt that he is just, even when he does what seems unjust to human beings and does what would be unjust if human beings did it."[176]

We must not doubt that He is just, therefore, even when He does what seems unjust by human standards. To this end, Saint Augustine fleshes this out by appealing to other biblical texts in which God repeats His words of *avon avot* at Sinai:

---

[175] Saint Augustine, *Answer to the Pelagians III*, 294–95.

[176] Saint Augustine, *Answer to the Pelagians III*, 295.

> I do not deny that a child ought not to be condemned in place of a parent or that a parent in place of a child when they have their own separate cases. But you do not want to hear the words in Leviticus, "They will perish on account of the sins of the parents" (Lv 26:39), and in the Book of Numbers, "Punishing the children for the sins of their parents to the third and fourth generation" (Nm 14:18), and in Jeremiah, "Exacting punishment for the sins of their parents upon the heart of their children after them" (Jer 32:18).[177]

That is, each person is held accountable for his own actions while at the same time being vulnerable to "inherited" effects from his own parents, which includes affliction from demons. While God is eternally faithful, there are consequences when we are not. This is not an isolated statement, but one found repeatedly in the Bible, he argues.

"All Souls are Mine": Julian and the Green Grapes Proverb

Typical of the Church Fathers, Saint Augustine reads the green grapes proverb within the entire history of salvation, and the prophets as foretelling the rebirth of the waters of Baptism, which makes all righteous and wipes away the guilt inherited from original sin. Moreover, as seen above, he uses the concept of an inherited, vicarious punishment as proof for the inherited guilt of original sin. The former is remitted with penance, he says, and the latter is removed by the waters of rebirth.

For proof that there is no hereditary guilt of any kind, original or familial, Julian countered by citing the prophets, specifically Ezekiel. Calling Saint Augustine "misguided" in

---

[177] Saint Augustine, *Answer to the Pelagians III*, 293.

his teaching of an inherited guilt passed on to children, Julian collapses human and divine justice into one: "But there may be someone so misguided as to want it to be proved by clear statements that God does not judge otherwise than he has commanded that we should judge." He then cites Ezekiel and the proverb of green grapes:

> Filled, therefore, with the Holy Spirit, the prophet Ezekiel said: "The word of the Lord came to me and said: Son of man, what is the meaning of those who speak this proverb in the land of Israel: Our parents have eaten sour grapes, and the teeth of the children are set on edge? As I live, says the Lord God, this proverb will no longer be spoken in Israel because all souls are mine, the soul of the child, just as the soul of the parent.[178]

The plain sense of the text, Julian argues, is that individual responsibility is now declared as superseding hereditary guilt, and that henceforth divine justice follows human justice. Notably, he makes no effort to address *avon avot* or reconcile this assertion with contrary prophecies, even within the prophetic books themselves.

Saint Augustine fires back by first contextualizing the proverb as echoing the giving of the Law at Sinai, asking: "But why did they say this except because they knew that God said: I shall punish the children for the sins of their parents (Ex 20:5)."[179] He then appeals to the nature of prophetic literature itself and its ultimate end in Christ. "The passage you mention from the prophet Ezekiel," Saint Augustine replies, "pertains to the New Testament in which is found the inheritance of the reborn [in the waters of Baptism]."[180] The promise of hope for liberation to the children now born into slavery and

178 Saint Augustine, *Answer to the Pelagians III*, 302–3.
179 Saint Augustine, *Answer to the Pelagians III*, 305.
180 Saint Augustine, *Answer to the Pelagians III*, 304–5.

exile (to wit, the righteous grandson in Ezekiel's explanation) is a foreshadowing of the rebirth that will come to humanity enslaved by sin and the devil. The captivity of Babylon is only a type of humanity's captivity to the devil through sin. Saint Augustine explains the proverb in the light of the revelation of Jesus Christ. He builds upon the theme of birth (that is, a generation born into slavery) as the key to understanding the theological meaning of the passage. He writes:

> And if one asks correctly, one will find that he said, "I shall punish the children for the sins of their parents" (Ex 20:5), on account of their birth into subjection, and from that birth there came the proverb about the sour grapes. But the New Testament was promised on account of the rebirth into freedom, and in it this proverb will no longer be said. For through the grace of Christ we renounce the inheritance that brings loss and comes from Adam, when we renounce this world in which it is necessary that the children of Adam be weighed down by a heavy yoke, and certainly not unjustly, from the day they emerge from the womb of their mother until the day of their burial in the mother of all (Sir 40:1). For this reason, the sacred mysteries give sufficient evidence of what is done since even the little ones make these renunciations.[181]

Thus, in the light of Christ, all humanity is born into the generation of slavery. The human race is enslaved not to Babylon, however, but to the devil and sin. We are born in exile and separated not from an earthly Jerusalem but a heavenly one (cf. Gal 4:26).

While stating that this passage ultimately refers to the hope of those to be reborn in the waters of Baptism as its ultimate fulfillment, he affirms that all humanity is under an inherited guilt. The prophet Ezekiel, he says, is "veiling

---

[181] Saint Augustine, *Answer to the Pelagians III*, 306.

the mystery, which was to be revealed in its own time, the prophet did not mention the rebirth by which each human being passes from Adam to Christ."[182] For Saint Augustine, moreover, those reborn in the waters of Baptism no longer carry the guilt of original sin or the punishment of the sins of the first parents, Adam and Eve.

He addresses how Jeremiah uses the green grapes proverb also in the context of the New Covenant:

> In those days they will not say: Parents have eaten sour grapes, and the teeth of the children have been set on edge. Rather, each will die for one's own sin, and the teeth of the one who has eaten the sour grapes will be set on edge (Jer 31:21–30). It is, of course, clear that this pertains to the day of the new planting about which he was speaking when he said this. But it had long been impressed upon the hearts of the people that it was written in the Old Testament, I shall punish the children for the sins of their parents (Ex 20:5). And so that no one would think that God's scripture contradicted itself, in order to show more clearly that the former statement belongs to the old and the latter to the new testament, he immediately added, "Look, the days are coming, says the LORD, and I will establish a new testament for the house of Israel and for the house of Judah, not in accord with the testament which I established with their fathers in the day I took their hand to lead them out of the land of Egypt" (Jer 31:31–32), and so on.[183]

For Saint Augustine, Jeremiah is pointing to the future—"In those days, they will no longer say"—is a future, not a present reality:

> Birth belongs to that former [old] testament, but rebirth to this latter [new]. Hence, in the former children are punished

[182] Saint Augustine, *Answer to the Pelagians III*, 304.
[183] Saint Augustine, *Answer to the Pelagians III*, 305.

> for the sins of their parents, but in the latter, in which the bonds of birth are broken by rebirth, it is not said: Parents have eaten sour grapes, and the teeth of the children have been set on edge (Ez 18:2), but the teeth of the one who has eaten sour grapes will be set on edge (Jer 31:29), because each person will not die for the sin of a parent, but for one's own sin, if one has committed sin. But you have not shown how the words of scripture, I shall punish children for the sins of their parents (Ex 20:5), are in harmony with the prophecy which says, Children will not inherit the sin of their parent (Jer 31:30). These will, of course, remain mutually contradictory unless each of these two is referred to one of the testaments, as the prophet Jeremiah showed with perfect clarity.[184]

Continuing the imagery of grapes, he states that the "new planting" is the New Covenant, and the ultimate fulfillment of the passage is in the light of Christ. Thus, "birth" is of the old, and "rebirth" (namely, Baptism) is of the new.

Saint Augustine also affirms that individual responsibility still applies to individuals with regard to personal sin. While original sin is passed down through natural generation, when it comes to individual sins of parents, beyond affirming *avon avot*, he is more nuanced. When pressed by Julian to read the green grapes proverb as ending any inherited guilt, he replied:

> I do not claim that the prophet's denial was false, but that you did not understand it. He, of course, foretold the rebirth [of Baptism]. The rebirth alone makes children to be free from their parents' sins, which fall under the judgment of God, not under the judgment of human beings. But when you deny that birth contracts from the parents the infection of the ancient death, you try to eliminate the very reason for rebirth [the remittance of original sin through baptism].

---

[184] Saint Augustine, *Answer to the Pelagians III*, 322–23.

Saint Augustine then draws a key parallel between the effects of original sin and the effects of personal sin, stating:

> For though the bath of rebirth washes away whatever sins it finds, other sins could also be healed by doing penance.[185]

This is a significant point of departure, as he moves from original sin as the negative effect of the sin of our first parents and into the effects of parents' sins upon their children. Thus, he presents the inherited guilt of personal sin as distinct from, but still following the pattern of, the original sin which is, as it were, archetypal. While the latter is remitted through "rebirth," the remedy for the former is "doing penance"—consistent with the language of Sinai and the need for satisfaction. This also is consistent with the words of Jesus concerning the boy possessed since infancy: "This kind can only come out through prayer" (Mk 9:29).

Saint Augustine then moves back to the penultimate meaning of the proverb and challenges the faulty logic of the heretic Julian to assert that God would change something so central to the identity of the people of God as the Law given at Sinai. While Julian pointed to the inconsistency of the biblical texts as proof, Saint Augustine points to the inherent inconsistency which would suggest that God changes. He asks:

> If then, after his declaration [at Sinai] God wants us to understand that no one will believe this, we must ask why before this declaration it was not wrong to believe that children were to be punished for the sins of their parents, but afterwards it is wrong.[186]

He asks, in effect, has God evolved and changed?

---

[185] Saint Augustine, *Answer to the Pelagians III*, 311.
[186] Saint Augustine, *Answer to the Pelagians III*, 306.

For Saint Augustine, this Ezekiel passage penultimately highlights that every soul has personal responsibility, that we cannot blame others for our own faults. "The prophet speaks the truth to children and parents who are living their separate lives," he says, telling Julian that "you slander with the Pelagian madness the Catholics who correctly understand the prophet by branding them as Manichees."[187] There is no contradiction, he says, because "God distinguishes according to their own actions if they are already adults, those who have been reborn from those who have been born. For those of whom he says, The soul of the parent is mine, and the soul of the child is mine (Ez 18:4), undoubtedly are leading their own lives."[188]

This prophecy only veils the ultimate meaning, which is hidden in Christ. He tells Julian, "This passage is the promise of the New Testament through the prophet Ezekiel, and you do not understand it." What was that prophetic promise "veiling the mystery" in prophetic language? For Saint Augustine, this passage points to the rebirth of Baptism:

> But veiling the mystery which was to be revealed in its own time, the prophet did not mention the rebirth by which each human being passes from Adam to Christ. But what he did not say at that time he wanted to be understood in this time in which the veil was going to be removed for those who pass over to Christ.

The answer is found not in the Old Testament but the New, "in which is found the inheritance of the reborn."[189]

This is prophetic discourse, he reminds Julian, and as such it points the Christian to Christ as its ultimate fulfillment:

---

[187] Saint Augustine, *Answer to the Pelagians III*, 313.
[188] Saint Augustine, *Answer to the Pelagians III*, 304.
[189] Saint Augustine, *Answer to the Pelagians III*, 304–5.

> When he says, "This proverb will no longer be spoken in Israel" he shows that it was customary to say: "Our parents have eaten sour grapes, and the teeth of the children have been set on edge" and he does not blame the fact that it was said but promises a time when it will no longer be said. But why did they say this except because they knew that God said: I shall punish the children for the sins of their parents (Ex 20:5).[190]

That time of ultimate fulfillment is the New Covenant where rebirth as "righteous grandchildren" comes not by means of circumcision and the Law but by the waters of Baptism (Col 2:11–15). As seen above, the plain sense of the proverb's usage is within the context of a promise of restoration to a people in exile and slavery (the children being punished for their parents' infidelity). Ultimately, it points to the salvific "passing over" the waters of rebirth as the "true Israelites," the baptized Christians. Accordingly, he tells Julian:

> You would be right in saying that it will no longer be spoken in Israel if you had in mind the true Israelites, those who have been reborn among whom this will no longer be spoken. For among these who are not reborn it is right to say it, since in accord with the apostle's words to the Romans they are not Israel: For not all who are descended from Israel are Israel (Rom 9:6), and here he surely wanted us to understand the children of the New Testament, that is, the children of the promise.

This foretells the freedom from slavery to sin due to the fall of Adam, and the rebirth of Baptism (cf. Rom 6:4).[191] The Exodus from Egypt is a metaphor for the mystery of Christ, the divine Warrior and Bridegroom. Just as God's people in

---

[190] Saint Augustine, *Answer to the Pelagians III*, 305.
[191] Saint Augustine, *Answer to the Pelagians III*, 306.

passed through waters and were freed from physical slavery, so now in Christ the Christian passing through waters and set free from spiritual slavery. As the *Catechism* states:

> The coming of God's Son to earth is an event of such immensity that God willed to prepare for it over centuries. He makes everything converge on Christ: all the rituals and sacrifices, figures and symbols of the "First Covenant." He announces him through the mouths of the prophets who succeeded one another in Israel. Moreover, he awakens in the hearts of the pagans a dim expectation of this coming. (CCC 522)

Thus, Saint Augustine affirms that Jeremiah's prophecy points to the new birth of Baptism which wipes away original and personal sin, at the same time not denying (or in the least way backing off from) the truth spoken directly by God, namely, "inflicting punishment for the fathers' wickedness on the children of those who hate me" (Ex 20:5).

Julian Appeals to Personal Responsibility

Julian responds by claiming that the explanation of Ezekiel that "All souls are mine" (Ez 18:4) means that the devil can only have dominion over a soul who grants it through personal sin. He states: "But all souls come under his [God's] dominion, and in this way, he shows that your claim is sacrilegious, namely, that the souls and bodies of the newborn fall under the dominion of the devil." In effect, to claim the green grapes proverb to be true is, in effect, to accuse God of being false or unjust.

Saint Augustine is direct in his reply: "Shame on you! You are most unjust. For he who said, 'I shall punish the children for the sins of their parents' (Ex 20:5) is not unjust." He reminds Julian that "God who says this [in Ezekiel] is the same God who says, "I shall punish the children for the sins of their parents" (Ex 20:5). Unless you understand how both of these are true, you should in no way believe that you have understood the truthful prophet, no matter how much wordiness I endure from you with your slanders."[192] He then counters by explaining that all souls do belong to God, but this means that sin introduces a defect in man, into the familial construct, not in God: "The whole human being, that is, soul and body, by its substance falls under the dominion of the creator. But by a defect, which is no substance, the human being was handed over to the devil, though under that same power of the creator under which the devil himself stands."[193] Here he makes a key point: the essence of inherited sin is that "by a defect, which is no substance, the human being was handed over to the devil." Thus, we can see here that a defect is a privation of the good and "generational curse" can be seen as a defect of the good of familial blessing. This in no way detracts from the sovereignty of God. Rather, it protects it.

Saint Augustine then points to the story of Ahab, the evil king of Judah (and husband of Jezebel) as proof that the effect of sins does actually carry down to the children. Ahaz not only embraced idols (2 Chr 28:1–4), but he also "even emulated his son by fire in accordance with the abominable practice of the nations, whom the LORD had cleared out of the way of the Israelites" (2 Kgs 16:2). For this and other grave sins, Ahab temporarily repented such that God told Elijah: "Since he has humbled himself before me, I will not bring the evil in his time. I will bring the evil upon his house during the reign of his son" (1 Kgs 21:29). Ahab's son Jehoram was just as evil, and "conducted himself like the kings of Israel, in the line of Ahab . . . he did evil in the LORD's sight" (2 Kgs

[192] Saint Augustine, *Answer to the Pelagians III*, 313.
[193] Saint Augustine, *Answer to the Pelagians III*, 308.

8:18). The punishment of Ahab, however, is recounted later where not only Jehoram but every male in his household were killed (2 Kgs 10:1, 7, 10–11; cf. 2 Chr 28:1–8). Here is how Augustine explains the connection:

> Heaven forbid that we should say that God does not punish children for the sins of other parents since God's scripture so often and by name testifies as to which children have been punished for the sins of which fathers to the point that God delayed punishment for a particular grave sin of King Ahab, sparing him but punishing his son.[194]

Notably, he points to the fact that God punished Ahab's sin in his son as proof that guilt can be inherited.

For him, moreover, the punishment of familial sin is reserved to God alone. As to whether there is such a thing as a generational curse, Saint Augustine assumes it to be so, according to the definition above. Speaking directly of the effects of familial sins in the context of original sin, he asks: "But who is able to search out the limit or plan and standard of God's justice in the case of sins of some parents for which their children are punished?" Again, this is not deterministic. That justice is reserved to God alone: "On this account God keeps to himself these judgments," he says, "but he forbade a human judge to exact such punishment."[195] This is because divine justice is not the same as human justice.

Julian, however, is unconvinced. Original sin, he says, "has nothing to do with inherited sin."[196] Julian appears to acknowledge that there was a time when God punished sins of fathers in their children, but not after Ezekiel and Jeremiah. Saint Augustine clarifies by arguing that God is

---

[194] Saint Augustine, *Answer to the Pelagians III*, 315.
[195] Saint Augustine, *Answer to the Pelagians III*, 315.
[196] Saint Augustine, *Answer to the Pelagians III*, 316.

unchanging, and that original sin sets the pattern for all sin. That is, familial sins parallel the mechanics of original sin.[197] To deny inherited guilt, he says, goes against the Law, reason, and prudence:

> To the detriment of the law you do not hear: I shall punish the children for the sins of their parents (Ex 20:5). To the detriment of reason you do not see that the evils which the little ones suffer, though they committed no personal sins in this life, have no just causes before God except for the sins of their origin. To the detriment of prudence you do not avoid bringing forth or defending a newfangled doctrine which denies original sin in opposition to the most ancient foundation of the Catholic faith.[198]

Thus, as cited above, certain sins of some parents are sometimes punished in some children, according to God's providence (to wit, "God's justice in the case of sins of some parents for which their children are punished"). God's perfect justice and mercy decides when, if, how, to whom, and to what extent. What is clear from the two prophets, however, is that righteous living brings the protection of blessing and sinful living brings a privation of protection, which here we follow the biblical language and definition of curse. Also made clear is that when a father sins, his children are vulnerable to repeat his sins—but not pre-determined to do so. When they do commit certain wicked sins, however, any operant curse is

---

[197] Augustine affirms the double consequence of sin seen in the archetypal sin of Adam: "We see the greatness of that misery imposed upon his offspring due to his sin by the judgment of God which is certainly not unjust. Because we are Christians, we say that, if no one had sinned, there also would not have existed in paradise, not merely the eternal death of the soul and body, but not even the temporal death of the body and all these great evils which we see that little ones suffer." Augustine, *Answer to the Pelagians III*, 317.

[198] Saint Augustine, *Answer to the Pelagians III*, 316–17.

ratified. Conversely, they can break the curse by living holy lives. The interplay between individual responsibility and hereditary guilt is thus always held in tension.

Unconvinced, Julian doubles down. "Even if you could prove," he says, "that the sin of Adam is held against his children, you would still agree that the crimes of other parents do not harm their offspring." Significantly, here Julian says that even if original sin were true, there is no such thing as an inherited guilt or generational curse. Specifically, he states that if this were the case, "the children were seen to be held subject to the sin of one parent before an unjust judge." Like those who cited the proverb of green grapes as they face exile, to claim inherited guilt is to declare oneself as innocent and God as guilty or unjust. Saint Augustine, however, calls this an "error" and refers him back to the words of God Himself: "Who would agree to this error but someone who does not believe God when he says, I shall punish children for the sins of their parents (Ex 20:5)."[199] He continues, "you most clearly call God unjust . . . for he most clearly says that he will punish children for the sins of their parents." Thus, for Saint Augustine, the answer is rather simple: inherited, familial guilt is true because God says it to be so.

Julian says such cases of a familial guilt must have "some other cause" than God because that would be unjust, in effect arguing the same as the people of Jerusalem to Ezekiel. He concludes that to say that if God punishes the sins of parents in their children, that "makes the devil appear to be the creator of human beings." He argues further that "it was clear that he whom we profess to be the true God can do nothing in judgment that is opposed to justice, and for this reason none can be held guilty for the sins of others." This is because "it

[199] Saint Augustine, *Answer to the Pelagians III*, 317.

would be unjust," Julian argued, "that guilt is passed on in the seeds."[200]

He appeals to the mercy of God and asks the very question which the reader of the Gospel of Saint Mark must ask. How can a loving God allow an innocent child to suffer demonic affliction? Julian argues that in the green grapes proverb, God is saying that He has "come to this degree of mercy that I pardon even personal sins of those who amended their lives." If that is so, Julian argues, "how is it possible that I hold the sins of others against the newborn?"[201] Amendment and forgiveness does not eliminate the need for reparation and satisfaction.

"A Punishment That Is Far Different and Far Less"

Saint Augustine tells Julian that he does not know "how to distinguish a defect from a nature, although a defect exists in a nature." Thus, personal sin follows the pattern of original in that inherited sin is a product of a defect in human nature, a privation. He points to physical defects as the privation of the fullness of health, and also the result of original sin: "Therefore, when we say: Human beings are born with a defect, you think that we are saying that the devil is their creator. You are so blind or stubborn that you cannot or will not notice even the bodily defects with which some are born."[202] Thus, he points to bodily defects as the result of the privation of the fullness of blessing lost in original sin. The physical points to the spiritual to highlight a "nature later damaged as a punishment for

[200] Saint Augustine, *Answer to the Pelagians III*, 288.
[201] Saint Augustine, *Answer to the Pelagians III*, 309.
[202] Saint Augustine, *Answer to the Pelagians III*, 318.

sin." By way of example, he points to "those defective bodies" of some infants born with disabilities as evidence to "you who deny that little ones contract any sin from their parents." He points to various ways in which infants suffer:

> **The case of penitents is one thing; that of the newborn is another.** For you do not, of course, find a way to show that God is just if even in the newborn he finds no sins and yet weighs them down with a corruptible body and with so many and such great troubles besides. **The evils that infants suffer are past counting:** fever, coughing, rashes, pains of various members, diarrhea, worms, and countless other woes stemming from the flesh, more torments from their cures than from their diseases, wounds externally inflicted, blows from beatings, **and attacks of demons.** But you wise heretics, you are ready to fill paradise with such flowers to avoid admitting original sin.[203]

Notably, not just physical sicknesses, but he mentions that demons attack children as punishment for the sins of their parents.

To that end, Saint Augustine acknowledges that the mechanics of inherited guilt work the same with regard to both original sin and personal sin, but he nuances the difference. "But even if other parents commit many sins," he says, "because they sin with a weak soul and in a corruptible body which weighs down the soul, nature does not become destined to die because of their sins." That is, nature "dies" (to the life of grace) because of original sin, but not in the same way as personal sins committed "with a weak soul." These, however, have an effect which must be recognized. With regard to familial sin, he says God's providence and merciful love are still at work: "By God's secret and just judgment the children

---

[203] Saint Augustine, *Answer to the Pelagians III*, 309.

receive for the sins of these parents a punishment that is far different and far less. For he arranges all things in measure and number and weight, and he truthfully says, I shall punish the children for the sins of their parents" (Ex 20:5). Here, he affirms the reality of generational curses but, notably, the effects are weighed and measured "by God's secret and just judgment" such that "the children receive for the sins of these parents a punishment that is far different and far less" than the parents receive.[204] That is, he assumes that not only original sin has an effect on children but private sins as well. Here Saint Augustine shows that inherited guilt of personal sins is not deterministic ("nature is not destined . . . even if parents commit many sins") but is a reality in our common human experience. He clarifies, significantly, that "for the sins of these parents a punishment that is far different and far less."

Ultimately, Julian argues that inherited guilt "attacks and destroys free choice." Saint Augustine shows that Julian is the one "who destroys free choice when you deny it the grace of God to restore and assist." Recall that a working definition of liberation is reconciliation with God the Father through Jesus Christ. Even in the extreme cases of generational curses, this is an extension of God's grace to restore the family to the state of grace and be reconciled to the Father. A key point here is how Saint Augustine uses the concept of inherited guilt of generational curse as proof of the original sin and the original inherited guilt of the sin of Adam. "By divine, not human justice children are also punished for the sins of other parents," he writes. "God, after all, knows when and how to do this with perfect justice, but human beings do not know this and must pass judgment in accord with their knowledge."[205] To say that

[204] Saint Augustine, *Answer to the Pelagians III*, 317.

[205] Saint Augustine, *Answer to the Pelagians III*, 319. He continues: "For, when they judge, they can know what each person has done, though they

Ezekiel denies any inherited guilt is to make the mistake of collapsing divine justice into human.

"Languishing on Account of One's Ancestors" (Lv 26:42): An Application for Today

In the passage Saint Augustine cites from Leviticus, God specifically gives promises for fidelity—"If you live according to my precepts and observe my commandments" (Lv 26:3)—to include temporal blessings of victory, abundance, peace, rest (Lv 26:4–12). Recall, however, that bodily actions have spiritual ramifications, and a curse is the privation of the protection and provision of blessing. In the same passage of Leviticus, God then gives a warning for infidelity—"But if you do not heed me, and do not keep all these commandments . . ." (Lv 26:14). The effects, notably also all temporal things, are the opposite of the blessing received for fidelity. We specifically read as part of the punishment for covenant disobedience:

> I will destroy your high places, and break your idols. You shall fall among the ruins of your idols, and my soul shall abhor you . . . I will scatter you among the Gentiles, and I will draw out the sword after you, and your land shall be desert, and your cities destroyed . . . You shall perish among the Gentiles, and an enemy's land shall consume you. And if of them also some remain, they shall pine away in their iniquities, in the land of their enemies, and **they shall be afflicted for the sins of their fathers, and their own: Until they confess their iniquities and the iniquities of their ancestors,** whereby they have transgressed me, and walked contrary

do not always know even this. But how do human beings know the sort of bonds by which a nature is linked to the nature from which it was born?"

> unto me. Therefore I also will walk them, and bring them into their enemies' land until their uncircumcised mind be ashamed: then shall they pray for their sins. And I will remember my covenant, that I made with Jacob, and Isaac, and Abraham. (Lv 26:30, 33, 38–42 DR, emphasis mine)

Implied here is that covenant fidelity brings the protection of blessing, while infidelity is a privation which is experienced generationally as a "languishing." Saint Augustine cites this passage in a way that builds upon what he had shown in his earlier writings that evil is not its own substance, *per se*, but rather the absence of a good (as darkness to light, or sickness to health).[206] Specifically, the passage shows that in the case of covenant infidelity (notably, Leviticus here lists increasingly grave sins as evidence), God withdraws the protection of blessing, thereby allowing the enemy to be the cause of division, defeat, and destruction.

On this passage of Leviticus where is mentioned "languishing" as the result of "the iniquities of their ancestors" (Lv 26:42), Father Ripperger notes three items of significance. One, this shows not only *that* "children will suffer from the sin of their parents" but also "*how* the sin of the parents will unfold in relationship to its effects." Two, Father Ripperger points out that it is not the fathers' sins themselves that carry down to the children but the effect of the sin. That is, the fathers are punished for their own sins, but the "effect of their sin . . . is passed on to the children, not the sin itself." Third, in this passage from Leviticus which describes the blessings of fidelity and the curses of infidelity, he notes how we see that "the children themselves have to confess their own sins and the iniquity of their ancestors." That is, there is a need for righteous living by the children and also a need for satisfaction

---

206 Saint Augustine, *Confessions*, Book 7, Chapter XII.

made by the children for their parents' iniquities. "In essence," Father Ripperger states, "the children need to correct or make reparation for the iniquities of their forefathers so that the effects of the sin do not continue."[207]

This passage from Leviticus brings to view, moreover, how a curse is a privation of the protection of blessing which opens the door to diabolic oppression. This was echoed by Moses at Sinai. In his final speech to the people of God before entering the Promised Land, moreover, Moses invokes the people suggestively of this: "I call heaven and earth today to witness against you: I have set before you life and death, the blessing and the curse. Choose life, then, that you and your descendants may live" (Dt 30:19). Curses are an inversion of blessings and the byproduct of free choice. Accordingly, spiritual oppression generally centers upon temporal goods and the interiority, with feelings of anxiety, dread, and unrest. Further, the way out is the children making satisfaction, confessing sin, and living faithful lives.

To that end, McCallum notes that "when addressing the question of why the child suffers, he [Augustine] provides the answer that the child's suffering is used by God to correct their parents." In an extreme example, Saint Augustine points out that the sins of some nations (in the land of Canaan, such as Sodom and Gomorrah, for example) were so great that God commanded they be blotted out, including children.[208] McCallum notes how Saint Augustine even suggests that God may compensate the suffering of infants in some way for having "suffered without having sinned," citing as an example the feast of the Holy Innocents.[209] The antiphon at the Magnificat for this feast day reads: "Innocent babes were slain for Christ, sucklings

207 Ripperger, *Dominion*, 176–77.
208 Augustine, *Answer to the Pelagians III*, 492.
209 McCallum, "Inherited guilt in Ss. Augustine and Cyril."

were killed by a wicked king: now they follow the Lamb without Spot, and cry, without ceasing: Glory be to Thee, O Lord." And the hymnody: "First to bleed for Christ, sweet lambs! What a simple death ye died! Playing with your wreathes and palms, at the very altar side."[210] That is, as St. Paul writes, "where sin increased, grace overflowed all the more" (Rom 5:20). Accordingly, when God allows a child to suffer the effects of a father's sin, God often offers more grace and more blessing to the child who makes satisfaction for his father's sins.

That this suffering (the "languishing" as the result of "the iniquities of their ancestors") is a corrective measure by God is seen in the next passage of Leviticus where God promises further suffering should the children not heed His warnings—namely, multiple "sevenfold fiercer punishments" of various afflictions (Lv 26:18–39). The goal of suffering is not vengeance, however, but conversion: "Thus they will have to confess that they and their families were guilty of having rebelled against me, and of having defied me, so that I, too, had to defy them, and bring them into their enemies' land. Then, when their uncircumcised hearts are humbled, and they make amends for their guilt, I will remember my covenant" (Lv 17:40–42). Here, we see the need for satisfaction to be made as a corrective measure to sin itself. As Saint Augustine said, "God punishes the sin from our origin."

Thus, the attacks of demons can even fall upon infants, such as the possessed boy in the Gospel of Saint Mark. This is consistent with Saint Bonaventure, who gives four primary reasons as to why God allows demons to afflict humans (to reveal God's glory, to punish sin, to rebuke a sinner, or to educate a person). When the effects of sin are felt within a family, one or more of those four reasons are generally at work. That is, God allows—by His own divine prerogative—all demonic

[210] Lefebvre, *St. Andrew Missal*, 163.

activity, whether ordinary or extraordinary, for some greater good.[211]

In addition, greater graces and rewards are often offered for those fighting. If an unholy spirit is operative in a familial line, broadly speaking, God has allowed it for a greater purpose. His justice, imbued with a holy zeal of the divine Bridegroom, demands it. Thus, His mercy will be present as well. However, God's mercy is, in a sense, severe in that He permits these things so as to call His people back to union with Him. He is calling not just the sinner but "they and their families" alike to a return of the nuptial embrace of holiness. Thus, even in cases where spiritual oppression or even possession are the result of some generational curse, God is allowing it for a greater good. The pathway out has always been the same: humbled hearts softened by divine love, making amends for sin until the cup of satisfaction is filled and God has mined every ounce of grace out of the suffering.

By way of example, let us say that a certain father who has a drinking problem is employed as a commercial truck driver. He stops at a bar on the way home one night and, as a result of heavy alcohol consumption, is involved in an unfortunate accident after he leaves the bar. He is arrested for drunk driving and vehicular homicide. Because of his actions, he loses his commercial driver's license and, consequently, his job and spends a period of time in jail. Due to his incarceration, his children suffer poverty (lack of provision) and no longer have the security of having a father in the home (lack of protection). In other words, he is punished for his own sin, but the effects of his actions mean his wife and children suffer a certain lack or want. That is, they specifically experience a privation of both provision and protection that comes with a

---

[211] Smit, *De Demoniacis,* 79. I discuss this as well in Schneider, *Manual,* 20.

father's blessing, seen in both a lack of temporal goods and his physical absence. They are now more vulnerable to negative influences due to that double privation. While the father—and the father alone—is punished for the crime, the children still suffer the temporal consequences of his actions. This distinction between the punishment of the sin and the effect of the sin is a key idea to grasp in understanding how generational spirits work.

Within the concept of the *generational* aspect of sin, Saint Augustine makes a key distinction. Inherited sin is not its own substance but a corruption or what he calls a "defect of a good substance."[212] Augustinian scholar J. Patout Burns summarized Saint Augustine's position on the effects of the Fall as twofold. Saint Augustine held that the first ramification of the sin of our first parents is that "God punished their sin by removing the gift that had protected them from death and bodily dissolution." Recall the above discussion and definition of a curse as the privation of the effects of blessing, filling the void where provision and protection are lacking. The second result, says Patout Burns, is "an urgency to satisfy the appetites that sustained mortal bodies," which meant "an affective shift away from heavenly and toward earthly goods." That is, as shown above, after the Fall, the corruption of bodily death and sin remain as the effect of the sin. Within that, there is an "affective shift," he says, to misuse those things which sustain human life (food, drink, sleep, and sex).[213] Where that "affective shift" has been the entry point of grave evil, the punishment for sin is found.

Along these lines, Saint Augustine distinguishes between personal guilt (the result of a volitional act) and natural guilt

---

[212] Saint Augustine, *Answer to the Pelagians III*, 302.

[213] Patout Burns, "The Late Augustine Against Julian on Inherited Guilt," 98.

(inherited by nature). According to McCallum, "throughout the debate Augustine is insistent that infants do not inherit personal sin."[214] They do, however, feel the effects of the personal guilt of their parents.[215] For Saint Augustine, this is borne of the effect of original sin upon human nature—namely, "the one made guilty by a man's action is man, but man is a nature." And that nature, he says, is vulnerable to the effects of sin: "Therefore, just as adults become guilty by a sinful action so minors become guilty by contagion from adults."[216] Original sin is not deterministic; that is, it is something inherited from the sin of others (*viz.*, "contracted not committed . . . a state not an act"). As he states:

> Learn if you can the sense in which original sins are understood as the sins of others and as our sins but are not the sins of others for the same reason that they are ours. They are, after all, the sins of others because each of us does not commit them in our own life, but they are ours because "Adam existed, and we all existed in him."[217]

Just as the cause is the same for all (the sin of Adam), so is the remedy—Baptism. Thus, the effect of the sin of our first parent is "contracted" and "a state" we find ourselves in, but not "an act" that we have "committed" (CCC 404). Notice the *Catechism* also uses the language of privation as a result of sin—namely, "human nature is deprived of" the goods that came with the blessing of man's original state. That is, original sin and its effects are *inherited* and not merely imitated (as Julian argued), the result of which is a privation of a greater good.

---

214 McCallum, "Inherited guilt in Ss. Augustine and Cyril."
215 Augustine, *A Treatise on the Merits*, 1.22.
216 Augustine, *Against Julian*, 117.
217 Augustine, *Against Julian*, 96.

Not Deterministic

Original sin, therefore, is the archetypal generational spirit which sets the pattern for all sin, in that there is a difference between the sin and the effect of the sin. Distinguishing between the sin and the effect, Father Ripperger states, "In relationship to the effects of original sin, there are generational spirits, in the sense that all humanity inherited spiritual warfare as a result of our forefather's, that is, Adam's sin."[218] Thus, in the example of the unfortunate truck driver above, the twofold effects are seen in (1) the punishment of his going to jail and losing his job, and (2) his children suffering the temporal consequences. His children do not go to jail, but they do suffer a privation of the protection of his presence and the lack of his provision. While his actions produced an evil effect, however, a greater good can be its result if satisfaction is made. The unfortunate father is, in a sense, punished further in seeing how his sins have made his children suffer—something which should drive him to conversion, penance, a life of virtue, and making amends/reparation. Is the judge unjust for putting him in jail? Or the employer for firing him because he is no longer employable because he lost his commercial driver's license?

According to Patout Burns, Saint Augustine "showed that divine judgment did hold descendants involuntarily responsible for the voluntary sin of an ancestor."[219] As will be fleshed out in the next chapter, Saint Thomas goes further and explains why. Since parents have natural law rights over their children, this is the mechanism whereby a "familial" curse is so-called. When there is a breach in that relationship of authority and its twofold ends (to provide and to protect), the effect of the

---

[218] Ripperger, *Dominion*, 174. Cf. CCC 409.

[219] Patout Burns, "The Late Augustine Against Julian on Inherited Guilt," 111.

sin of the father can be transmuted to the children as part of the double consequence of sin (the spiritual and temporal dimensions). This extends, says Saint Thomas, even to animals and temporal goods, which means that the generational spirits can also manifest themselves in the oppression of property and other temporal goods. This can (but not always) occur when one in authority commits grave sin, granting a permission to the demon who enticed that sin.[220]

This is why the effects of a generational curse are manifested as spiritual oppression. As I stated elsewhere, oppression is "a form of extraordinary diabolic influence in which a demon attacks one's externals"—that is, temporal goods such as finances, possessions, relationships, vocation, etc. Interiorly, spiritual oppression is often marked by "a heaviness, malaise, melancholy, or depression," and the person under oppression experiences an increasing diabolic influence, to include "the individual begins to lose focus, especially on vocational obligations."[221] The demon, then, exploits (under God's providential will) the lack of protection of blessing. In the end, the devil is God's instrument of the temporal punishment due to sin.

Even this is allowed so that more grace will flow into the family. If the spiritual guilt (and not the temporal punishment) were to pass to the children, this would be deterministic and unjust, but this is not the case. Thus, sometimes a demon is allowed to afflict the children as part of the temporal punishment so that a descendant can drive the demon out of the familial line. "In relationship to the generational spirits," says Father Ripperger, "the successor can then adequately deal with the demon that was introduced into the line in order to expel him from the line."[222] This leads Fr. Ripperger to

220 See Ripperger, *Dominion*, 179–80.
221 Schneider, *Manual*, 19–20. For an in-depth exploration of spiritual oppression, see Ripperger, *Dominion*, 258–66.
222 Ripperger, *Dominion*, 179.

conclude, "The second thing of importance is that someone can be punished by the temporal punishment due to the sin." That is, he says, "the effects of the sin can be passed to another individual. So even though the sin does not pass, the effects of the sin can pass."[223] This, he says, is given by God as a "corrective measure" and is, in fact, "an act of mercy on God's part."[224]

Notably here, Father Ripperger asserts that "the effects of the sin *can* pass"—not that it *will* pass down the family line. This is consistent with Saint Augustine who states that, unlike original sin, generational guilt is not deterministic. The way he caveats this is significant. He points to the mystery of how inherited guilt is not just the logical continuance of the effects of original sin but also falls squarely within the perfect providence of God. God decides if, when, where, and how to punish sin. To this end, Saint Augustine states:

> In some way, nonetheless, **some sins of certain parents are passed on to their children, not by imitation, but by generation, and [the parents] are punished in them.** And for this reason he does not say: To the third and fourth imitation, but generation (Ex 34:7). You, of course, do not like this, but whether you like it or not, you hear it.[225]

A significant point here is that the process is not deterministic. "In some way," he says, "some sins of certain parents are passed on to their children . . . and [the parents] are punished in them." Saint Augustine admits that how this works is a mystery. The effects of some sins of certain parents are passed on to their children, not every sin of every parent to every child. Here, he affirms that generational spirits are real yet mysteriously fall under divine Providence. God alone decides how this plays out in a family line.

---

223 Ripperger, *Dominion*, 177.
224 Ripperger, *Dominion*, 179.
225 Saint Augustine, *Answer to the Pelagians III*, 292. Emphasis mine.

That is, whether or not the effects of personal sins are passed on depends on God. Here, Saint Augustine also distinguishes between original sin of our first parents and the personal sins of other parents. He says that "even if other parents commit many sins because they sin with a weak soul and in a corruptible body which weighs down the soul, nature does not become destined to die because of their sins." God ultimately decides if, when, and to what extent He will punish the personal sins of parents. Here is another key point: the punishment experienced by the children of parents who sin is "far different and far less." That is, the effect of the sin differs in both essence and in degree from how the one who committed the sin itself is punished.

Saint Augustine's argument implies the existence of generational spirits, that is, he assumes that not only original sin has an effect on children, but private sins do as well. As he states:

> But who is able to search out the limit or plan and standard of God's justice **in the case of sins of some parents** for which their children are punished? On this account God keeps to himself these judgments, but he forbade a human judge to exact such punishment.

Again, this is not deterministic. He appeals to God's providence in that the "sins of some parents" (notably, not all sin of all parents, but some sins of some parents) are being punished in their children. He repeats elsewhere that "nature is not destined . . . even if parents commit many sins." Of note, moreover, is his assertion that "for the sins of these parents" even here is seen the mercy of God in that He often renders "a punishment that is far different and far less."[226] Just because someone's father committed this or that sin, therefore, what

[226] Saint Augustine, *Answer to the Pelagians III,* 315.

passes down is a vulnerability, not necessarily that the negative effects will automatically pass down to the children. God's providence determines if, when, and to what extent He will punish sin.

An Example

Although Saint Augustine was primarily arguing against the Pelagians on the concept of original sin, he assumes the concept of an inherited guilt and *avon avot* and even uses it to argue *for* an original sin. When he speaks of "generational" effects of sins, moreover, he is referring to sin's effects along familial lines. When someone in authority commits a grave sin, he abdicates the responsibilities of his office which creates a negative effect upon those under his authority with regard to that provision and protection. This lies at the heart of the concept of inherited guilt, and thus generational spirits, because to inherit something implies a natural law relationship.

Father Charles Hugo Doyle cites an interesting study in Germany (from the 1950s) which shows how the effects of the sins (not the sins themselves) of parents can be passed down to their children. This study examined blindness in children and found one peculiar subgroup of thirty thousand German children who suffered blindness who all shared a common factor. As Father Doyle reports, these children "owed their sightlessness to parents with social diseases." The study he cites notes the direct connection between adults with venereal diseases and the birth defect of blindness. This study highlights the mechanics of generational curses in that the effect of the parents' sexual sins was punished not only in themselves (social diseases) but also in their children (blindness). As for the personal and spiritual guilt for the sexual sins, the individuals who committed the fornication are individually responsible. Nonetheless, in this stark example, we see how the effect of the sin carries down to the children in a bodily way (Saint Thomas will explain why in the next chapter).

Father Doyle even cited as an example Saint Augustine himself, who strayed for many years into a sinful lifestyle before his conversion to Catholicism. Saint Augustine, says Father Doyle, laid the blame for his youthful errors, and his great sin, directly upon his parents, saying, "My family took no care to save me from this moral destruction by marriage; their only concern was that I should make as fine and persuasive speeches as possible."[227] Perhaps this personal sentiment is what makes Saint Augustine so keenly aware of inherited guilt and original sin. Perhaps, as well, this gives insight into the prayers of his saintly mother, Saint Monica, who spent many years in prayer and wept many tears for her wayward son. The child of those tears, a bishop told her, shall never perish. Whether they made him a saint, we do not know. But they made her a saint.

A similar, recent story shows the power of grace, the advantages of a family led in prayer by the father, and the graces obtainable from the sacraments. A young woman had suffered the traumatic experience of sexual assault at the age of sixteen. The mother was devout, and her father was a good man, but not Catholic or religious. The mother reported having Freemasonry in their family. The daughter, now twenty-six, had fallen into hard times. She had same-sex ideation, thoughts of self-harm, and had completely abandoned her faith. The level of her affliction was a high-level spiritual obsession, and on a very quick path to full possession. Through the course of her suffering, however, the father came into the Catholic faith and began a life of prayer and sacrifice for the daughter.

---

[227] Doyle, *The Sins of Parents*, xv.

At long last, the daughter indicated that she wanted help, so the family reached out to a team that worked with their local exorcist. With the permission of the exorcist, the team gave instruction to the girl over Zoom (she was in a different diocese). The parents asked the entire family, including siblings and spouses, aunts and uncles, to pray the assigned prayer regimen.[228] The family also did the Freemasonic renunciations together. After thirty days, the young woman began weekly catechesis. In due time, she wanted to go to confession, so the team sent her to a priest in her diocese who also did minor exorcisms, just in case. He would know what to do, they thought.

She arrived at the parish to line up a meeting with the priest, only to find out that he was on sabbatical for six months. "There's a visiting priest here," the office lady told her, "and he's not busy if you would like to talk to him." She agreed. What took place in the confession, the team was not told (nor did they ask). But there, on an ordinary Tuesday afternoon somewhere in suburban America, an unnamed, substitute priest assisted a suffering woman in making a deep and heartfelt confession. In the course of that simple confession, part of the ordinary means of grace, this woman who had been tormented by demons for ten long years was totally and completely liberated of a high-level spiritual obsession. She is now happily married in the Church to a good, Catholic man and the mother of several children.

The Hope

If a man is alive, he has a chance. "Hope," says Saint Paul, "does not disappoint" (Rom 5:5). The above story gives witness to the incredible mercy of God. Her healing is also testimony to the power of the ordinary means of obtaining grace, the sacraments

[228] For the Liber Christo Protocol, see Schneider, *Manual*, 313–14.

of the Catholic Church. When a father leads the family in prayer and sacrifices as a spiritual leader, the heavens move. When a suffering soul pushes back with simple faith, humility, and commitment to growing in holiness above all else, the heavens move and hell trembles. We must not underestimate the power of a life ordered to prayer, spiritual discipline, and a family united in prayer. They are accelerants to the holy fire of the ordinary graces offered through the sacraments.

A Prayer

O my God! this is the grace which, above all others, I ask through the merits of Jesus Christ: grant that throughout my life, and especially in time of temptation, I may recommend myself to Thee, and hope for Thy help through the love of Jesus and Mary. O holy Virgin! obtain for me this grace on which depends my salvation.[229]

O my Jesus! as Thou hast had so great patience with me in waiting for me, and so great love in pardoning me, as I trust I would love Thee with all my heart; but this love Thou must give me. Give it me! O my Lord! and little honor is it to Thee that I, a sinner so favored by Thee, should love Thee in some little degree. O my Jesus! when shall I begin to be grateful to Thee, as Thou hast been gracious to me? For the past, instead of being grateful to Thee, I have offended Thee and despised Thee. Shall I, then, hereafter ever live thus turned away from Thee, who hast spared nothing to gain my love? No, my Saviour! I would love Thee with all my heart; I would never displease Thee. Thou commandest me to love Thee, and I desire nothing but to love Thee. Thou seekest me, and I seek nothing

[229] Saint Alphonsus Liguori, *The Way of Salvation and of Perfection*, 195.

but Thee. Give me Thy help, without which I can do nothing. O Mary, O Mother of Mercy! draw me altogether to God.[230]

O Mary, because you are so merciful, I have recourse to you. Only two things will keep me from receiving mercy, my failure to ask you or little confidence in your intercession. Therefore, help me always to ask and to seek with confidence.[231]

Acts of Rejection

I reject any dedication, consecration, vow, pact, promise, contract or blood contract, covenant or blood covenant to Satan for myself (and insert names of others if you have made generational consecrations or included anyone else when making an offering to Satan), my heart, spirit, soul, body, mind, memory, imagination, intellect, will, dreams, inner thoughts, subliminal thoughts, touch, taste, smell, sight, hearing, stomach, blood, healthy bacteria, immune system, nervous system, and all other internal processes, especially through (insert list at this time) in the Name of the Father and of the Son, ✠ and of the Holy Spirit. Amen. (Thrice) I consecrate myself and my heart, spirit, soul, body, mind, memory, imagination, intellect, will, dreams, inner thoughts, subliminal thoughts, touch, taste, smell, sight, hearing, stomach, blood, healthy bacteria, immune system, nervous system, and all other internal processes, to the Sacred Heart of Jesus and the Immaculate Heart of Mary, in the Name of the Father and of the Son, ✠ and of the Holy Spirit. Amen.

(After the person has made his rejection, he can then reconsecrate himself to the Trinity and the Blessed Mother.)

---

230 Saint Augustine, *Answer to the Pelagians III*, 225.
231 Saint Alphonsus Liguori, *Glories of Mary*, 49.

V.

Vicarious Punishment for Sin in St. Thomas Aquinas

By this point, we see that sin has spiritual and temporal ramifications, both of which require satisfaction. We have also seen how the *Catechism* affirms that God punishes sin not out of vengeance but out of love so as to remove the attachments to sin which impede our union with Him. Accordingly, there remains satisfaction to be made to restore balance, which is the remission of the "temporal punishment due to sins" which are already "forgiven as far as the guilt is concerned" (Pope Saint Paul VI, above). To assist in that satisfaction, the Church invites us to share in the treasury of merit by acquiring indulgences, by making acts of voluntary, vicarious atonement, and having Masses said for our ancestors in purgatory. In addition, the Fathers of the Church have taught that God uses angels (glorified and fallen) as His instruments of purification of the temporal effects of sin and also His instruments to punish sin. That is, He uses angels, and even demons, not for remission of the guilt of sin but to assist in the satisfaction for the penalty of sin. The effect of the Fall meant not only physical effects of sin but spiritual as well, and Saint Augustine affirms that even infants can suffer at the hands of demons. What remains, then, is to explore whether the latter is also consistent with *avon avot*. Namely, we know *that* God punishes sin, but *why* do the temporal effects of a father's sins carry down to his children? For that, we turn to Saint Thomas Aquinas.

The Divine Physician: Penal Versus Medicinal Punishments for Sin

In both his early and later writings, Saint Thomas comments on God's words to Israel at Sinai: "For I, the LORD, your God, am a jealous God, inflicting punishment for their father's wickedness on the children of those who hate me, down to the third and fourth generation" (Ex 20:5). In his earlier writing, he confirms the error of Traducianism and affirms that only original sin is handed down from parents to children. That is, he states, "no deficiency is passed down necessarily from parent to offspring, most of all one existing on the part of the soul." He weighs in against the intergenerational sin hypothesis and affirms Catholic doctrine that "the actual sins of the immediate parents in no way pass into their children." He reiterates that "the sins of the immediate parents do not introduce any corruption into the nature precisely as nature." He continues by affirming, moreover, that original sin has created a privation. He states that "the first sin led to a deficiency pertaining to the nature alone, since it disrupted man's clinging to God." Sin has created "a disturbance in the order among the lower powers in relation to reason and of the soul in relation to the body followed."[232]

That "disturbance" among the "lower powers" of the soul means that soul-body dichotomy is then the point of departure for a discussion of the spiritual versus the temporal effects of sin and of Exodus 20:5 and *avon avot* directly.

[232] Saint Thomas Aquinas, *II Sent.*, d. 33, q. 1, a. 1.

Asking "whether the fault of the immediate parents redounds to their children as far as punishment is concerned," he begins with a distinction:

> Now, a child is something of the parent's as regards his body, which he has from his father, and as regards worldly affairs, in which the child is bound to assist his father. But as regards the soul, which is created immediately by God, the child is not something of the parents but belongs to God himself. This is what Ezekiel 18:4 means: *the soul of the father as well as the soul of the son is mine.*[233]

Here he builds upon Saint Augustine and lays the foundation for the *Catechism*'s assertion that sin has a "double consequence" in affirming that sin has two effects and, therefore, two punishments—namely, the spiritual and the temporal. Accordingly, to restore the harmony with God destroyed by sin, he distinguishes these two punishments as "essential" and "incidental."[234] In this context, Saint Thomas discusses how the sins of a father, due to the nature of the authority structure, can have a temporal effect upon the children, according to God's providence:

> Therefore, it should be known that there are **two punishments that follow on sin**. One is the **essential** punishment, which pertains to the soul, both in the present—such as the loss of grace, a troubled conscience, and things of this sort—and in the future—such as the punishment of hell. And a child is never punished with this kind of punishment for his father's sin, since this punishment does not regard him insofar as he is something of his father's. The other punishment follows on sin, as it were, **incidentally**, such as bodily infirmities **and other temporal punishments**.

[233] Saint Thomas Aquinas, *II Sent.*, d. 33, q. 1, a. 1.
[234] Saint Thomas Aquinas, *II Sent.*, d. 33, q. 2.

He affirms, therefore, that a child is never punished for his father's sins. By "essential punishment," he means that punishment pertaining to the essence of the person's autonomous self, a spiritual soul who has individual responsibility and culpability for his or her own sins.

Here is where the transgenerational sin thesis lacks clarity. On the one hand, the effect of personal sin carries with it an essential punishment (to wit, essential, primarily spiritual) that each person bears individual responsibility. On the other hand, with regard to the temporal effects of sin, however, Saint Thomas affirms that the temporal (to wit, incidental, or accidental/secondary) punishment remains and can carry down. He continues:

> **Hence it is also not the case that such punishments are always inflicted on those who sin. Rather, this takes place in accord with the direction of divine providence, which governs all things.** And a child **is sometimes punished** with this kind of punishment for his father's sin, **unless there is an impediment on the child's part**, such as being contrary to the father's sin by way of a good life. For this punishment befalls him as being something of his father's, just as for a man's sin animals are sometimes killed and houses demolished, and there is no fault in these.

Notice that this secondary effect of sin: (1) can include a vicarious punishment, (2) that punishment is confined to within the familial construct and temporal goods, (3) is not deterministic, but rather completely under divine providence, and (4) the effect of the sin can be resisted by the "impediments" of a life of virtue. "Hence it is also not the case," he states, "that such punishments are always inflicted on those who sin. Rather, this takes place in accord with the direction of divine providence, which governs all things." Thus, while the sin does not pass down, the effect of the sin does, according to Saint Thomas.[235]

Accordingly, he affirms that God sometimes does, in fact, allow affliction to rectify the sin of an ancestor, affirming *avon avot*. "A child is sometimes punished," he states, "with this kind of punishment [the incidental, or temporal] for his father's sin." This is not random, but rather because the child is under the authority of the father: "For this punishment befalls him as being something of his father's." He distinguishes, moreover, between human and divine justice and affirms that "in accord with divine justice, too, children are punished for their fathers' sins." To those who cite Ezekiel and the green grapes proverb, he states:

> Human justice does not punish the child for the father's sin in what the child has already received from the father, but in that which he would be going to receive, as regards either body or possessions. For just because his father sins, a child already born is not maimed, nor is a subject child disinherited. **But incidentally, a father's punishment does redound to the child, when what was supposed to go to the child from the father is taken away from the father**, such as an inheritance or even a limb, since from maimed people a maimed person is born.[236]

The phrase "that which he would be going to receive" is consistent with the above definition of a curse as the privation of the protection and provision which come with blessing. Here, the father's sins present a vulnerability in his children.

That vulnerability means a tendency of a child to imitate the sins of the father as part of the effects of the father's sin, as certain behaviors, good or bad, are learned and can be habituated

---

[235] Saint Thomas Aquinas, *II Sent.*, d. 33, q. 2., art.2.

[236] Saint Thomas Aquinas, *II Sent.*, d. 33, q. 2., art.2.

by the demon as part of his ordinary activity of temptation. "Imitation is not posited as the first cause for which temporal punishment is inflicted." Rather, "it is a sort of intermediate cause, through which the influence of the first cause is connected to the effect. For the power of the parent's sin does not reach it if it is opposed to the sin. But through imitation, it, in a way, becomes continuous. Hence by this fact the child's being punished for his father's sin in a certain way is not taken away."

The passing down of the effect of sin is not deterministic; that is, it is not inevitable that a sinful father's sin will be punished in his children. The effect of the father's sin does pass down, he says, "unless there is an impediment on the child's part, such as being contrary to the father's sin by way of a good life." Although a child may have a vulnerability due to his parents' sins, they also have free will and can offer resistance. "For the power of the parent's sin does not reach it [the next generation]," he states, "if it is opposed to the sin. But through imitation, it, in a way, becomes continuous. Hence by this fact the child's being punished for his father's sin in a certain way is not taken away."[237] Accordingly, when the parent's sin is continued by imitation, and the sin is not opposed, the punishment upon the father continues. This suggests that God allows the incidental effect to be upon a family so that someone in the family line will oppose the sin and break its effects. A life of virtue and maintaining the state of grace, even in the face of a certain vulnerability presented to the child, can block the effects of sins.

In his mature thought, moreover, Saint Thomas further fleshes out the topic. In the *Summa Theologica,* he asks: *Whether the debt of punishment is an effect of sin?* He begins by affirming that sin has secondary effects regardless of a person's intentions. "Just as evil is accidental to the sinner's act being beside his intention," he says, "so also is the debt

---

[237] Saint Thomas Aquinas, *II Sent.*, d. 33, q. 2., art.2.

of punishment."[238] That is, regardless of whether a person intends an ill effect for their actions, the debt of punishment remains as sin's direct effect. This is because sin, he says, "incurs a further punishment through disturbing the order of the Divine or human law."[239]

Notably, Saint Thomas expands on his earlier writings by connecting the two punishments as satisfaction for sin with the two systems of justice, divine and human. He further reaffirms the concept as an imbalance created by our sinful actions. Sin, he says, "incurs a debt of punishment through disturbing an order. But the effect remains so long as the cause remains. Wherefore so long as the disturbance of the order remains the debt of punishment must needs remain also."[240] This echoes the words of *avon avot* and *visitans* as punish and *iniquitas* as an imbalance which needs remedies.

The Greek word for justice is *dika*, which means "balance, harmony, and satisfaction for sin"—that is, the restoration of balance. That is, paying the debt of punishment (whether through suffering, prayers, indulgences, and the like) is a corrective to the disturbance of right order.[241] This is seen in that the symbol for the justice system is the scales, and the phrase "the balance of justice" derives itself from an ancient Greek concept. The base meaning of the word is *balance*. Sin can be seen as a fourfold alienation from God, the self, others, and one's environment. Sin creates a disorder, and punishment makes satisfaction and, as a result, brings or restores proper balance to those four.

In the *Summa*, Saint Thomas expands on his earlier writings and notes the distinction between spiritual and temporal punishment. The former, he says, "pertains to the soul" and thus

---

[238] Saint Thomas Aquinas, *ST* I–II, q. 87, art. 1.
[239] Saint Thomas Aquinas, *ST* I–II, q. 87, art. 1.
[240] Saint Thomas Aquinas, *ST* I–II, q. 87, art. 3.
[241] Saint Thomas Aquinas, *ST* I–II, q. 87, art. 1.

this spiritual punishment does not pass from one person to another. Temporal punishment, however, is different. He states that in "temporal punishment, sometimes one is punished for the sins of another." This is because, he says, "one man is the temporal good (*res*) of the other, and so in his punishment the other is also punished, as the children are, according to the body, a certain thing belonging to the father."[242] Notably here, Thomas places the temporal effects of sin within the authority structure of natural law. Thus, the children of a drunk driver suffer the effects of their father's punishment, while he alone stands trial. "In other words," states Fr. Ripperger, "even if the father is condemned to hell or loses his state of grace, this does not cause his children to be condemned to hell or to lose their state of grace."[243] That is, while they do not go to jail on behalf of their father, they can suffer the effects of his sin.

On the effects of sin, Saint Thomas says, "the withdrawal of grace is a punishment, and is from God . . . the result is that the sin which ensues from this is also a punishment accidentally." Thus, the withdrawal of grace, like the privation of blessing, is the natural consequence of sin. God honors our free will, even allowing us to fall into grave sin when we so choose. Here is where the evil spirits exploit the familial vulnerabilities while also being God's instruments of purification.

He always does so, as discussed above, to bring about a greater good. "Even when God punishes men by permitting them to fall into sin," Saint Thomas says, "this is directed to the good of virtue. Sometimes indeed it is for the good of those who are punished, when, to wit, men arise from sin, more humble and more cautious."[244]

The punishment is for a greater good. "God does not delight in punishments for their own sake," he affirms, "but He does

---

242 Saint Thomas Aquinas, *ST* II–II, q. 108, art. 4.
243 Ripperger, *Dominion*, 177.
244 Saint Thomas Aquinas, *ST* I–II, q. 87, art.1.

delight in the order of His justice, which requires them."[245] To that end, he further asks whether the debt of punishment remains after sin.[246] He answers in the affirmative but further distinguishes between the "punitive" (spiritual) and the "medicinal" (temporal) effects of sin and the general theological concept of inherited guilt within the familial structure. To show what he means, he points to a story in the life of King David (2 Sm 12:13–14) as an example:

> "David said to Nathan: I have sinned against the LORD. And Nathan said to David: The LORD also hath taken away thy sin; thou shalt not die. Nevertheless, because thou hast given occasion to the enemies of the LORD to blaspheme . . . the child that is born to thee shall die." Therefore, a man is punished by God even after his sin is forgiven; and so the debt of punishment remains, when the sin has been removed.

I will flesh out the story of David in a later chapter, but for now note that after "the LORD hath taken away thy sin," the punishment for David's sin was upon the next generation, his offspring which bore the punishment for his sin of adultery and murder. In what finds echo in our understanding of the inner logic of indulgences and the need for satisfaction for sins, he affirms: "We must, therefore, say that, when the stain of sin has been removed, there may remain a debt of punishment, not indeed of punishment simply, but of satisfactory punishment."[247] That is, for Saint Thomas, David's life is an example of satisfaction for sin.

Saint Thomas builds upon Saint Augustine (who said that "human beings are born with a defect") by asserting that "evil is a privation of good." Even when God allows demons to

---

[245] Saint Thomas Aquinas, *ST* I–II, q. 87, art.1

[246] Saint Thomas Aquinas, *ST* I–II, q. 87, art. 6.

[247] Saint Thomas Aquinas, *ST* I–II, q. 87, art. 6.

afflict children, this too is "medicinal punishment," says Saint Thomas, "because a medical man prescribes bitter potions to his patients, that he may restore them to health." Punishment of sin, therefore, is salutary (that is, producing good results) because of its beneficial effect of both healing and preventing further evil in individuals, families, and communities. For Saint Thomas, God allows this suffering to heal the soul "so that . . . the disorder may be remedied by the contrary of that which caused it." In addition, the "punishment is requisite in order to restore the equality of justice, and to remove the scandal given to others, so that those who were scandalized at the sin may be edified by the punishment, as may be seen in the example of David quoted above."[248] David, Saint Thomas says, exemplified how satisfaction is made by directly militating against the vice of a generational spirit by developing the requisite virtue.

Having affirmed *avon avot*, Saint Thomas then turns to the topic of vicarious punishment, asking, *Whether anyone is punished for another's sin?*[249] He alludes to original sin as archetypal for all sin and further builds on Saint Augustine when he states that "human nature needs a treatment of penal medicines . . . due to the corruption of nature which is itself the punishment of original sin."[250] With regard to individual responsibility for sin, he affirms that "each one is punished for his own sin only, because the sinful act is something personal." The spiritual punishment for personal sins, he says, is "penal." Accordingly, he says, "With regard to spiritual punishments, these are not merely medicinal, because the good of the soul is not directed to a yet higher good. Consequently no one suffers loss in the goods of the soul without some fault of his own."

[248] Saint Thomas Aquinas, *ST* I–II, q. 87, art. 7.
[249] Saint Thomas Aquinas, *ST* I–II, q. 87, art. 8.
[250] Saint Thomas Aquinas, *ST* I–II, q. 87, art. 7.

That is, with regard to the spiritual effects of sin, each soul has personal responsibility, citing Ezekiel. Following Saint Augustine, he notes that children are not punished penally for the sins of their fathers. "Punishments are *not* inflicted on one for another's sins," he says, "because, as regards the soul, the son is not the father's property. Hence the Lord assigns the reason for this by saying (Ezekiel 18:4): 'All souls are Mine.'" Nonetheless, he says, "it does happen that one is punished for another's sin" and that he calls punishment "medicinal" because they are "intended for the health of the soul." With regard to Exodus 20:5 and *avon avot,* he affirms that this refers to "temporal or bodily punishments, in so far as children are the property of their parents, and posterity, of their forefathers."[251]

With regard to this temporal punishment visiting the children, he brings it back to the punishment of the father: "The text adds, 'to the third and fourth generation,' because men are wont to live long enough to see the third and fourth generation, so that both the children can witness their parents' sins so as to imitate them, and the parents can see their children's punishments so as to grieve for them." Thus, it is through the authority structure that the debt of punishment enters the familial construct because, Saint Thomas says, since children are the "property" of the father, the product of his body and under his authority (with its two ends to provide and to protect), God can punish a father's sins in his children. In that sense, it is *familial* (or, *generational* in that the effect of the sin flows down from father to child, according to Saint Thomas). Hence:

> Those who are near of kin are said to be punished, rather than outsiders, for the sins of others, both because the punishment of kindred redounds somewhat upon those who sinned, as stated above, in so far as the child is the father's

[251] Saint Thomas Aquinas, *ST* I–II, q. 87, art. 8.

> property, and because the examples and the punishments that occur in one's own household are more moving.[252]

Accordingly, the phenomenon may be correctly termed generational spirit (and even generational sin), only if one is clear in distinguishing what is passed down—the sin or the effect of the sin, since only original sin is passed down by natural generation.

Life of David as Example

By this point, the reader may see more deeply the mechanics of how even after the forgiveness of sin "the temporal punishment of sin remains" (CCC 1473). Perhaps nowhere in Scripture is original sin seen as archetypal of the double consequence of sin more clearly than in the life of David, specifically his infamous affair with Bathsheba, found in 2 Samuel 11–12. We do not live in a vacuum, and our personal sins have an effect on those around us. Specifically, the result of the sin of King David follows the same twofold effect of mortality (i.e., which was both a physical and a spiritual death in Adam and Eve) and a privation of the protection of blessing experienced in temporal matters (which, as was seen, were both familial and communal). Lastly, sin demands satisfaction, and often the graver the sin, the graver the need for satisfaction. Thus, embedded in the story of David's sin is that redemptive suffering not only makes satisfaction for sin but also breaks the effects of sin. That is, a volitional act purifies the effects of a volitional act. In his story is also seen the effects of a father's sins as a vulnerability passed down to his children, in this case Solomon.

"At the turn of the year, when kings go out on campaign," the Scripture says, King David sent out his army to battle

[252] Saint Thomas Aquinas, *ST* I–II, q. 87, art. 8.

with his general Joab. The reader is alerted with a key detail: "David, however, remained in Jerusalem" (2 Sm 11:1). The reader is told in some detail what the king was doing while his men waged war without him. Was he conducting important affairs of governance? Building alliances to help end the war? No. David was taking a siesta, something which he seems to have been doing routinely: "One evening David rose from his siesta and strolled about on the roof of the palace" (2 Sm 11:2). Siestas are not in of themselves bad, but remember this was the springtime, when kings led their armies in battle after the winter months of garrison and resupply. His men are at war, but David drifts into softness and neglects his vocational duties. The temptation to selfishness, avoidance of suffering, and lack of mortification is always the first movement of sin.

The next movement for David was an unholy curiosity. This patterns Eve's curiosity about the "tree of the knowledge of good and bad" and the forbidden fruit it contained (Gn 2:9, 17) as well as Adam's neglect of his duties, which mirror the two ends of the authority structure in the responsibility given to Adam "to cultivate (provide) and care (protect)" for the garden of Eden (Gn 2:15). The care of the paradisal garden was entrusted to Adam, as was the punishment for the violation of this prohibition—namely, death ("you will be surely doomed to die" should he eat its fruit, Gn. 2:14). In the primordial garden, Adam was silent while Eve conversed with the talking serpent. Similarly, instead of performing his kingly duties, David too was negligent. Like the garden scene where God "strolled" in the "cool, breezy time of the day" (literally, "in the evening," Gn 3:8) and finds that Adam and Eve had eaten the forbidden fruit as seen in their covering of their nakedness with loincloths (Gn 3:7, 11), so David "took a stroll" on the roof of his palace "in the evening" and sees a naked woman.

As it happened, on his "evening time" stroll, that time of day when the cool breeze of Palestine gently blows, David had a clear view of "a woman bathing," who, we are told, "was very beautiful" (1 Sm 11:2). The various trees in the garden were also "beautiful to look at" (*kalon* in Greek, Gn 2:9). When Eve (and Adam silently beside her) saw the tree of knowledge of good and evil, she "saw the tree was good for food, pleasing to the eyes, and desirable" (Gn 3:6). Similarly, we are told that Bathsheba is "exceedingly beautiful" (*kalon*) and pleasing "to David's eyes" (2 Sm 11:2). Are we to believe that this was a chance encounter? The reader is not told, but our common human experience suggests that it is highly unlikely that this was a first for either of them (although the text itself is silent). The lexical parallels between the first sin and that of David and Bathsheba suggest that the latter sin will follow the pattern of the former, its archetype. Like Eve at a place where she was not supposed to be, lingering around "the tree of knowledge of good and evil" and pondering the fruit, so David put himself in a place to be tempted. Bathsheba may well have placed herself there as that very fruit, as both were recounted as "very beautiful and pleasing to the eye." The stage was set for the demon to set up the fall of the king through a sin that would have familial ramifications.

Other lexical parallels with the first sin are found in key words/phrases that link both accounts:

The original sin of Adam and Eve	**The sin of David**
Eve is curious of the forbidden fruit and the serpent "inquires" from the woman (Gn 2:9)	David is curious about the woman and sent "inquiries" about her (2 Sm 11:3)
God "strolls" in the garden in the evening breeze and finds the man and the woman ashamed because they were "naked" (Gn 3:8, 10)	Adam "took a stroll" on the rooftop of his palace in the evening and sees a "naked" woman (2 Sm 11:2)

The trees of the garden were "beautiful to the eyes and good for food" (Gn 2:9); and "the woman saw that the tree was good for food, pleasing to the eyes, and desirable" (Gn 3:6)	The bathing woman was "exceedingly beautiful to the eyes" of David (2 Sm 11:2)
Adam and Eve eat the fruit and results in death and strife in the family line (Gn 3:1, 19; 4:8–10)	David tastes the fruit of the mortal sin, the child dies and David refuses to eat or drink (2 Sm 11:4; 12:17, 8); strife enters his family line (2 Sm 12:11)
God "rested from his work on the seventh day" and blessed it (Gn 2:2–3)	The child died "on the seventh day" and God cursed the offspring of David's house (2 Sm 12:18; 11)
The serpent tells Eve, "You certainly will not die" (Gn 3:4)	Nathan tells David, "The LORD has forgiven your sin, you shall not die" (2 Sm 12:13)
Adam is created "from the ground" (Gn 2:7)	David rises "from the ground" (2 Sm 12:20)
God said to the woman, "What is this thing you have done?" (Gn 3:13)	David's servants said to him, "What is this thing that you have done?" (2 Sm 12:21)
Adam tells God, "I was afraid because I was naked, and I hid myself" (Gn 3:10)	God tells David, "You have done this in secret/hidden" (2 Sm 12:12)
"The man had relations with his wife Eve, and she conceived and bore Cain" (Gn 4:1)	David "had relations" with the wife of Uriah the Hittite "and the woman conceived" (Sm 11:4–5); David also "had relations" with Bathsheba and "she conceived and bore him a son . . . Solomon" (2 Sm 12:24)

Notably, we see in both accounts the transgression followed by death and strife in the family line (Gn 3:1, 19; 4:8–10; 2 Sm 11:4; 12:17, 8; 12:10,11). Both involve eating/not eating (Gn 3:6). While God "rested from his work on the seventh day" and blessed creation (Gn 2:2–3), David's child died "on the seventh day" and God cursed the offspring of David's house (2 Sm 12:18; 11). In both, there is the phrase "you shall not die" (Gn 3:4; 2 Sm 12:13). After the sin of Eve, God said to the woman, "What is this thing you have done?" (Gn 3:13). The exact phrase is used by David's servants to David ("What is this thing that you have done?") in 2 Samuel 12:21. Both accounts mention the shame of sin with a cognate word meaning "secret/hidden" (Gn 3:10; 2 Sm 12:12). In the garden, "the man had relations with his wife Eve, and she conceived and bore Cain" (Gn 4:1). In the exact same phrase, David "had relations" with the wife of Uriah the Hittite "and the woman conceived" (2 Sm 11:4–5). David later "had relations" with Bathsheba and "she conceived and bore him a son . . . Solomon" (2 Sm 12:4–5). These parallels suggest that the account of David's sin follows the pattern of the original sin.

The prophet Nathan gives a parable about a rich man who took a poor man's ewe lamb out of greed as a metaphor for David's sin (2 Sm 12:1–6). The rich man had "flocks and herds" from which to choose. God blessed David with abundance, to include kingship, wealth, and victory over his pursuers (2 Sm 12:7–8). Mention of "flocks and herds" recall the blessing upon Abraham: "And the LORD hath blessed my master greatly; and he is become great: and he hath given him flocks, and herds, and silver, and gold, and menservants, and maidservants, and camels, and asses" (Gn 24:35). Yet David was greedy for the wife of Uriah like the rich man in the parable was greedy for the poor man's prized ewe. Upon hearing the parable, David responded with indignation: "As the LORD lives, the man who has done this deserves to die; and he shall restore the lamb fourfold, because he did this thing, and because he had no pity" (2 Sm 12:6). That "fourfold" restitution hints at the temporal satisfaction due to sin. An additional allusion to the effect of the sin of Adam and Eve upon their offspring is seen in mention of prize firstlings and "flocks." Like Cain who killed his brother Abel who offered to the LORD "the best firstlings of his flocks," so in Nathan's parable the rich man takes the prize ewe and "merits death" (2 Sm 12:5). Nathan then informs David that the parable is about what he did to Uriah, saying to the king, "You are the man!" (2 Sm 12:7). The Hebrew word for man or husband is *adam*. In another subtle play on words, Nathan says to David: *You are Adam*.

Perhaps the most interesting key phrase which highlights the inherited guilt is an allusion not to creation, however, but to Sinai. Through Nathan, God speaks:

> Why have you **despised** the word of the LORD, to **do what is evil in his sight**? You have struck down Uriah the Hittite with the sword and have taken his wife to be your wife and have killed him with the sword of the Ammonites. Now therefore the sword shall never depart from your house, because you have **despised me** and have taken the wife of Uriah the Hittite to be your wife.' Thus says the LORD, 'Behold, I will raise up evil against you out of your own house. And I will take your wives before your eyes and give them to your neighbor, and he shall lie with your wives in the sight of this sun." (2 Sm 12:9–10 ESV)

The repetition here of "hating me" is used as emphasis, to recall the warning of *avon avot* in Deuteronomy 5:9, where God promises that He will punish the sins of the father "to those who hate/despise me." We see here that the effects of grave sin include not just idolatry, but also adultery. The punishment will follow along the familial lines. The story continues:

> Thus says the LORD, "Behold, I will raise up evil against you out of your own house. And I will take your wives before

> your eyes and give them to your neighbor, and he shall lie with your wives in the sight of this sun. For you did it secretly, but I will do this thing before all Israel and before the sun." David said to Nathan, "I have sinned against the LORD." And Nathan said to David, "The LORD also has put away your sin; you shall not die. Nevertheless, because by this deed you have utterly scorned the LORD, the child that is born to you shall die." (2 Sm 12:11–154 ESV)

Here, the "double consequence of sin" is seen as the spiritual and the temporal. As in the discussion on St. Thomas above, the death of the child is the spiritual (essential/penal) punishment for the sin (2 Sm 12:14). The temporal (incidental/medicinal) punishment is the effect of the sin that carries down to the familial line (the "sword" of strife and rebellion and sexual sins, as per 2 Sm 12:10–12). The story continues:

> And the LORD afflicted the child that Uriah's wife bore to David, and he became sick. David therefore sought God on behalf of the child. And David fasted and went in and lay all night on the ground. And the elders of his house stood beside him, to raise him from the ground, but he would not, nor did he eat food with them. On the seventh day the child died. And the servants of David were afraid to tell him that the child was dead, for they said, "Behold, while the child was yet alive, we spoke to him, and he did not listen to us. How then can we say to him the child is dead? He may do himself some harm." But when David saw that his servants were whispering together, David understood that the child was dead. And David said to his servants, "Is the child dead?" They said, "He is dead." Then David arose from the earth and washed and anointed himself and changed his clothes. And he went into the house of the LORD and worshiped. He then went to his own house. And when he asked, they set food before him, and he ate. Then his servants said to him,

> **"What is this thing that you have done?"** (2 Sm 12:15–21 ESV)

The phrase "what is this thing you have done" echoes the words of God to Eve after the Fall in Genesis 3:13, suggesting that inherited guilt (*avon avot,* the sins of the father are punished in the children) follows the pattern of original sin. The twofold effect of spiritual death and concupiscence as part of the temporal punishment due to sin according to the *Catechism* as we have seen above. Thus, original sin is archetypical for all subsequent sin. In David's case, there is the death of his infant son and the effect of the sin seen in the sword which would visit his household in the form of strife, continued sexual sin, etc.

The child himself is not cursed but lived under the effect of the curse—that is, the privation of the protection of a blessing. The next offspring of David and Bathsheba was Solomon: "Then David comforted his wife, Bathsheba, and went in to her, and lay with her; and she bore a son, and he called his name Solomon. And the LORD loved him, and sent a message by Nathan the prophet; so he called his name Jedidiah, because of the LORD" (2 Sm 12:25). The child's name means "Beloved of the Lord."

The Life of Solomon and the Effect of David's Sin

The story ends by closing the loop where it began, with Joab "sending word" to David (2 Sm 12:27) just as David had "sent word" to Joab to kill Uriah (2 Sm 11:6). At long last, David departs from Jerusalem and returns to the battlefield and leads his troops to victory in battle against the Ammonites, as a king should do. He captures the capital city of Rabbah (2 Sm 11:11; 12:29) before returning to Jerusalem with his army (2 Sm 11:1; 12:31). Ironically, the principal deity of Rabbah, the "water-city" (2 Sm 12:27), was Molech (also known as Milcom). Combined with Astarte, these were the demon-gods of the Canaanites. Molech—ironically, whose name means "king"—was a fertility deity who was appeased by human sacrifice, specifically children (Lv 18:21; Ez 16:21; Jer 32:35). In this cultic practice, children were placed into an effigy of the god, which was an image of the human body with a bull's head with horns (similar to images of Baphomet seen today) and burned alive. A second principal deity of the Canaanites was Astarte, the mother goddess of Sidon to whom ritualistic sex was performed in groves and sacred poles (Ez 16:24). This activity is condemned by God Himself and evokes the "jealousy" of God (Ex 34:13), who alone is the Beloved of Israel.

Lest the reader think these are coincidental occurrences, when the child of David and Bathsheba became king, the twofold effect of the sin of David—familial strife and sexual sin—gradually overtook his reign. The combination of first and sixth commandment violations is often what is seen in cases of diabolic affliction, and often when generational curses are operative. These, in a sense, ratify the curses and now have the willful participation. We see this in the life of Solomon: "King Solomon loved many foreign women besides the daughter of pharaoh (Moabites, Ammonites, Edomites, Sidonians, and Hittites), from nations which the LORD had forbidden the Israelites to intermarry, 'because,' he said, 'they will turn your heart to their gods'" (1 Kgs 11:1–2).

Solomon is reported to have had "seven hundred wives and three hundred concubines" (1 Kgs 11:3). What began with sexual deviancy, however, gradually "turned his heart to strange gods" away from "the LORD, his God as the heart of his father David had been" (1 Kgs 11:4). Accordingly, and perhaps ironically, Solomon is said to have introduced into Isreal the same demons of the Canaanites that his father had conquered ("Astarte, the goddess of Sidonians, Milcom, the idol of the Ammonites . . . [and] Chemosh, the idol of Moab," 1 Kgs 11:4–8). Further, Solomon introduced, "on the hill opposite Jerusalem" the cultic human sacrifice of "the idol of the Ammonites" (1 Kgs 11:7). For these offenses to God, the generational curse sinks into the familial line. God honors the free will and allows us to suffer the consequences of our decisions:

> So the LORD said to Solomon: "Since this is what you want, and you have not kept my covenant and my statutes which I enjoined on you, I will deprive you of the kingdom and give it to your servant. I will not do this during your lifetime, however, for the sake of your father David; it is your son whom I will deprive. Nor will I take away the whole kingdom. I will leave your son one tribe for the sake of my servant David and of Jerusalem, which I have chosen. (1 Kgs 11:11–13)

We see here the compounding effect of inherited guilt, and the twofold punishment of David's sin was disorder and division in the family. David will retain Judah (and its capital, Jerusalem) and Benjamin, the tribe geographically beneath Judah.

The life of David highlights how sin offends God and damages our relationship with Him, requiring satisfaction be made. In discussing the need for satisfaction for sins, the *Catechism of the Council of Trent* taught that "sin carries in its train two evils, the stain which it affixes, and the punishment which it entails." On a spiritual level, "to satisfy is also to cut all occasions of sin, and to close every avenue of the heart against its suggestions . . . [and is] a cleansing, which effaces whatever defilement may remain in the soul from the stains of sin, and which exempts it from the temporal chastisements due to sin."[253] The same *Catechism* then cites the life of David as evidence from Scripture as a "most conspicuous and illustrious" example of the remittance of the temporal punishment and satisfaction for sin. To wit:

> Already had Nathan announced to him: "The Lord hath taken away thy sin, thou shall not die" (2 Kgs 12:13) yet the royal penitent voluntarily subjected himself to the most severe penance, imploring, night and day, the mercy of God, in these words: "Wash me yet more from iniquity, and cleanse me from my sin, for I know my iniquity and my sin is always before me" (Ps 51:4–5). Thus did he beseech God to pardon not only the crime, but also the punishment due to it, and to restore him, cleansed from the stains of sin, to his former state of purity and integrity. This is the object of his most earnest supplications to the throne of God, and yet the Almighty punishes his transgression with the death of his adulterous offspring, the rebellion and death of his beloved son Absalom, and with other heavy chastisements, which his vengeance had already threatened him.[254]

Notably, and as Saint Thomas noted above, the punishment for David's sin was upon the next generation, his offspring, which bore the punishment for his sin of adultery and murder.

Imitation or Personal Responsibility?

As noted in the previous chapter, the imitation and personal responsibility arguments of Julian still do not answer the problem found in the New Testament of children afflicted by demons. One could reasonably argue that the Syrophoenician woman's daughter in chapter seven of the Gospel of Saint

[253] *Catechism of the Council of Trent*, 286.
[254] *Catechism of the Council of Trent*, 287–89.

Mark was of a sufficient age; "little girl" was diminutive and not indicative of her age, and therefore she could imitate the sins of her mother or commit mortal sin. But what of the boy in chapter nine of the Gospel of Saint Mark who was possessed "since infancy"? The argument from imitation, quite simply, falls short. Accordingly, by way of summary, when we look at the exchange between Saint Augustine and Julian in light of Saint Thomas on vicarious punishment, the mechanics of generational spirits (not sin) begin to emerge.

Saint Augustine makes a key response to Julian, who continually claimed that God does not visit the iniquities of the father upon the children, that only the one who sins suffers for his own sins, when a child suffers, it is because of imitation of the parent's sins, and that there is neither an original sin nor any generational effect of personal sins. Saint Augustine acknowledges that the effect of the sin of Adam and Eve means that even infants suffer. In response to Julian, who claimed that to say that a child suffers because of his parents is to imply that God is unjust, he points out the generational effect of the fall on infants. He distinguishes between one who suffers affliction for his own sins and the suffering of infants. "The case of penitents is one thing," He says, "that of the newborn is another." In addition to bodily ailments being passed down generationally as the result of original sin, Augustine also lists "attacks of demons."[255] Demons attack even infants, he argues, but in a list of otherwise bodily sufferings. This is a key point when understanding the potential mechanics of generational spirits through a patristic and theological lens. Original sin has introduced evil into the human condition, to include attacks by demons upon infants, he says.

Saint Thomas both affirms and builds on this when he makes the connection between the passing down of the

---

[255] Saint Augustine, *Answer to the Pelagians III*, 309.

effects of sins and the familial authority structure, and the punishment of the sins of the father as able to pass to their children in the form of "temporal or bodily punishments." This is because, Saint Thomas says, the children as part of the bodily goods of parents, to wit, "in so far as children are the property of their parents, and posterity, of their forefathers," can be afflicted in this way.[256] While the spiritual effects and punishment for sins are retained upon the individual who alone is punished and who alone is personally responsible for making satisfaction, the "double consequence" of sin (CCC 1472) means that sin also has a bodily/temporal component. Saints Thomas and Augustine both affirm *avon avot* and personal responsibility, and both also hold that what is passed down, or generational, is not the sin or its personal punishment (as the traducianists hold), but rather the effect of the sin itself. The Church affirms that all sin requires satisfaction ("the temporal punishment due to sin" even after forgiveness, as per CCC 1471), and that the purpose of temporal punishment is to remove obstacles to union with God (CCC 1471–73).

Children are a part of the bodily goods of parents, and the satisfaction for parents' sins can be punished vicariously in them. This is not deterministic, however, as ultimately God knows what is best for the soul, and the family gives the medicinal remedy according to His perfect mercy and justice. God sometimes uses demons to serve as His instruments of punishing sin, the salutary effect of which also serves to purify a person and family of sin and any obstacles to union with God, as Saint Bonaventure affirms. This is experienced as "languishing" resulting from "the iniquities of their ancestors" (Lv 26:42) which is experienced as an oppression upon temporal goods. Ultimately, God honors free will, and to each

[256] Saint Thomas Aquinas, *ST* I–II, q. 87, art. 8.

generation he calls His people of the new covenant to fidelity as He did to those of the first covenant (cf. Dt 11:22).

Saint Thomas's explanation on the inner logic of vicarious punishment bears reading at length:

> I answer that, punishment may be considered in two ways. First, under the aspect of punishment, and in this way punishment is not due save for sin, because by means of punishment the equality of justice is restored, in so far as he who by sinning has exceeded in following his own will suffers something that is contrary to this will. Wherefore, since every sin is voluntary not excluding original sin as stated above; it follows that no one is punished in this way, except for something done voluntarily. Secondly, punishment may be considered as a medicine, not only healing the past sin, but also preserving from future sin, or conducing to some good, and in this way a person is sometimes punished without any fault of his own, yet not without cause.[257]

Here, notably, he evokes the language of *iniquitas* (sin as creating an imbalance which needs to be remedied through satisfaction) of *avon avot*. He also distinguishes between personal responsibility for sin, while also affirming that sin can be punished vicariously. In the case of the latter, it is medicinal—that is, healing the effects of past sins, preserving us from future sins, and always ordered to some greater good according to divine providence.

The goods of the soul are more important than the goods of the body. As Saint Paul writes, "We hold this treasure [of divine life on us] in earthen vessels" (2 Cor 4:7). Thus, "this momentary light affliction is producing for us an eternal weight of glory beyond all comparison" (2 Cor 4:17). Saint Thomas echoes this and continues:

[257] Saint Thomas Aquinas, *ST* II–II, q. 79, art. 6.

> And since spiritual goods are of the greatest consequence, while temporal goods are least important, sometimes a person is punished in his temporal goods without any fault of his own. Such are many of the punishments inflicted by God in this present life for our humiliation or probation. But no one is punished in spiritual goods without any fault on his part, neither in this nor in the future life, because in the latter punishment is not medicinal, but a result of spiritual condemnation.[258]

Here he affirms that vicarious punishment of *avon avot* is upon the temporal goods while the spiritual punishment for sin is personal to each sinner who is culpable for his own sins. Suffering produces the fruits of humility and perseverance.

He then affirms *avon avot* and reminds us not to dismiss it as anthropomorphic; rather, this bespeaks of the mystery of God:

> The saying of the Lord, "Visiting the iniquity of the fathers upon the children unto the third and fourth generation," seems to belong to mercy rather than to severity, since He does not take vengeance forthwith, but waits for some future time, in order that the descendants at least may mend their ways; yet should the wickedness of the descendants increase, it becomes almost necessary to take vengeance on them.[259]

"Visiting the iniquities" is ultimately an extension of the unbounded mercy of God, who allows each generation free will. When the children repeat the sins of their fathers, God's punishments become necessary so as to stop the continuation of evil.

---

[258] Saint Thomas Aquinas, *ST* II–II, q. 10, art. 4.
[259] Saint Thomas Aquinas, *ST* II–II, q. 87, art. 1.

He concludes by showing that the punishment for sin falls within the realm of divine, not human, law. He also limits the effects of sins to temporal goods as a preventative measure:

> By the judgment of God children are punished in temporal matters together with their parents, both because they are a possession of their parents, so that their parents are punished also in their person, and because this is for their good lest, should they be spared, they might imitate the sins of their parents, and thus deserve to be punished still more severely.[260]

Ultimately, what Saint Thomas adds to the discussion sheds light on both the *why* and the *how* of this phenomenon of generational spirits as part of the temporal punishment for sins. This, then, would also explain how the demons are passed on from one parent to the child based upon the fact that the demon is actually attached to the parent's body and the child is part of the bodily goods of the parents and under their authority. Even in cases of possession, where the demon influences the higher faculties of the intellect and will, what he possesses is only the body, properly speaking. This, then, is the mechanics of how spirits can pass from father to child in that he can afflict the parent and that the parent allows the demon to be present bodily, such that he can then be passed on bodily through the authority structure. As Saint Thomas notes, since children are of the body of the parents and in a sense their "property" or part of the temporal, bodily goods of parents, then they can suffer not the spiritual punishment but the bodily punishment of their parents. This would also indicate why a generational spirit can be passed on by parents once it has gotten into a family, which is technically speaking a physical or a bodily entry, that he can then start picking

[260] Saint Thomas Aquinas, *ST* II–II, q. 10, art. 4.

away at the children as a result. This suggests that by both an imitation and a certain vulnerability created, it is passed on through that mechanism as well.

This is a much clearer understanding of the familial effects of personal sin and why the sins of parents do have a negative effect on their children. Saint Thomas both refutes the modern error of "intergenerational sin" and affirms that there is such a thing as a generational passing down of the effects of sin. If a person has the sin of anger (or infidelity, or gossip, or alcoholism, etc.), that sin does not pass down like the sin of Adam and Eve passed down through natural generation. The punishment for sin, however, can pass down along the family line because of the sins of the father. That breach of the protection which comes through blessing makes the child "more prone to sin," says Saint Thomas, due to the privation of the protection which comes with blessing and the poor example of the father. This, in turn, means a greater propensity to imitation because of a disordering in the child's socialization.

Notably, it is not deterministic, says Saint Thomas, since the child can offer impediments of a life of holiness and the state of grace. "For the power of the parent's sin does not reach [the children]," he says, if it is opposed to the sin." Nonetheless, with the vulnerability that comes from a lack of paternal spiritual protection as well as negative socialization, a child is conditioned, in a sense, to commit the sins of his father. In that case, he says, "through imitation [the sin] in a way, becomes continuous. Hence by this fact the child's being punished for his father's sin in a certain way is not taken away."[261]

Perhaps the problems lie in the fact that many of us live as if semi-habituated by modernism, which tells us that there are no effects of sins if we do not intend them. Accordingly, as stated above, original sin sets a pattern for all sin in that

[261] Saint Thomas Aquinas, *II Sent.*, d. 33, q. 2.

there are twofold consequences and twofold punishments, the spiritual and temporal. Original sin is, as the *Catechism* states, "'the reverse side' of the Good News" (CCC 389) and it sets the pattern for all sin. The developed tradition is clear that each person has a personal responsibility for his own sins and sins themselves are not intergenerational. Nonetheless, with regard to the temporal effect of the sins of a father that can be experienced by the children, according to divine providence. Both Saint Augustine and Saint Thomas are clear on that. This is quite different than an intergenerational sin and healing the family tree by using the Mass in a superstitious way.

Just as darkness is not light's equal but the privation of light, so also a curse in this sense is not the equal opposite force to blessing, but rather the privation of the effects of blessing. In this sense we can rightly speak of the *effects* of sin as *generational* not because the sin is "generated" but due to both the nature of sin (CCC 1471) and the *familial* construct of authority whereby God Himself states: "For I, the LORD, your God, I am a jealous God, inflicting punishment for their fathers' wickedness on the children of those who hate me, down to the third and fourth generation" (Ex 20:5). Also in the section on the need for satisfaction for sins, the *Catechism of Trent* recalls these words from Sinai:

> In Exodus too the Almighty, although yielding to the importunity of Moses, he had spared the idolatrous Israelites [referring to the Golden Calf incident in Exodus 32], threatens the enormity of their crime with heavy chastisements (Ex 32:8–9); and Moses himself declares, that the Lord will take vengeance on it, even to the third and fourth generation. *That such was, at all times, the doctrine of the Fathers, a reference to their writings will place beyond the possibility of all doubt.*[262]

[262] *Catechism of the Council of Trent*, 288.

Notably, here the Council of Trent affirms *avon avot* as firmly embedded in the theological tradition of the Church, and lists Saints Augustine, Gregory, Chrysostom, and Ambrose as evidence.[263]

The Fathers, then, provide the correct theological context for the phenomena of familial spirits. God honors our free will and withdraws His blessing when we commit grave sins, such as idolatry. Human free will is a gift from God, but it carries with it serious consequences. Thus, "man is . . . subject to the laws of creation and to moral norms that govern the use of freedom" (CCC 396). God allows us to live with the consequences of our sinful actions. Even in darkness, however, God uses the evil spirits as the instrument of reparation (to restore balance) and satisfaction (temporal debt due to sin). Accordingly, the phenomenon may be correctly termed "generational" only if one is clear in distinguishing what is passed down—not the sin, but its effects, which requires satisfaction.

Thus, we can affirm that while sin does not hand down, the effect of sin can carry down as part of the temporal punishment and can (not always, as this is under divine providence) be experienced along the family line. The entry point can be a curse by the father or mother or simply the temporal effect of a grave

---

263 *Catechism of the Council of Trent*, 288–89. Father Peter Joseph is correct in his assessment of McCall and the healing the family tree in his assertion that "no Father, no Doctor of the Church, no Saint, no Pope, no Council ever taught or even implied any such thing." Nonetheless, in his rejection of McCall's intergenerational theory, Father Joseph also rejects *avon avot*, stating that God's words at Sinai are a "provisional Revelation" in which "God changed this arrangement" whereby the children can suffer the effects of the sins of parents. This position is not only contrary to Saint Augustine's own thoughts expressed in the debate with Julian of Eclanum, but in direct contradiction to the unanimous voice of the Fathers as cited here from the Council of Trent. See Joseph, "False Religion." *In Where Peter Is* (November 21, 2024). Father Alcántara-Mendoza similarly dismisses *avon avot* as hyperbole and says it is anthropomorphic to claim that God punishes sin in this way. See Alcántara-Mendoza, "La llamada oración de 'sanación del árbol genealógico.'"

sin where God uses, as noted above, Saints Bonaventure and Ambrose both assert, angels (both fallen and glorified) to punish sin. Thus, the *Catechism* asserts that there remains the need for "patiently bearing sufferings and trials of all kinds . . . prayer and the various practices of penance" (CCC 1473), which break the effects of, and makes satisfaction for, sin. This is consistent with what Father Amorth noted above: family members should "make whatever sacrifices are necessary to break each evil spell." This, in turn, gives a foundation for the two instances in the New Testament where children are afflicted by demons.

Blessing means provision and protection and closeness to Him, cursing means languishing in the effects of His absence. To this generation, too, He says, "I set before you here, this day, a blessing and a curse: a blessing for obeying the commandments of the LORD, your God, which I enjoin on you today; a curse if you do not obey the commandments of the LORD, your God, but turn aside from the way I ordain for you today, to follow other gods, whom you have not known" (Dt 11:26–28). Joshua laid out the same challenge before entering the Promised Land and reminded the people that being a part of the covenant people of God is a family affair, and with him said: "As for me and my household, we will serve the LORD" (Jo 24:15).

An Example

In speaking of the religious identity and gods of the foreign nations that surrounded Israel, the psalmist states clearly that "all the gods of the Gentiles are demons (*daimonia*, Ps 96:5).[264] Thus, whether someone offers a sacrifice (petitioning a favor, etc.) or worship of any kind to a false god,

[264] The NRSV translates Psalm 96.5: "For all the gods of the peoples are idols, but the Lord made the heavens." The Latin Vulgate: *Quoniam omnes dii gentium dæmonia; Dominus autem cælos fecit*. The Greek Septuagint (LXX 95.5) reads similarly.

they are offering it to a demon. This holds as much cosmic import today as it did then and occurs whether knowingly or unknowingly by the participant. Accordingly, whether so-called white magic is used for good ends like love or healing or the dark arts are summoned for evil purposes, both are an intrinsic evil. Father Amorth notes that "there are no such things as 'white' or 'black' magic. Every form of magic is practiced with recourse to Satan."[265]

The "surrender" posture of yoga, for example, or channeling of chakras through Reiki or reflexology, are common entry points since these modalities offer worship (in the form of petitioning) to cosmic entities other than the One, True God. In the common experiences of exorcists, the demons take these petitions very seriously (and do not like to let go once given permission in). As I mention elsewhere, this is referred to as interactive diabolic activity, this describes,

> activities in which a person invokes—whether through incantation, pledge, or bodily ritual—a power other than the One, True God. The *interactive* component is meant that such invocations involve an exchange between participants and the demons. These can be seemingly innocuous things like the Ouija board of a previous generation, tarot cards and fortune tellers, or some (but not all) modern video games where real curses and spells have been coded into the game's script. Thus, tarot cards and Ouija boards, for example, invoke evil spirits for some favor and open the persons to diabolic affliction by giving permissions to the demons called upon.[266]

---

[265] Amorth, *An Exorcist Tells His Story*, 60.
[266] Schneider, *Manual*, 60.

As Father Hardon notes, these can include "Satanism, fetishism, black and white magic, spiritism, theosophy, divination, and witchcraft."[267]

When a person has their faculties properly ordered and in a state of grace, however, it is much easier to discern the diabolical. An example of this is a woman who was experiencing health issues and her doctor recommended she do yoga. The woman was a cradle Catholic, and she raised a Catholic family and lived in a Catholic household. She lived her Catholic faith in an exemplary way. She was in her fifties and married over thirty years when her doctor made the recommendation.

About six to eight weeks into having done the yoga, she began to have invasive thoughts of impurity which were completely foreign to her. She had never had any issues with infidelity or impure thoughts, but began to have increasingly perverted thoughts. She began to have thoughts of infidelity, which made her realize these were not her thoughts but rather diabolic projections. She was astute enough to look for a pattern, "*Okay, when does this happen?*" She came to realize that it always happened in correlation with the times that she would participate in yoga. As she investigated further, she began to pray, *Is this wrong? What did or how is this happening?* Perhaps providentially, she happened upon a pamphlet on Catholicism and yoga, which laid out all of the Scripture references with regard to deviant practices, specifically the psalm that states, "*The gods of the Gentiles are demons.*" While there was nothing obvious in the visible realm, she was very aware of the invisible realm where the action of the fallen angels was associated with yoga and with the practices that body positions in the incantations of yoga. She began to realize and correlate that the thoughts that accompanied certain positions had a negative connotation. She asked the yoga instructor about the spiritual

[267] Hardon, *Modern Catholic Dictionary*, 387.

ramifications of the yoga body positions, but her instructor was emphatic that none of these sessions involved any spirit of the yoga. What they did, she said, was simply exercises.

The woman discussed it with her husband, and both went to confession that following weekend. She chose another form of exercise and began to pray more. The malicious thoughts quickly ceased.

The Hope

Spiritual author Jean-Pierre de Caussade counselled: "To escape the distress caused by regret for the past or fear about the future, this is the rule to follow: leave the past to the infinite mercy of God, the future to His good Providence, give the present wholly to His love by being faithful to His grace."[268] The enemy is an apex predator and uses every means to lead us astray. As the experience of this woman shows, however, when we stay in the state of grace, form a Catholic conscience, and spend time in prayer, we can discern the enemy's traps and make our way back to God. Jesus has left to the Church the means to defeat the enemy. The two things to which we hold fast are the infinite mercy of God and the merits of Jesus Christ. All else is vanity. God even uses sin for a greater good:

> God, says St. Augustine, would not allow any evil to happen, if He were not sufficiently powerful and good to turn it all to the greater good of His elect. Let us make use of our present evils, to escape those that are eternal, and to merit the rewards promised to faith and patience. The time will come, and it is at hand, when we shall say with David, "We have rejoiced for the days in which Thou hast humbled us for the years in which we have seen evils" (Ps 89:15).[269]

[268] De Caussade, *Abandonment to Divine Providence*, 110.
[269] De Caussade, *Abandonment to Divine Providence*, 203.

A Prayer

O my most amiable Jesus, how much have I too caused You to suffer during Your lifetime! You have shed Your blood for me with so much sorrow and love, and what fruit have You hitherto drawn from me, but contempt, offenses, and insults? But, my Redeemer, I will no longer afflict You; I hope that in the future Your passion will produce fruit in me by Your grace, which I feel is already assisting me. I will love You above every other good; and to please You, I am ready to give my life a thousand times. Eternal Father, I should not have the boldness to appear before You to implore either pardon or graces, but Your Son has told me, that whatever grace I ask of You in His name You will grant it to me: If you ask anything of the Father in My name, He will give it to you. I offer You the merits of Jesus Christ, and in His name I ask of You first a general pardon of all my sins; I ask holy perseverance, even unto death; I ask of You, above all, the gift of Your holy love, that it may make me always live according to your divine will. As to my own will, I am resolved to choose a thousand deaths sooner than offend You, and to love You with my whole heart, and to do everything that I possibly can to please You. But in order to do all this, I beg of You, and hope to receive from You, grace to execute what I purpose. My Mother Mary, if you will pray for me, I am safe. Oh, pray for me, pray; and cease not to pray till you see that I am changed, and made what God wishes me to be.[270]

O compassionate Mother, look at this traitor who kneels at your feet. My sins increase my confidence because your compassion is even greater to great sinners. I do not fear my sins because you give the remedy. I do not fear the devil because

[270] Saint Alphonsus Liguori, in *The Road to Bethlehem*, 57–58.

you are more powerful. I do not fear your Son because your words appease Him. O Mary, I hope all things from you because you are all powerful with God.[271]

Fatima Prayer

(The Fatima prayer is also a prayer of reparation against the offenses against God that occult practice brings.)

My God, I believe, I adore, I hope, and I love Thee! I ask pardon for those who do not believe, do not adore, do not hope, and do not love Thee.

Most Holy Trinity—Father, Son, and Holy Spirit—I adore Thee profoundly. I offer Thee the most precious Body, Blood, Soul, and Divinity of Jesus Christ, present in all the tabernacles of the world, in reparation for the outrages, sacrileges, and indifferences whereby He is offended. And through the infinite merits of His Most Sacred Heart and the Immaculate Heart of Mary, I beg of Thee the conversion of poor sinners.

O my Jesus, I offer this for love of Thee, for the conversion of sinners, and in reparation for the sins committed against the Immaculate Heart of Mary.

O My Jesus, forgive us our sins, save us from the fires of Hell, lead all souls to Heaven, especially those who have most need of Thy mercy.

---

271 Saint Alphonsus Liguori, *Glories of Mary*, 16.

VI.

Women and Children First: A Look at the New Testament

The concept of the holy jealousy of God and nuptial and bridal imagery to describe His covenant people did not end with the Old Testament. Our understanding of the Church as the "bride" of Christ is most directly found in the writings of Saint Paul, who echoes the words of God who revealed Himself as "Jealous One" in holy betrothal at Sinai. "For I am jealous of you with the jealousy of God," Saint Paul writes, "since I betrothed you to one husband to present you as a chaste virgin to Christ" (2 Cor 11:2). He links the nuptial imagery and its corruption back to the original couple in the next verse: "But I am afraid that, as the serpent deceived Eve by his cunning, your thoughts may be *corrupted* from a sincere (and pure) commitment to Christ" (2 Cor 11:3, emphasis mine).

Saint Paul's choice of the Greek word for "corruption" (*ftheiro*) is curious—meaning to destroy, to corrupt (morally), and to bribe, specifically to seduce, as in seducing a woman to corrupt her morally. In the Old Testament, this term was used by the prophets to describe the seduction-that-leads-to-corruption—that is, idolatry. Saint Paul's mention of corruption, moreover, echoes the "corruption" found in the writing of the prophets. Ezekiel uses the word to describe the idolatry of the "sinful sisters" of both Samaria, what remained of Israel after those tribes in the north fell to the Assyrians, and Judah and Jerusalem in the south (Ez 16:52). Jeremiah describes the "corruption" of the "hubris" of the idolatry of both the ten northern tribes of Israel and the two southern tribes of Judah (Jer 13:9, 11). Hosea uses the term as well: "They have sunk to the depths of *corruption*, as in the days of Gibeah; God will remember their iniquity and punish their sins" (Hos 9:9). Gibeah refers to the rape and sodomy found in Judges 19:22–30. Hosea then denounces their fathers for the sexual revelry to Ba'al (read: "husband/lord/master") and "they became as abhorrent as the thing they loved" (Hos 9:10).

For Isaiah, the world "languishes," having been "corrupted" because its inhabitants have "broken the ancient covenant" (Is 54:4–5), echoing the punishments for covenant infidelity in Leviticus that "they will languish for their own and their fathers' guilt" (Lv 26:39).[272] Thus, Saint Paul's mention of the chaste virgin and the jealousy of God in the face of and seduction away from worship of the true God into the false worship and deviant sexual practices of idolatry begs the question: Has anything changed?

Saint Paul also uses the metaphor of human love to describe the relationship between God and His people:

> Wives should be subordinate to their husbands as to the LORD. For the husband is head of his wife just as Christ is head of the church, he himself the savior of the body. As the church is subordinate to Christ, so wives should be subordinate to their husbands in everything. Husbands, love your

[272] Thus, for Isaiah, "a curse devours the earth" and "inhabitants pay for their guilt" (Is 54:6). The result is all joy has "disappeared" and "the streets cry out for a lack of wine" (Is 54:11), echoing the messianic joy and abundance of wine in the Song and prophets as symbolic of the messianic age.

> wives, even as Christ loved the church and handed himself over for her to sanctify her, cleansing her by the bath of water with the word, that he might present to himself the church in splendor, without spot or wrinkle or any such thing, that she might be holy and without blemish. (Eph 5:22–27)[273]

"This is a great mystery," Saint Paul says, "but I speak in reference to Christ and the Church" (Eph 5:32). Saint Paul, the Apostle to the Gentiles (see Eph 3:1–12; 1 Thes 2:16, et al.), elsewhere in Ephesians speaks of "the mystery of Christ" that "the Gentiles are coheirs, members of the same body, and copartners in the promise in Christ Jesus through the gospel" (Eph 3:6; cf. Rom 1:16). Gentile "dogs" included in covenant union with God? For a faithful adherent of the Law, this is more than a mystery, this is scandalous.

Saint John also recounts a bridal and nuptial imagery connected to Christ and the Church. John the Baptist gives two titles of significance to Jesus: He is both Passover Lamb and Bridegroom. When the Baptizer first sees Jesus approaching, he cries out: "Behold the Lamb of God who takes away the sin of the world" (Jn 1:29). Then, when his mission was completed, John reveals a second title of Jesus, the divine Bridegroom who seeks His bride: "The one who has the bride is the bridegroom; the best man, who stands and listens to him, rejoices greatly at the bridegroom's voice. So this joy of mine has been made complete. He must increase, I must decrease" (Jn 3:29–30).

The images of a "bridal" church, divine Bridegroom, and the Passover Lamb are found elsewhere in Saint John's writings. In Revelation, for example, he uses Exodus imagery to include the same signs performed by Moses in Egypt such as boils (Rv

[273] The Greek word *upotasso* here translated to "be subordinate to" is a military term and is relevant to the discussion on inherited guilt and vicarious suffering of children for the sins of their fathers. It means to be *ordered under*, and in military usage means to be *under the protection of.*

16:2; Ex 9:1–4), water to blood (Rv 16:3; Ex 7:17–18) darkness (Rv 16:10; Ex 10:21–22), frogs (Rv 16:12; Ex 8:1–4), hailstones (Rv 16:21; Ex 9:22–23), the same signs performed by Pharaoh's magicians as signs performed by "demonic spirits" (Rv 16:14; Ex 7:11–12), cosmic signs echoing the Great Theophany at Sinai (Rv 16:18; Ex 19:16–20), and also "the song of Moses" (Rv 16:3–4; Dt 32:1–29). In that context, he uses the same prophetic imagery of harlotry to describe the unfaithful, the apostates; they are "the great harlot" (Rv 17:1).

Saint John then sees "the great city" Jerusalem comprised of "holy ones, apostles and prophets" and, like Ezekiel, pronounces a prophetic judgment (Rv 18:20). He hears from heaven a victory song (Rv 19:1–18) not unlike Moses's victory song after the Exodus (Ex 15:1–21). That victory song emanating from heaven denounces "the great harlot" and the sounds of a "great multitude" like the people who left Egypt (Rv 19:6; Ex 12:38) as if "rushing water" like the water that flowed from the rock (Rv 19:6; Ex 17:6). What Saint John then describes echoes the betrothal imagery of Sinai:

> Then I heard something like the sound of a great multitude or the sound of rushing water or mighty peals of thunder, as they said: "Alleluia! The LORD has established his reign, (our) God, the almighty. Let us rejoice and be glad and give him glory. For the wedding day of the Lamb has come, his bride has made herself ready. She was allowed to wear a bright, clean linen garment." (The linen represents the righteous deeds of the holy ones.) Then the angel said to me, "Write this: Blessed are those who have been called to the wedding feast of the Lamb." And he said to me, "These words are true; they come from God." (Rv 19:6–9)

Finally, at the climax of Revelation, John sees the Church in all her nuptial beauty and glory: "I also saw the holy city, a new Jerusalem, coming down out of heaven from God, prepared as a bride adorned for her husband" (Rv 21:2).

The One who has the Bride is the Bridegroom. Hold these concepts in mind as this chapter explores the divine Bridegroom seeking His bride from among both the Jews and the Gentiles. Here, I examine two New Testament stories, which are the problem of this inquiry—namely, children possessed by demons, which is what initially sparked my interest in this topic. Specifically, if the Catholic Church affirms that the Gospels are historically accurate, then we accept that Jesus walked on water, multiplied loaves, healed the sick, and even raised the dead. If those events are historically factual, however, then we also accept at face value that a little girl and an infant were possessed by evil spirits. Only after several years of working cases, which included afflicted children and even infants, did these two New Testament stories begin to make more sense. Without an understanding that children can suffer (inherit) the effects of the sins of their fathers (not inherit the sins themselves), as the previous chapters have shown from the Catholic tradition, then these two stories defy explanation. This has led some to search for other, scientific explanations such as epilepsy for these two children that the evangelists recount as afflicted by an evil spirit.[274] Behind the literal and historical meaning, however, are spiritual and theological truths which I hope to explore here with a view toward understanding how the effects of sin can pass to children.

A Little Dog: A Hariot's Price

The account of the exorcism of the daughter of a Gentile woman is found only in Mark and Matthew. Perhaps Luke

[274] See, for example, Father Wilfrid Harrington, who states that "the distressing symptoms of epilepsy" recounted by the evangelist was "in accordance with the ideas of the time" that "the recurrent convulsions and fits are prescribed to the periodical assault of an evil spirit." That is, the boy's convulsions had a natural, not a preternatural, causality. Harrington, *Mark*, 141.

omitted the story as his Gentile audience may have been a bit turned off being referred to as "little dogs," while Matthew's Jewish audience and Mark's mixed congregation in Rome would not have found it offensive, rather, they would have found it true. The two evangelists give slight differences in the detailing of the event:

Mark 7:24–30	Matthew 15:21–28
From that place he went off to the district of Tyre. He entered a house and wanted no one to know about it, but he could not escape notice. Soon a woman whose daughter had an unclean spirit heard about him. She came and fell at his feet. The woman was a Greek, a Syrophoenician by birth, and she begged him to drive the demon out of her daughter. He said to her, "Let the children be fed first. For it is not right to take the food of the children and throw it to the dogs." She replied and said to him, "LORD, even the dogs under the table eat the children's scraps." Then he said to her, "For saying this, you may go. The demon has gone out of your daughter." When the woman went home, she found the child lying in bed and the demon gone.	Then Jesus went from that place and withdrew to the region of Tyre and Sidon. And behold, a Canaanite woman of that district came and called out, "Have pity on me, LORD, Son of David! My daughter is tormented by a demon." But he did not say a word in answer to her. His disciples came and asked him, "Send her away, for she keeps calling out after us." He said in reply, "I was sent only to the lost sheep of the house of Israel." But the woman came and did him homage, saying, "LORD, help me." He said in reply, "It is not right to take the food of the children and throw it to the dogs." She said, "Please, LORD, for even the dogs eat the scraps that fall from the table of their masters." Then Jesus said to her in reply, "O woman, great is your faith! Let it be done for you as you wish." And her daughter was healed from that hour.

The basics of both accounts are essentially the same. Jesus travels into pagan territory where a Gentile mother seeks help for her daughter who is afflicted by evil spirits. Jesus resists, referring to them as "little dogs," before delivering the absent daughter with a command and commending the woman's faith. For Matthew, the daughter is "cruelly/evilly tormented/possessed by a demon" (Mt 15:22), while for Mark, she "had an unclean spirit" (Mk 7:26). The focus is on the mother and the interplay between her and Jesus, as if two characters on stage. Only in Matthew does the mother persist in "calling out" and "keeps shouting" (Mt 15:22–23). Matthew's Jewish audience would have taken notice that she asked for "pity" (or mercy). Jesus says nothing in reply to her seeking of mercy, something Matthew's Jewish audience would have immediately identified as *hesed*, God's covenant fidelity toward Israel. Essentially, she is not owed *hesed* as she is not part of the covenant people, thus making Jesus's response even more significant. The woman represents the pagans, and the story shows the divine Bridegroom seeking His Bride even among the Gentile nations. They and their children need first to be purified of their uncleanliness before a new covenantal union with God.

The location has historical and spiritual significance. Matthew has Jesus coming from Galilee (Mt 13:54) before he "withdrew to the region of Tyre and Sidon" (Mt 15:21). Matthew further recounts that the woman was "a Canaanite" (Mt 15:22). Notably, the word "Canaan" means "to be subjugated" or "to make low." In the table of nations, Moses recounts that Canaan was the son of Ham and grandson of Noah (Gn 10:6). Sidon was Canaan's firstborn son (Gn 10:15). Tyre was a nearby, fortified rocky peninsula and port city. From the rocky terrain, Tyre derives its name (the Hebrew *sor* means "rock").[275] When David was made king over Israel and took his throne, "Hiram, king of Tyre, sent ambassadors to David. He furnished cedar wood, as well as carpenters and masons, who built a palace for David" (2 Sm 5:11).[276]

[275] Wilhelm Gesenius, *Hebrew Lexicon*, 1833.
[276] Incidentally, here is where the Freemasons claim the origins of the master mason and third degree of Masonry.

As Irene Nowell notes, the "apocalyptic worldview, which arose around the second century BCE, presents a clearer view of demons as superhuman malevolent spiritual beings." She further notes, "In the earlier books of Scripture the gods of the other nations are sometimes understood as demons, or sometimes these foreign people are themselves demonized."[277] This forms the backdrop of this story and underpins the two accounts in the Gospels, but also drives us to a deeper, symbolic, and theological understanding. Of significance here, Canaan was the Promised Land given to the people of God after the Exodus, the place where Moses warned the Israelites that they "will prostitute themselves by following the foreign gods among whom they will live in the land they are about to enter" (Dt 31:16). Recall from a previous chapter that Canaanite religion was principally a fertility religion whose cultic practices were primarily animal and human sacrifice as well as ritualistic acts of sexual perversion.

Accordingly, a common slur of the Gentiles (the Hebrew word is *goyim*) is that they are dogs, pointing to their pagan sexual ethics and cultic, ritualistic prostitution. Like pigs (which were unclean to the Jews), dogs were scavengers that roamed feral in the outskirts of towns (cf. Ps 59:6). Interestingly, certain pagan rituals of antiquity utilized dogs, and "particularly puppies," in ceremonies enacted "for the elimination of impurity and disease" and even to eliminate certain curses, to include spirits of family discord, and even in exorcisms. Another son of Canaan was Heth, the younger brother of Sidon, who was the founder of the Hittites (Gn 10:15; 1 Chr 1:13; Gn 23:3).[278] Ancient Hittite texts describe a certain cultic function, found also in Phoenicia, of "dog men" which "may have been male prostitutes of some sort."[279] Notably,

277 Nowell, *101 Questions & Answers on Angels and Devils*, 61.
278 *Anchor Bible Dictionary* vol 6, 1143–44.
279 *Anchor Bible Dictionary* vol 6, 1144.

Jesus refers to the woman and her daughter not just as dogs but as "little dogs" in both accounts, perhaps an allusion to the puppies used in the Hittite cult. This is the only place in all of Scripture where "little dog" is used.

In giving the holiness code of Leviticus, moreover, Moses gives specific instructions from God on preserving the sanctity of sex: "You shall not do as they do in the land of Egypt, where you once lived, nor shall you do as they do in the land of Canaan, where I am bringing you; do not conform to their customs" (Lv 18:3). What were some of those customs? A cult of ritualistic sex with temple prostitutes, male and female, which may have included one's mother (Lv 18:6–8) or sister or niece (Lv 18:9–10), or daughter, aunt, or sister-in-law (Lv 18:14). Other sexual practices (which made their way into cultic worship) included male homosexuality (Lv 18:22) and even bestiality (Lv 18:23). With a religion and culture so depraved sexually, we must not be surprised that they also immolated their children in human sacrifice (Lv 18:21). Due to their ritualistic prostitution and unclean sexual practices, therefore, the Gentiles were considered "dogs." Like dogs, the Canaanites copulated indiscriminately and, like dogs, even ate their own young.

Thus, Moses gave as law to the community, "there shall be no temple harlot among the Israelite women, nor a temple prostitute among the Israelite men. You shall not offer a harlot's fee or a dog's price as any kind of votive offering in the house of the LORD, your God; both these things are an abomination to the LORD, your God" (Dt 23:18–19). He also warns the Israelites of the effects of the customs in the land of Canaan:

> Do not defile yourselves by any of these things, because by them the nations whom I am driving out of your way have defiled themselves. And so the land has become defiled, and

> I have punished it for its wickedness, and the land has vomited out its inhabitants. You, however, must keep my statutes and decrees, avoiding all these abominations, both the natives and the aliens resident among you—because the previous inhabitants did all these abominations and the land became defiled; otherwise the land will vomit you out also for having defiled it, just as it vomited out the nations before you. (Lv 18:24–28 NABRE)

In Revelation, Saint John similarly links "dogs" with "the sorcerers, the unchaste, the murderers, the idol-worshipers, and all who love and practice deceit" (Rv 22:15). A dog, therefore, is synonymous with unclean, shameless and unabashed. For the Jews, it was synonymous with cultural, social, moral, and ritual impurity. This is the underpinning of Jesus's words to the Canaanite woman whose daughter was possessed.

For Matthew, the demonic possession was quite extreme. Her daughter was "severely tormented by a demon," causing the woman to beg Jesus for mercy by calling Jesus by the messianic titles of "Lord" and "Son of David" (Mt 15:21–22). The prophets had foretold of the restoration of the house of David (Am 9:11), of the Messiah who would come and liberate Israel and rule on the throne of David (Is 9:6), and who would be born in Bethlehem, David's birthplace, and ruler over Israel (Mi 5:2). Ironically, this Gentile woman recognizes Jesus as the awaited Messiah, the Anointed One of the Jewish people. That she, a pagan woman, is evoking mercy or *hesed*, the covenant fidelity promised by God to His people, must have struck a chord with the disciples, who immediately asked Jesus to "send her away, for she keeps calling out after us" (Mt 15:23). The reader is not told whether Jesus was testing her faith, simply that He ignores her pleading and keeps walking: "But he did not say a word in answer to her" (Mt 15:23).

Perhaps Jesus wanted to show the disciples why He brought them to this historic and pagan place in the first place, as the location itself suggests what is at stake. Jesus deliberately goes to a place called "rock" (Tyre) in a pagan territory that means "to be subjugated" (Canaan) where the ancient Israelites had fallen into pagan idolatry and subjugation. The sister city is named after the firstborn son of subjugation, Sidon. In this place, their ancestors revealed what diabolic subjugation looks like: their gods demanded the appeasement by human sacrifice, particularly their children, to the Canaanite Ba'al, a name which means "husband, lord, and master." They abandoned the divine Bridegroom and joined themselves to a cruel and powerful demon who became their master and subjugator.

Meanwhile, this pagan woman calls out to Jesus for *hesed* to the One who alone is Son, Rock, Liberator, and Lord. Jesus, the divine Bridegroom, has gone into the heart of idolatry to extract His bride from the same place where their ancestors were given the Promised Land but prostituted themselves by imitating the cultic rituals of the Canaanites. He initially ignores the woman, reminding His disciples that "I was sent only to the lost sheep of the house of Israel" (Mt 15:24). He, not Tyre, is the true Rock ("The Rock—how faultless are his deeds, how right all his ways! A faithful God, without deceit, just and upright is he!" Dt 32:4). He, not Sidon, is the true Son of the Father, not of subjugation but of freedom. He was sent to lead His bride not to an earthly kingdom but to a heavenly one. There in the Promised Land, He, not Ba'al, shows Himself as divine Lord, the true Husband. He comes not to subjugate, like the Canaanites, but to liberate from spiritual oppression and the slavery of sin and its effects.

In antiquity, the word "dog" was also synonymous with shameless audacity, and so she persists with dog-like ferocity (as mothers are wont to do when their children suffer). In her persistence, however, the woman shows that she knows something that her co-religionists yet do not—namely, that Jesus is not just another healer or exorcist but God and Lord. In Mark, she "fell at his feet" in supplication (Mk 7:25). Matthew recounts that she "did him homage" (Mt 15:25). The Greek word he uses is *proskuneo*, a word which means "to fall down and worship, prostrate oneself before, pay homage by kissing"—something a Gentile would only do either in worship of their gods or before their kings who, in their pagan understanding, embodied the gods, or were the children of the gods. This was the posture Moses found the Israelites in when worshipping the golden calf (Ex 32:8). Mordecai refused to do this posture or worship before the pagan king and his wicked official, Haman (Est 3:5). This is a posture of worship reserved for the true God alone, as the people did during the Exodus before God's presence (Ex 33:10). As the psalmists cried out: "Exalt the LORD, our God; bow down before his footstool; holy is God!" (Ps 99:5).

She prostrates herself in adoration and supplication, as if before the presence of God in the holy Temple. To her, however, Jesus further resists, as if to test the purity of her faith, by pointing out that "it is not right to take the food of the children and give it to the little dogs" (Mt 15:26). Her boldness is palpable, however, as she reminds Jesus that "even the little dogs eat the scraps that fall from the table of their masters" (Mt 15: 27). Mention of "dog" and "table" evokes another type, or image, of dog in antiquity—that is, the house or table dog (the *kunes trapezeis*) that fed while their master was at table. She counters Jesus's claim of her being a scavenger-dog and impure like her ancestors by claiming to be a "table dog" at her master's feet.[280] This was the response He was waiting for. She admits that she and her daughter are "little dogs" that are

[280] LSJ, *Greek-English Lexicon*, 401.

unclean, yet due to her faith ("O woman, great is your faith!"), Jesus grants her request. Matthew tells us that "her daughter was healed from that hour" (Mt 15:28).

For Mark, Jesus had been teaching in Bethsaida and Gennesaret, cities on the northeast shore of Galilee of northern Israel (Mk 6:45, 53). Mark notes that Jesus then "went off to the district of Tyre" (Mk 9:24). He simply tells the reader that the absent daughter "had an unclean spirit" (Mk 9:25), and only later states that the possessing entity was a "demon" (Mk 7:26, 29, 31). The Greek word for "unclean" is *akathartos*, which means either being ritually or morally unclean—that is, the state of moral guilt that results from sin.[281] Technically, an unclean spirit is "an evil supernatural spirit which is ritually unclean and which causes persons to be ritually unclean." This title reveals their task—namely, to lead man to immoral and irrational behavior which, in turn, renders one ritually unclean as well.[282] In addition, the mention of demon (*daimon* in Greek) three times in six verses perhaps echoes the words of the psalmist, "the gods of the Gentiles are demons" (*daimonia*), and "tremble before God, all the earth; say among the Gentiles, the LORD is king" (Ps 96:5, 10).

The use of the word "unclean" while in Gentile territory would also evoke the holiness code of Leviticus (Lv 11–26), which, as mentioned above on the sanctity of sex, goes into detail on the clean versus the unclean—from food and hygiene to sexual and cultic practices. In the ancient Jewish mind, moreover, those who lived in this Gentile region were descendants of the Canaanites and unclean in every way. The ancient Jews also held what was called the "semitic totality concept" which thought in terms of totalities, or parts in relation to the

---

[281] DiFransico, "Guilt" in John D. Barry et al. eds., *The Concise Lexham Bible Dictionary*.

[282] Louw and Nida, *Greek-English Lexicon*, 145–46.

concrete whole.[283] Thus, an individual person can be a representative character for the broader group. At the Transfiguration, for example, Moses and Elijah appear alongside Jesus (Mt 17:3; Mk 9:4; Lk 9:30), which indicates that Jesus is the fulfillment of both the Law (symbolized by Moses) and the Prophets (symbolized by Elijah). A Jewish hearer of Mark, therefore, would take note that when Mark mentions "the woman was a Greek, a Syrophoenician by birth" (Mk 7:26) as opposed to Matthew, who simply said that she was "a Canaanite woman" (Mt 15:22), he is inviting his reader to move from the literal and historical to something deeper. When a Greek noun lacks the definite article ("the"), it often indicates the subject is a particular example of a category or class, in this case the class of "a Greek, a Syrophoenician by birth" (Mk 7:26). The extra details given by Mark suggests he is using this semitic totality concept—namely, that this unnamed woman is not only Canaanite but also thoroughly and wholly pagan in upbringing, religiosity, customs, and manners. This would further enhance Jesus's previous teachings on purity and defilement (Mk 7:14–23; Mt 15:10–20).

Mark narrates another key detail not found in Matthew. While in both accounts the mother herself called her child "my daughter" and begged Jesus to drive out the unclean spirit, Mark notes that it was not just her daughter (which can be a female child of any age) but her "little daughter" (Mk 7:25). His use of the rare diminutive ("little daughter") is found only twice in the New Testament, here and in Mark's version of the healing of Jairus's daughter (Mk 5:21–34). There, Mark makes note that the "little daughter" of Jairus was "a child of twelve" (Mk 5:42). Admittedly, this could be a term of endearment in Greek, so it could read as "my precious, little daughter" of any age. But why would Mark, and not the mother, give

[283] See Lefrois, "Semitic Totality Thinking," 195–203.

us that detail, if not to give the reader a clue? The reference here is likely a narrative insert to indicate the age of the girl as pubescent or pre-pubescent. In fact, Jesus's response suggests that He also gleans that she is a child. "Let the children be fed first" (Mk 7:27). Here the word for "children" is *teknia*, "offspring, child" (as in a "young one"), to contrast with the woman's emphasis on "little daughter" and "little dog."

If this is the case, what could a girl of middle-school age have done to warrant not only an unclean spirit but to be "severely tormented by a demon"? Was she so gravely sinful in her willful acts at such a young age so as to be "extremely afflicted" and "tormented" to the point of diabolic possession? Mark gives us a clue in the seemingly harsh and non-pastoral words of Jesus: "Let the *children* be fed first. For it is not right to take the food of the *children* and throw it to the little dogs" (Mk 7:27). In Scripture, repetition is often used by the sacred authors to indicate a concept of importance to the author as well as to distinguish two ideals: in this case, the contrasting ideals of the baseness of paganism and the dignity of divine sonship. This twice repetition of "children" contrasted with the twice repeated "little daughter" and "little dogs" suggests that those inside the covenant family of God are children of the father and those outside are dogs, the children of Canaan, the lowest insult in the mind of the Jewish people. In addition, the familial imagery is unmistakable, and when combined with the thrice repetition of *daimonian,* the text suggests that there is something *familial* about the unclean spirit that is afflicting the little girl. The text is silent on how it got there, but clear that a child is possessed, potentially affirming *avon avot* and spirits as familial.

The literary technique of repetition—children, little dogs, little daughter, demons—has two other purposes. One, it is used to introduce a new doctrine imbued with mystical meaning, and two, it alerts the reader in preparation for further doctrine. Here, the repetition in Mark reveals that Jesus does the unthinkable: He is including the Gentiles into the new covenant family of God. In both Gospel accounts, moreover, this is reinforced by the subsequent healings where the infirmities themselves take on a symbolic import. In Matthew, Jesus departs to other Gentile regions where great crowds of Gentiles came to Him, and He healed "the lame, the blind, the deformed, the mute, and many others" (Mt 15:29–30). As a result, the Gentiles "glorified the God of Israel" (Mt 15:29–31). For Matthew, the Gentiles reflect the human condition apart from Christ: lame (unable to walk the path of righteousness), blind (unable to see the truth), deformed (ritually impure), and mute (unable to proclaim the gospel).

For Mark, Jesus immediately heals a deaf-mute, which points more directly to the mission to the Gentiles. Those people, on the borders of Israel, who were deaf to the true God will now hear the proclamation of the gospel and proclaim faith and believe in the true God. Like the deaf-mute, Jesus will open their ears to the gospel and free their tongues to "speak plainly" and to "proclaim" the good news of Jesus Christ (Mk 7:31–35). Here, in the pagan territory of the Decapolis, Jesus drives out demons, and now the deaf-mute stands as representative of what will then happen in and through the Church.

Saint Thomas comments on this passage, with focus on Matthew's version, and specifically, "five things are noted of this woman of Canaan which availed for the liberation of this demoniac." These are a formula for anyone (parent or child) suffering under demonic possession:

1. Her *humility*: "Yet the dogs eat."
2. Her *patience*: since she patiently endured the seeming reproaches of Our Lord.
3. Her *prayer*: "Have mercy on me, O Lord."

4. Her *perseverance*: she did not cease asking till she obtained what she desired.
5. Her *faith*: "O woman, great is thy faith."

"If we had had these five qualities," Saint Thomas says, "we should be delivered from every devil, that is, from all sin."[284]

For Jerome, "The Gentiles are called dogs because of their idolatry."[285] Saint Anselm focuses on Mark's version, and begins by recalling the titles she uses for Jesus: "The great faith of this Canaanite woman is herein showed. She believes Him to be God, in that she calls Him Lord; and man, in that she calls Him Son of David. She claims nothing of her own desert but craves only God's mercy." He shifts to the familial aspect of the possession, noting that "she says not, 'Have mercy on my daughter,' but 'Have mercy on me.'" This is, he says, "because the affliction of the daughter is the affliction of the mother."[286] Recalling Hosea ("Yet though I stopped to feed my child, they did not know that I was their healer," Hos 1:14), Saint Anselm states: "And the more to excite His compassion, she declares to Him the whole of her grief, My daughter is sore vexed by a demon; thus unfolding to the Physician the wound, and the extent and nature of the disease; its extent, when she says is sore vexed; its nature, by a demon."[287]

Here I highlight three things. One, Saint Thomas equates "deliverance from every devil" with deliverance "from all sin." Sin is what attracts the demon to us. Two, Saint Anselm notes that the daughter's affliction is the mother's affliction, suggesting a familial component of the spiritual affliction, over and above a mother's concern for her daughter. Three, his

[284] Saint Thomas Aquinas, "Homily IV: The Sinful Soul," 10. in John M. Ashley, trans., *Ninety-nine Homilies of S. Thomas Aquinas Upon the Epistles and Gospels for Forty-nine Sundays of the Christian Year*. London, UK: Church Press Company, 1867.

[285] Cited in Saint Thomas Aquinas, *Catena Aurea* I–II, 564.

[286] Cited in Saint Thomas Aquinas, *Catena Aurea* I–II, 562.

[287] Saint Thomas Aquinas, *Catena Aurea* I–II, 562.

pathway out of affliction is lived out by the Gentile woman: humility; patience in the face of suffering; prayer, specifically, calling upon God's mercy; perseverance unceasing in prayer; and, most importantly, faith in Jesus, who is God, Messiah, Physician, and Bridegroom.

Since Infancy: The Boy with a Demon

I return now to the problematic of this book; namely, how can an innocent child be possessed or afflicted by a demon if there is *avon avot* and familial effect of sin? As Saint Augustine noted above, many things—to include affliction by demons—befall infants even after Baptism. Here are the three accounts of the event:

Matthew 17:14–21	Luke 9:37–43	Mark 9:14–29
And when they came to the crowd, a man came up to him in kneeling before him said, "Lord, have mercy on my son, for he is an epileptic, and he suffers terribly; for often he falls into the fire, and often into the water. And I brought him to your disciples, and they could not heal him." Jesus said in reply, "O faithless and perverse generation, how long will I be with you? How long am I to	On the next day, when they came down from the mountain, a great crowd met him. And behold, a man from the crowd cried, "Teacher, I beg you to look upon my son, for he is my only child; and behold, a spirit seizes him, and he suddenly cries out; it convulses him till he foams and it shatters him, and will hardly leave him; And I begged your disciples to cast it out, but they could not."	And when they came to the disciples, they saw a great crowd about them, and scribes arguing with them. Immediately all the crowd, when they saw him, were greatly amazed, and ran up to him and greeted him. And he asked them, "What are you discussing with them?" And one of the crowd answered him, "Teacher, I brought my son to you, for he has a dumb spirit; and wherever it seizes him, it dashes him down; he foams and grinds his teeth and becomes rigid; and I asked your disciples to cast it out, and they were not able." And he answered them, "O faithless generation, how long am I to be with you? How long am I to

Matthew 17:14–21	Luke 9:37–43	Mark 9:14–29
be with you? Bring him here to me." And Jesus rebuked him and the demon came out of him, and the boy was cured instantly. Then the disciples came to Jesus privately and said, "Why could we not cast it out?" He said to them, "Because of your little faith. For truly, I say to you, if you have the faith as a grain of mustard seed, you will say to this mountain, "Move hence to yonder place," and it will move; and nothing will be impossible to you. [But this kind never comes out except by prayer and fasting.]" (RSVCE)	Jesus answered, "O faithless and perverse generation, how long am I to be with you and bear with you? Bring your son here." While he was coming, the demon tore him and convulsed him. But Jesus rebuked the unclean spirit, and healed the boy, and gave him back to his father. And all were astonished at the majesty of God. (RSVCE)	bear with you? Bring him to me." And they brought the boy to him; and when the spirit saw him, immediately it convulsed the boy, and he fell on the ground and rolled about, foaming at the mouth. And Jesus asked his father, "How long has he has this?" And he said, "From childhood. And it has often cast into the fire and into the water, to destroy him; but if you can do anything, have pity on us and help us." And Jesus said to him, "If you can! All things are possible to him who believes." Immediately the father of the child cried out [with tears], and said, "I believe; help my unbelief!" And when Jesus saw that a crowd came running together, he rebuked the unclean spirit, saying to it, "You dumb and deaf spirit, I command you, come out of him, and never enter him again." And after crying out and convulsing him terribly, it came out, and the boy was like a corpse; so that most of them said, "He is dead." But Jesus took him by the hand and lifted him up, and he arose, and when he had entered the house, his disciples asked him privately, "Why could we not cast it out?" And he said to them, "This kind cannot be driven out by anything but prayer and fasting." (RSVCE)

The tendency of modern, biblical scholars is to look to scientific, rather than supernatural, causality to explain (and, therefore, dismiss) such uncomfortable passages as a demon-possessed child. Accordingly, there are two possible answers to this dilemma. The modern, historical critics claim that the boy was not possessed but rather was having an epileptic seizure, as described in the text: "Whenever it seizes him, it throws him down; he foams at the mouth, grind his teeth, and becomes rigid" (Mk 9:18). Matthew (and only Matthew) does say the boy has *lunacy* (NAB), sometimes also translated as having *epilepsy* (RSVCE). In antiquity, epilepsy was considered a sacred and prophetic state whereby the gods were manifested in this trance-like, convulsive state, believed to be the effect of the moon.[288] Immediately prior to this event, Jesus is transfigured and a voice from heaven says, "This is my beloved Son, with whom I am well pleased; listen to him" (Mt 17:5), which Jesus refers to as a "vision" (Mt 17:9).

Mark and Luke describe how some *thing*, in fact, does seize the boy when Jesus approached. For Mark: "when the spirit saw him [Jesus] immediately it [the spirit] convulsed the boy and he [the boy] fell on the ground and rolled about, foaming at the mouth" (Mk 9:20). And Luke: "While he [Jesus] was coming, the demon tore him and convulsed him" (Lk 9:42). If this were either physiological (epilepsy) or psychological (lunacy or mental illness), however, Matthew would not have recounted that Jesus rebuked *it*. Jesus's command to "bring him to me" could also be read as "bring it (the demon) to me" (Mt 17:17).[289] The Greek personal pronoun used here can be either *it* or *him*. Certainly, the context does not suggest that

[288] *Anchor Bible Dictionary*, vol. 6, 12.

[289] The personal pronoun here could mean either *him* or *it* and seems to anticipate the demon in the next verse. See Zerwick and Grosvenor, *Grammatical Analysis*, 56.

Jesus rebukes either the father or the boy. That it is a demon (not a "spirit" as in Mark and Luke) is verified in Matthew's next sentence—namely, that Jesus's rebuke resulted in not a healing but "a demon came out of him" (Mt 17:18). If this were epilepsy, moreover, Matthew would have recounted a healing miracle, not an exorcism.

In all three versions, Jesus chastises "this faithless generation" (Mt 17:17; Mk 9:19; Lk 9:41). The Greek word used is *genea,* which means "race, family, age, or time," and thus a *generation.* For Matthew and Luke, not only is this generation faithless, but they are also "perverse," an allusion to the Canticle of Moses: "Yet basely has he been treated by his degenerate children, a *perverse* and crooked *race*" (*genea,* Dt 32:5). In that canticle, recall from above, the generation brought out of Egypt "scorned their saving Rock" (Dt 32:15, 16) by taking false gods as their "rock" (Dt 32:37). They "offered sacrifice to demons, to 'no gods'" (Dt 32:17), something Jeremiah's scribe Baruch recalled his own green-grapes generation in exile also did ("For you provoked your Maker with sacrifices to demons, to no gods," Bar 4:7). The once-beautiful bride was God's "darling" but has now "[grown] fat and frisky ... gross and gorged" because they "spurned the God who made them and scorned their saving Rock" (Dt 32:15). Thus, when Jesus decries this "unfaithful and perverse generation," He is recalling the sins of their ancestors.

Saint Jerome includes in the Vulgate a final verse in both Matthew and Mark which reinforces that this was not only a demon but also one of a specific kind. Matthew states that "this kind [of demon] never comes out except by prayer and fasting" (Mt 17:21). Similarly, Mark states: "This kind [of spirit] cannot be driven out by anything but prayer and fasting" (Mk 9:29). The word used here is *genos,* which means "race or kind," but in the sense of *direct descent, collateral relationship, offspring, posterity, hereditary, familial* (as in *house* or *clan* or *tribe*), *age*, or *generation*. The evangelists could have used a better word for a distinct category, class, or kind (*eidos*) but did not. Both used *genos*, a word imbued with familial undertones, suggesting the hereditary and familial aspect of this demon possessing the boy. Inferred, then, is a type of spirit that is generational.

As the boy fell to the ground, Mark recounts that "he began to roll around and foam at the mouth" (Mk 9:20). While this may be consistent with an epileptic seizure, this is also consistent with a diabolic manifestation for anyone who has ever witnessed one. Notably, a physiological illness does not have intentionality and, therefore, does not "throw" a child "into the fire and into the water" with the purpose to "kill him" (Mk 9:22). For Pseudo-Jerome there is symbolism connected to idol worship in this verse:

> Further, in his being vexed from his infancy, the Gentile people is signified, from the very birth of whom the vain worship of idols arose, so that they in their folly sacrificed their children to devils. And for this reason it is said that "it cast him into the fire and into the water;" for some of the Gentiles worshipped fire, others water.[290]

Like the Syrophoenician woman, therefore, there is an historic and spiritual symbolism in the father and his possessed son. This unnamed father and son echo not just their race or generation, but humanity in general: unfaithful and perverse, subjected to the bondage of slavery to the evil one. Where the Syrophoenician woman believed, however, this father had doubts.

This is reinforced by the words of the boy's father that only Luke recounts: "Teacher, I beg you to look upon my son, for

[290] Cited in Saint Thomas Aquinas, *Catena Aurea* II, 178.

he is my only child" (Lk 9:38). Jesus had just been transfigured where the Father announces: "This is my chosen Son" (Lk 9:35) and "my beloved Son" (Mt 17:5; Mk 9:6). To Matthew's Jewish audience, that father asks for "pity" from Jesus (Mt 17:15) would evoke *hesed,* God's mercy and covenant fidelity. That the father "knelt" before Jesus echoes Solomon, who "knelt" before the temple and praised God because "you keep your covenant and show kindness to your servants who are wholeheartedly faithful to you" (2 Chr 6:16), asking, "Can it indeed be that God dwells with mankind on earth? If the heavens and the highest heavens cannot contain, how much less this temple which I have built!" (2 Chr 6:16).

Another detail unique to Luke reinforces this. Not only does Jesus drive the demon out but also "gave him back to his father" (Lk 9:43). Jesus's purpose is to do the same—that is, to give all of the sons of men back to the heavenly Father by healing them of their sins. That only Luke, who was writing to Gentiles, mentions that "all were astonished at the majesty of God" (Lk 9:43) is a likely echo of the prophecy of Jeremiah where God promises the restoration of Israel and Judah: "I will return the exile of Iouda and the exile of Israel and build them as they were before. And I will cleanse them from all their injustices which they sinned against me, and I will not remember their sins which they sinned against me and they withdrew from me" (Jer 40:7–8, NETS). As a result of the restoration of the two kingdoms, God's "greatness [majesty]" will be "for all the people of the earth" and "peace which I shall make for them" (Jer 40:7–9, NETS).

When read together, moreover, we get a glimpse of what a possessed person experiences when a demon manifests. The Latin verb *manifesto* means "to make public, discover, show clearly, exhibit, manifest, or reveal." By diabolic *manifestation* is meant the appropriation of the bodily senses by a demon whereby he is revealed and publicly seen. For Matthew, the boy "suffers terribly" (RSVCE) or "severely" (NAB). Luke and Mark give more details as to what suffering terribly looks like. For Luke, the spirit "seizes him" and (still the subject of the sentence) the spirit "shrieks, screams, cries out" (Lk 9:39). The evil spirit also "convulses" the boy, a word which means "to mangle, rend in pieces, tear, or retch." These convulsions are so forceful that the boy foams at the mouth and only "with great difficulty" (literally, "with toil and pain") does it depart from the boy (Lk 9:39).

The Greek word Luke uses for to "shatter him" (RSVCE) or to "wear him out" (NAB) to "maul" (NASB) literally means "to rub together sand to wear out," but in the sense of grind, beat to a jelly and, therefore, shatter, crush, or bruise. In Mark, when they bring the boy to Jesus, the manifestation immediately worsens: "And when he [the evil spirit] saw him [Jesus] the spirit immediately threw the boy into convulsions. As he fell to the ground, he began to roll around and foam at the mouth" (Mk 9:20). Literally, the evil spirit "tore him asunder, mangled, tore him to pieces" and "rolled [him] about." The word for "roll about" is only used here in all of the New Testament. This word means to roll about, move an object about by turning over and over. Often, this is what manifestations look like—rolling on the ground in snake-like movements, hissing and foaming at the mouth.

Mark gives the additional information on diabolic manifestations that the boy "grinds his teeth" and "becomes rigid" (Mk 9:18). The latter literally means "to dry up, parch, or wither" and, therefore, become dried and waste away. This word is used in the Old Testament to describe the "dryness" of the lack of the provision of the fruitfulness of blessing that comes with covenant fidelity. If water is a metaphor for Torah (i.e., "All you who are thirsty, come to the water!" Is 55:1), then to wither in dryness is a metaphor for what happens when one lives apart from the refreshment and fruitfulness of the righteous living of the Law. This was heard in Ezekiel, who spoke of "your mother" who was "like a vine, planted by the water" who once bore fruit and was stately, but now due to her infidelity "withered up" (Ez 19:10, 12). Ezekiel also had a vision of "*dry* bones" which foretold of a time of restoration to those in exile when the spirit of the Lord will raise them up (Ez 37:1–14). Also, this echoes Lamentations, where Jeremiah described the once beautiful daughter-Jerusalem as now lacking the waters of blessing: "their skin shrinks on their bones, as dry as wood" (Lam 4:8). When a possessed person manifests, these realities are made present as well.

Accordingly, Mark gives the additional detail that the crowd said that "he is dead" (Mk 9:26). In addition, for Mark, liberation means reconciliation with the Father, as in Luke, but also a salvific encounter. After driving the demon out, Jesus "took him by the hand and lifted him up, and he arose" (Mk 9:27). This is just as God had spoken to those in exile: "For I the LORD, your God, who grasp your right hand . . . I will help you, says the LORD; your redeemer is the Holy One of Israel" (Is 41:13, 14). This passage from Isaiah not only evokes the holiness of God but also alludes to both the Jealous One and divine Warrior zealously seeking His wayward bride: "For your husband is your Maker; the LORD of hosts is his name, your redeemer, the Holy One of Israel, called God of all the earth" (Is 54:5). Thus, for Mark, this action shows that liberation is not just being demon-free but an encounter of redemption and personal ("he took him by the hand") resurrection through the resurrection of Jesus Christ where He conquered sin and death.

Only Mark gives the detail that the spirit renders the boy "mute" (*alalos*), and only in Mark is this word used in the

New Testament. The psalmist uses this word as the prayer of an afflicted sinner crying to God for mercy ("LORD punish me no more in your anger, in your wrath do not chastise me," Ps 38:1). In humility, the penitent appeals to the LORD for mercy: "But I am like the deaf, hearing nothing, like the dumb, saying nothing" (Ps 38:16). Accordingly, Jesus adds "deaf" to the father's statement that the spirit makes his son "mute" when he drove out the demon: "You dumb and deaf spirit, I command you, come out of him, and never enter him again" (Mk 9:25). By analogy, all the nations will, through faith in Jesus Christ, hear the Good News and proclaim it.

One last detail of importance is given by Mark not found elsewhere. As the demon was manifesting in front of him, Jesus notably does not panic or rush into the offensive. He first shows the importance of finding the root cause or entry point of the demon. He immediately addresses the father, as if to highlight the necessity to work within the authority structure, asking, "How long has this been happening to him?" (Mk 9:21). "Since childhood," the father replies. The Greek adverb *piadiothen* means "since birth," implying since the boy was an infant, long before the age of reason or even the development of discernible personhood. If this were in southern Ohio, the father's response would have been "since he was a little feller." Saint Jerome translates the Greek *ek piadiothen* into Latin with *ab infantia*—since infancy. Interestingly, Mark adds the preposition *ek*, which means "since, from that time." This preposition is redundant and superfluous—literally, "from that time, since [his] infancy"—and is utilized in Greek as an emphatic to impart the realism of the situation. Thus, the father tells Jesus that this has been going on in the child his entire life, as long as the boy has been alive, since it could be discernible.

Jesus then sets the stage for what is needed for the power and authority of the Church to be made manifest—namely, faith: "O faithless generation" (Mk 9:19). Doubting whether Jesus could deliver his son, and perhaps in a moment of pure despair, he says to Jesus, "but if you can do anything, have pity on us and help us" (Mk 9:22 RSVCE). He does not ask for pity and help for just his son or himself but, curiously, "on us." The son suffers in the father and the father in the afflictions of the son. Reiterating the need for faith, Jesus mildly rebukes him with, "If you can! All things are possible to him who believes" (Mk 9:23 RSVCE). "The boy's father cried out, 'I do believe, help my unbelief'" (Mk 9:24). That Mark uses the present tense implies an ongoing condition; that is, Jesus's help would be needed both at the present and constantly from now on.[291] A father's authority must be fueled by faith before his son is healed.

Regarding the father, Saint John Chrysostom notes that he was "weak in faith" and that "although his want of faith was the cause of their [the disciples] not casting out the devil, he nevertheless accuses the disciples."[292] Here we see the importance of a father's faith as locking or unlocking the power of the Church in liberation of an afflicted child. Contrary to what is seen today in many Protestant and charismatic models of deliverance, one's power and authority are to be exercised within the bounds of our sacramental relationship with God in and through the Church.[293] Our prayer of deliverance

[291] Zerwick and Grosvenor, *Grammatical Analysis*, 137.

[292] Cited in Saint Thomas Aquinas, *Catena Aurea* II, 174.

[293] Saint Thomas discusses the liceity of invoking the divine Name in command or adjuration, concluding it is based on one's relationship vis-à-vis the person (or demon). See *ST* II–II, q. 90. On the distinction between solemn and private adjurations and the application of this section of the *Summa*, see McHugh and Callam, *Moral Theology*, 360–62. On the right to bless as based on one's office within the Body of Christ, see USCCB, *Book of Blessings*, p. 26, 22.

must begin with faith and hope, while flowing from our own authority within the Church and familial construct.

If not an epileptic seizure, what could the entry point be in this case if not something familial? The only other option is to affirm the historicity of the gospel and accept the story at face value. That is, either he had epilepsy or he was possessed since birth and was having a diabolic manifestation. If the latter, Mark's "since infancy" gives evidence of a possession of a child before the age of reason (and, therefore, no culpability). When combined with Jesus's words of "this type" with its flavor of familial/hereditary nature, we also have a potential pathway for families to find liberation. His story, then, is the lens through which we see a potential *why* and *how* of the mechanics of familial spirits.

Avon Avot Elsewhere in the New Testament

Finally, the argument could be made that the green grapes proverb applies only to the Old Testament but is no longer applicable in the New (apart from a possible reference to Baptism). Saint Augustine affirms that this is a prophecy of the new birth of Baptism which wipes away original sin, which had set humanity's "teeth on edge." That is, we inherit original sin from our parents and suffer the effects. At the same time, he does not deny, or in the least way back off from, the truth spoken directly by God: *I shall punish the children for the sins of their parents* (Ex 20:5). If Julian were correct in asserting that the explanation of the Ezekiel and Jeremiah passage meant that God's words at Sinai were made null and void, moreover, then we would expect to hear no mention of any inherited guilt in the New Testament. Nonetheless, we do on three occasions.

A first passage in the New Testament also reveals the popular belief in inherited guilt at the time of Christ is found at the trial of Jesus before Pilate. When Pilate washed his hands and declared himself "innocent of this man's blood" (Mt 27:24), the account affirms the received history of inherited guilt at the time: "And the whole people said in reply, 'His blood be upon us and our children'" (Mt 27:25). Only Saint Matthew, who was writing to a Jewish audience, records these words of Jesus, as they would have been foreign to a Gentile audience. Matthew's Jewish audience would have heard the words of Jeremiah, who spoke to a similar angry mob of inhabitants of Jerusalem who also faced destruction. "But mark well," Jeremiah said, "if you put me to death, it is innocent blood you bring on yourselves, on the city and its citizens. For in truth it was the LORD who sent me to you, to speak all these things for you to hear" (Jer 26:15). Within the span of a generation, Jerusalem would again be under siege by a Gentile nation (the Romans in AD 70) just like the people in Jeremiah's time were taken captive by the Babylonians.

When the Romans sieged Jerusalem, the Jewish historian Josephus reported that the inhabitants resorted to cannibalism before the city fell by fire.[294] The sevenfold woes given by Jesus (Mt 23:1–9, see below) echo the sevenfold woes (viz, curses) given by Moses for covenant infidelity: "If, despite all this, you still persist in disobeying and defying me, I, also, will meet you with fiery defiance, and will chastise you with sevenfold, fear or punishment for your sins, till you begin to eat the flesh of your own sons and daughters" (Lv 26:27–29). The language Jesus uses evokes imagery of the fiery siege of Jerusalem at the time of Jeremiah at the hands of the Babylonians,

---

[294] Flavius Josephus, *The Complete Works*, 1474.

which included cannibalism (cf. Jer 19:9), is a divine judgment against them. As Jeremiah warned, the Babylonians will "enter this city and set fire to it, burning it and its houses" (Jer 32:29).

Like the inhabitants of Jerusalem who resisted the prophet's words "submit your necks to the king of Babylon" (Jer 27:12) but were led into captivity, so will this generation of inhabitants of Jerusalem. Saint John makes a subtle twist that echoes this in recording the words of the chief priests in reply to Pilate: "We have no king but Caesar" (Jn 19:15), which is an admission of apostasy according to the Law ("a foreigner, who is no king of yours, you may not sit over you [as king]," Dt 17:15). As to Saint Matthew's recounting of "May his blood be upon us and our children," Father Ripperger notes that passage as evidence of the belief in *avon avot* in the Second Temple period, which was approximately the return from the Babylonian exile by the decree of King Cyrus in 538 BC and the destruction of Jerusalem by the Romans in AD 70. He states this verse as evidence of the belief in "the notion that the effects of a particular person's sins can pass from the parents to the children." Certainly, if Julian were correct in his literal reading of the green grapes proverb, then the Jewish people would have had no such inklings after six hundred years.

A second mention is found in a chapter of Saint Matthew where Jesus denounces the religious leaders of His day. There, Jesus condemns not only their false religiosity and oppression of the people, but in a prophetic judgment against them, He declares:

> Woe to you, scribes and Pharisees, you hypocrites. You build the tombs of the prophets and adorn the memorials of the righteous, and you say, "If we had lived in the days of our ancestors, we would not have joined them in shedding

> the prophets' blood." Thus, you bear witness against yourselves that you are the children of those who murdered the prophets; now fill up what your ancestors measured out! (Mt 23:29–32)

According to Jewish tradition, the prophets Isaiah, Jeremiah, Ezekiel, Micah, and Amos were all martyred.

That in Saint Matthew Jesus also mentions "Zechariah, the son of Berechiah whom you murdered between the sanctuary and the altar" (Mt 23:35) recalls the time leading up to the Babylonian exile, when, according to Ian Boxall, "God sent messengers and prophets to his people in a compassionate attempt to avert the Babylonian exile" (2 Chr 36:15–17). Jesus is setting the stage, in the language of prophetic judgment in the tradition of Ezekiel and Jeremiah, for the woes that will befall Jerusalem again, as it did before its fall to the Babylonians. Accordingly, as Boxall concludes, "Christs sends to his contemporaries 'prophets and wise men and scribes' (23:43a; Lk 11:49 has 'prophets and apostles'), his missionaries who will be crucified, or scourged in synagogues and pursued from town to town (23:34b; 10:17, 23)."[295] This generation of inhabitants of Jerusalem will not only kill Jesus like their "fathers" killed the prophets, but also kill the ones He sends after Him.

Mention of "Zechariah, the son of Berechiah," therefore, recalls the time of great apostasy in Jerusalem at the time of the green grapes proverb and the lives of Jeremiah and Ezekiel. As the chronicler recounts:

> They forsook the temple of the Lord, the God of their fathers, and began to serve the sacred poles and the idols; and because of this crime of theirs, wrath came upon Judah

[295] Boxall, "Matthew" in *The Jerome Biblical Commentary for the Twenty-First Century*, 1222.

> and Jerusalem. Although prophets were sent to them to convert them to the Lord, the people would not listen to their warnings. Then the spirit of God possessed Zachariah, son of Jehoida the priest. He took his stand above the people and said to them: "God says, 'Why are you transgressing the Lord's commandments, so that you cannot prosper? Because you have abandoned the Lord, he has abandoned you.'" (2 Chr 24:18–20)

For this "they stoned [Zechariah] to death in the court of the Lord's temple" (2 Chr 24:21). Jesus reminds the Jewish leaders of His day that they are acting just like their wicked ancestors who killed the prophets and sharing in their behavior and their guilt. Jesus here neither directly affirms nor denies inherited guilt but does show the generational aspect of guilt: "Amen, I say to you, all these things will come upon this generation" (Mt 23:36). By "these things" He means the "seven woes" of prophetic indictment He just pronounced (Mt 23:13, 15, 16, 23, 25, 27, 29) which are the antithesis of the nine beatitudes (Mt 5:1–12) that Jesus gave while "up a mountain" (Mt 5:1) as if a new Moses giving a new Law. Jesus is both Law and Lawgiver, Word and prophet. Saint Matthew presents Him within the prophetic tradition in His condemnation of this generation. Jesus is saying they are like their fathers who rejected and killed the prophets and, as a result, "Behold, your house will be abandoned, desolate" (Mt 23:38).

Commenting on these two passages, however, Father Ripperger notes that this "gives us an indication that in the mind of the Jews during the time of Christ, there was a clear indication that the children can suffer from the sins of the parents."[296] As Boxall comments: "Inspired by the prophetic antecedents (e.g., Jer 16:15), he [Matthew] interprets the city's

---

[296] Ripperger, *Dominion*, 176.

destruction as due to Jerusalem's rejection of Jesus."[297] That is, this verse gives evidence in the belief that evil can befall a people who reject God. Again, this is consistent with the four reasons given by Saint Bonaventure as to why God allows evil. Sometimes, evil is allowed to punish sinful behavior.

A third allusion to inherited guilt in the New Testament is found in the story of the man born blind (John 9). When Jesus was asked by His disciples, "Rabbi, who sinned, this man or his parents, that he was born blind?" (Jn 9:1), Jesus's answer is telling: "Neither he, nor his parents sinned; it is so that the works of God might be made visible through him" (Jn 9:2). Not every evil that is suffered is the direct result of one's personal sin or that of his parents. Too often, people blame others for their suffering and fail to recognize that, since the Fall and original sin, the negative effects of evil cover humanity, including the physical realm (here, blindness as the privation of a good).

God allows suffering, however, for a greater good. As Jesus said, sometimes evil exists "so that the works of God might be made visible." Recall another of the four reasons that Saint Bonaventure gives as to why God allows man to be afflicted by evil is so that God may be glorified. When we endure suffering and offer it to God, we glorify God and bring the light of Christ into the world (cf. Jn 9:4). In this passage, Jesus neither confirms nor denies inherited guilt, but the story does show that the belief was still held at the time of Christ, five to six hundred years after Jeremiah and Ezekiel.

In the *Summa,* Saint Thomas rebuffs those who cite the man born blind (Jn 1–41) as evidence that Jesus rejects the notion of inherited guilt. He states:

---

[297] Boxall, "Matthew" in *The Jerome Biblical Commentary for the Twenty-First Century*, 1233.

> It would seem that not every punishment is inflicted for a sin. For it is written (John 9:3,2) about the man born blind: "Neither hath this man sinned, nor his parents . . . that he should be born blind." In like manner we see that **many children, those also who have been baptized, suffer grievous punishments**, fevers, for instance, **diabolical possession**, and so forth, **and yet there is no sin in them after they have been baptized**. Moreover before they are baptized, there is no more sin in them than in the other children who do not suffer such things. Therefore not every punishment is inflicted for a sin.

He begins by acknowledging (as did Saint Augustine) that infants suffer physical and spiritual ailments alike, even being possessed by evil spirits. These, he says, are the result of original sin: "Such like defects of those who are born with them, or which children suffer from, are the effects and the punishments of original sin . . . and they remain even after baptism." For Saint Thomas, God allows evil (even child possession by evil spirits) to afflict even infants so as to bring greater glory. Citing this passage from the Gospel of Saint John, Saint Thomas states:

> Such like defects of those who are born with them, or which children suffer from, are the effects and the punishments of original sin, as stated above (I–II:85:5); and they remain even after baptism, for the cause stated above (I–II:85:5 ad 2): and that they are not equally in all, is due to the diversity of nature, which is left to itself, as stated above (I–II:85:5 ad 1). Nevertheless, they are directed by Divine providence, to the salvation of men, either of those who suffer, or of others who are admonished by their means—and also to the glory of God.[298]

[298] Saint Thomas Aquinas, *ST* I–II, q. 87, art. 7.

These types of sufferings such as a man born blind, he says, "are directed by Divine providence to the salvation of men, either of those who suffer, or of others who are admonished by their means—and also to the glory of God." This is again consistent with Saint Bonaventure, who states this as one of four reasons as to why God allows demons to afflict us but also that, ultimately, the goal of bodily suffering is to lead our souls to salvation.

While this pericope from Saint John's Gospel is often used to argue that Jesus is nullifying *avon avot* ("inflicting punishment for their father's wickedness"), Saint Thomas echoes Saint Augustine and says otherwise. In fact, Jesus is neither affirming nor denying the ancient Jewish belief. As Father Ripperger comments:

> The Apostles also ask Christ regarding the man who is blind whether it is the sin of the parents or his own sin that caused him to be blind (John 9). Christ's response does not deny that the effects of sins of parents could have caused it, but merely that in this particular case, the man's blindness was permitted for the glory of God.[299]

Notably, Saint Thomas here links the man's blindness to original sin. Recall, moreover, that the story of the healing of the blind man is read at the rite of Baptism, for sacramental Baptism washes away original sin and "illuminates" the soul with the life of grace, suggestive of Saint Augustine's own teachings on the inherited guilt of original as remitted in the rebirth in baptismal waters.

Thus, in the *Summa*, Saint Thomas cites the man born blind (Jn 9:3) notably linking the man's blindness to original sin, which is consistent with that pericope read at Baptism. In addition, he notes two reasons besides punishing sin as

---

[299] Ripperger, *Dominion*, 182.

to why God allows man to be afflicted, also consistent with Saint Bonaventure's four reasons why God allows the demon to afflict us. Here physical maladies are the effect of original sin and directed by providence with the end of salvation. Accordingly, Saint Thomas says, they are allowed by God to admonish and to glorify God, as ultimately suffering leads us to salvation.

Saint Augustine immediately allegorizes the blind man and narrows in on original sin. "That blind man," he says, "is the human race; for this blindness had place in the first man, through sin, from whom we all draw our origin, not only in respect of death, but also of unrighteousness." For him, "unbelief is blindness, and faith enlightenment," and in as much as the evil of original sin "has so taken root within us, every man is born mentally blind." When Jesus anointed him, it was "a sacramental act," he says, and in that anointing, Jesus "made him a catechumen," and he was made a Christian when he washed in the waters of Baptism.[300] His blindness, moreover, was not the direct result of personal sin of his parents:

> For his parents had sin; but not by reason of the sin itself did it come about that he was born blind. If, then, it was not through the parents' sin that he was born blind, why was he born blind? Listen to the Master as He teaches. He seeks one who believes, to give him understanding. He Himself tells us the reason why that man was born blind: Neither has this man sinned, He says, nor his parents: but that the works of God should be made manifest in him.

Here Saint Augustine distinguishes between original and personal sin and reminds his listeners that Jesus was not declaring the parents or the blind man sinless. Rather, he affirms

[300] Saint Augustine, *Tractate (John 9)*, 44.14, in NPNF, vol. 7.

that all are "children of wrath" by nature because of original sin (citing Eph 2:3). "If children of wrath," he says,

> then children of vengeance, children of punishment, children of hell. For how is it by nature, save that through the first man sinning moral evil rooted itself in us as a nature? If evil has so taken root within us, every man is born mentally blind. For if he sees, he has no need of a guide. If he does need one to guide and enlighten him, then is he blind from his birth.

As for the literal meaning, he qualifies his commentary on Jesus's response with "but only in respect to the point on which he was questioned" that neither he nor his parents sinned that the man was born blind.[301] He rhetorically asks: "Was he himself either born without original sin, or had he committed none in the course of his lifetime?"[302]

Saint John Chrysostom focuses on a literal reading with emphasis on personal responsibility and the words of Jesus. He affirms that the essential punishment for sins is proper to the individual and states that "it cannot be that when one sins another should be punished." He cites the green grapes proverb and Moses's communal laws (Dt 24:16) to support Jesus's response that the child is not suffering because of his parents' sins. He also denies that the blindness can be the result of the man's personal sins, since he was born blind and before he could have committed personal sin. Suffering is not always the direct result of personal sin. "For if we allow this," he says, "we must also allow that he sinned before his birth. As therefore when He declared, neither has this man sinned, He said not that it is possible to sin from one's very birth and be

---

[301] Saint Augustine, *Tractate (John 9)*, 44.14, in NPNF, vol. 7.
[302] Saint Augustine, *Tractate (John 9)*, 44.9, in NPNF, vol. 7.

punished for it; so when He said, nor his parents, He said not that one may be punished for his parents' sake."[303]

Saint John Chrysostom is explaining the literal sense of the passage and also suggesting the continual sin theory of punishment in light of personal responsibility. He limits *avon avot* to the generation that came out of Egypt who committed the same sin of idolatry as their parents who received the Law at Sinai. Despite the fact that they themselves saw "signs and wonders," they nonetheless "have become worse than their forefathers who saw none of these things, they shall suffer, it says, the same that those others suffered, since they have dared the same crimes." Thus, he argues, we cannot blame *avon avot* for his blindness. Turning to the words of Jesus and the literal sense, he concludes: "And that it was spoken of those men, anyone who will give attention to the passage will more certainly know. Wherefore then was he born blind? That the glory of God should be made manifest, He says."[304]

In his *Commentary on the Gospel of Saint John*, Saint Thomas cites both Saints John Chrysostom and Augustine and further distinguishes, consistent with his other writings:

> Note that people are punished with two kinds of punishment. One is spiritual and concerns the soul; the other is bodily and concerns the body. A child is never punished on account of his father with a spiritual punishment, because the soul of a child is not from his father but from God: *all souls are mine*, that is, by creation, *the soul of the father as well as the soul of the child is mine: the soul that sins will be punished* (Ez 18:4). Augustine also says this in one of his letters.

---

303 Saint John Chrysostom, *Homily 56, On the Gospel of John*, in NPNF, vol. 14.

304 Saint John Chrysostom, *Homily 56, On the Gospel of John*, in NPNF, vol. 14.

Thus, he begins to explain the passage of the man born blind by separating between the essential/penal (primary, spiritual) and accidental/medicinal (secondary, bodily) effects of sin and the punishments proper to each. He continues:

> But a child is punished on account of his father with a bodily punishment, since he is of his father as far as his body is concerned. This is expressly shown in Genesis (c 19) where when Sodom was destroyed the children of the inhabitants of Sodom were killed on account of the sins of their parents. Again, the Lord very often threatened to destroy the children of the Jews on account of the sins of their parents.[305]

Here he again links the bodily suffering of children as sometimes part of the temporal punishment of and satisfaction for the sins of parents.

He then acknowledges Saint John Chrysostom's assertion of continual sin and focus on divine justice and individual responsibility but further expands. For Saint Thomas, he mentions Saint John Chrysostom to show the nuances of sin's effects: "One is spiritual and concerns the soul; the other is bodily and concerns the body." Thus, "to understand why one person is punished on account of the sins of another," he explains, "we must realize that a punishment has two aspects: it is an injury and a remedy." Drawing an analogy from medicine, he reminds his reader that "sometimes a part of the body is cut off to save the entire body." This, he states, is for the greater good of the entire body:

> And a punishment of this kind causes an injury insofar as a part is cut off, but it is a remedy insofar as it saves the body itself. Still, a doctor never cuts off a superior member to save one which is inferior, but the other way around. Now in human matters, the soul is superior to the body, and the

[305] Saint Thomas Aquinas, *Commentary on the Gospel of John*, 2–3.

> body is superior to external possessions. And so it never happens that someone is punished in his soul for the sake of his body, but rather he is punished in his body as a curing remedy for his soul. **Therefore, God sometimes imposes physical punishments, or difficulties in external concerns, as a beneficial remedy for the soul. And then punishments of this kind are not given just as injuries, but as healing remedies. Thus, the killing of the children of Sodom was for the good of their souls: not because they deserved it, but so they would not be punished more severely for increasing their sins in a life spent in imitating their parents. And in this way some are often punished for the sins of their parents.**[306]

Thus, in answering why the blind man suffered, he reiterates here several key points in building upon Saints Augustine and John Chrysostom. The temporal and bodily suffering as punishment for sin is a corrective measure. Punishments are "healing remedies" for the higher purpose of healing the soul and its end of salvation. Also, we glean that this process is not deterministic; that is, "some" children are "often punished for the sins of their parents." He says neither "all children are always punished" nor no children are ever punished, but "some" and "often" (indicating that the divine Physician knows which remedy is best for each soul).

Saint Thomas then cites Saint Gregory specifically to expand upon Saint Augustine's allegorical and Saint John Chrysostom's literal reading of the man born blind. Turning to the question presented by the disciples which alluded to *avon avot,* he mentions Gregory as giving five reasons. "It should be noted," Thomas says, "as Gregory says in *I Morals,* that God sends afflictions to men in five ways."[307] Those five are as follows:

---

[306] Saint Thomas Aquinas, *Commentary on the Gospel of John,* 2–3.
[307] Saint Thomas Aquinas, *Commentary on the Gospel of John,* 4–5.

1. Sometimes they are the beginning of damnation, according to Jeremiah: "Strike them with a double punishment." A sinner is struck with this kind of punishment in this life so that without interruption or end he might be punished in the other life. For example, Herod, who killed James, was punished in this life and also in hell (Acts 12:23).
2. Sometimes afflictions are sent as a correction, as we read: "Your discipline will teach me" (Ps 17:36).
3. And sometimes a person is afflicted not to correct past wrongs but to preserve him from future ones, as we read of Paul: "And to keep me from being too elated by the abundance of revelations, a thorn was given me in the flesh, a messenger of Satan, to harass me, to keep me from being too elated" (2 Cor 12:7).
4. Again, sometimes it is done to encourage virtue; as when a person's past sins are not being corrected, nor future ones hindered, but he is led to a stronger love by knowing the power of the one who unexpectedly delivered him from some difficulty: "Virtue is made perfect in infirmity" (2 Cor 12:9); "Patience has a perfect work" (Jas 1:4).
5. And finally, sometimes afflictions are sent to manifest the divine glory; thus we read here that the works of God might be made manifest in him.[308]

The five reasons that Saint Gregory the Great gives as to why God allows evil to afflict us can be summarized as: (1) punishment for sin and prelude to damnation, (2) chastisement for past wrongs which acts as a corrective measure, (3) admonishment to preserve us from falling into sin, (4) neither as punishment nor a corrective, but to help us grow in virtue, and (5) to glorify God, which is the reason Jesus gives in this instance of the man born blind. Saint Gregory's five reasons, notably, are very similar to Saint Bonaventure's four reasons

[308] Saint Thomas Aquinas, *Commentary on the Gospel of John*, 4–5.

why God allows demons to afflict us. Saint Gregory's last reason, Saint Thomas shows, is consistent with the exegesis of Saint Augustine and Saint John Chrysostom on this passage.

An Example

While we see the effects of sins can pass down to children, the process is not deterministic. When the children live virtuous lives, the words of Saint Paul resound: "Where sin increased, grace overflowed all the more" (Rom 5:20). An example of this is found in a young man who was abandoned by his father and grew up very poor in Mexico, raised by his mother. The father led a dissolute life and wanted nothing to do with his son, placing the boy in a very painful and vulnerable position.

The boy's mother did what she could to make sure her son would not follow in his father's footsteps. She did her best to make sure the boy did not have a "father wound" and become angry at God. She consecrated him to Our Lady of Guadalupe and taught him to pray and prayed daily for her son. The boy discerned a vocation to the priesthood at an early age, and the mother nurtured his vocation through prayers and sacrifices. While always desiring to see his father, he knew it was out of his control, so he committed continually to pray for him that he would reconcile with God someday. The family informed the father of his son's ordination day, but the father refused to attend. Meanwhile, he consecrated his priesthood to the Blessed Mother. After ordination, the now-young priest moved to the United States and served in a missionary diocese, offering his priesthood in thanksgiving for his mother and in reparation for his father. He would occasionally try to contact his father, but to no avail.

After completing his first assignment, the local diocesan exorcist was removed from the priesthood for sufficient cause, and the diocese had no exorcist. This was particularly hard on the young priest because the now-former priest and exorcist was his friend and mentor, and in many ways a father figure to him. But he continued serving the people of God in whatever capacity the Lord asked, always in thanksgiving for his mother and in reparation for his father.

Not long after the diocesan exorcist was removed from office, the priests in his diocese all went on their annual retreat, together with their bishop, in a sparse, desert retreat center. To his surprise, his bishop approached him at the beginning of the retreat. "Father," he said, "would you consider serving as the diocesan exorcist for me? I have no one, and there is much need." The priest was taken by surprise by the bishop's request but said he would pray that week and give him an answer. Everyone was shocked, not to mention a bit frightened, that the previous exorcist had been compromised and removed, and this priest surely had no desire to be the next in line.

That same afternoon, the priest was walking quietly and praying the Rosary when he heard a commotion—squealing and grunting—in the distance. He looked up just in time to see a wild boar burst out of the sage bushes in a dead run straight toward him at a distance of about fifty feet. He was in the middle of the desert, so there were no trees to climb and no structures to run into for safety. Meanwhile, the boar was gaining speed and quickly closing the distance. The priest knew he could not outrun the angry beast, so he planted his feet under him and raised his hand. The boar was now within fifteen feet, and the priest could see his tusks bared and fur spiking along the animal's back. Another priest heard the wild sounds coming from the boar and ran over, but it was too late to stop the inevitable collision. The animal was now within ten feet of the priest and lowering his tusks to slash into him. Heart racing, the priest stood his ground and with his hand still raised, shouted:

"In the name of Jesus Christ, I command you to stop! Creature of God, in the name of Jesus Christ, stop!"

At that command, the angry boar suddenly and immediately slid to a stop, panting, directly at the feet of the priest. The priest, meanwhile, continued to stand his ground, hand outstretched atop the panting animal, who looked directly back at him. His adrenaline racing, and the boar not moving away, the priest continued:

"I am a priest of the living God," the priest bellowed, "it is not I who command you, but it is Jesus Christ who commands you! And you must obey!"

At that command—*It is not I who command you, but it is Jesus Christ who commands you!*—the boar slowly dropped his front legs to the ground and bowed his head in supplication before the priest. The other priest who had heard the commotion now arrived, just in time to snap a picture of the miraculous event.

With a wild boar kneeling before him, the priest stood there for a moment, shaking, until his brother priest told him, "Tell it to leave."

"In the name of Jesus Christ, be gone."

At that, the boar stood up, turned, and trotted away, disappearing into the sagebrush. The priest told his bishop that he would serve as his mandated exorcist and continues to do so to this day.

The most amazing story in the life of this priest, however, is not the wild boar. Years later, as the father lay dying in a hospital in Mexico, he felt remorse for abandoning his family and leaving God. He reached out to family members and asked for the son that he had abandoned, to ask if he would consider visiting him. The priest got on a plane immediately, and there in a simple Mexican hospital room lay a man who had spent his best years in dissolute living. Filled with shame and guilt, when his priest-son arrived to his bedside, the father begged his forgiveness. They both wept as the son forgave him. Then the true miracle occurred. "Father, I forgive you. And so does your heavenly Father. Let us prepare you to meet Him." The priest then heard his father's confession and gave him Last Rites. The father peacefully died soon afterwards, in a state of grace. The prodigal son was reconciled to the heavenly Father by the same son he had abandoned many years ago.

The Hope

Sometimes what seems like our greatest tragedy turns out to be our greatest triumph. "For this momentary light affliction," says Saint Paul, "is producing for us in eternal weight of glory beyond all comparison, as we look, not is seen, but to what is unseen; for what is seen as transitory, but what is unseen is eternal" (2 Cor 4:17–18). The story of this ordinary priest shows how God's great mercy is always at work, as well as the glory of holy priesthood. He is an example of how the privation of protection and provision of blessing of a father is not deterministic. We are all called to holiness and virtue, and to do battle with the weapons of faith (even as small as a mustard seed), prayer and penance. His story also shows the beauty of motherhood in a mother who trusted God above all else.

A Prayer

Most sweet Jesus, pierce the interior of my soul with the sweet wound of Thy love, that my soul may ever languish and be dissolved with Thy love and with the desire of possessing Thee, and long to quit this life, that it may come to be perfectly united with Thee in a blessed eternity. Grant that my soul may ever thirst after Thee, speak only to Thee, find Thee, and do all for Thy glory. Grant that my heart may be ever fixed on Thee, who art my only hope, my riches, my peace, my refuge, my confidence, my treasure, and my inheritance.[309]

O eternal God! I know that I am poor in all things; I can do nothing, I have nothing, save what comes to me from Thy hands; all I can say to Thee is, Lord, have mercy upon me. My misery is that to my poverty I have added the sin of having answered Thy graces with the sins I have committed against Thee. But, notwithstanding, I would hope from Thy mercy this twofold blessing: first, that Thou wouldst pardon my sins; and then that Thou wouldst give me perseverance together with Thy holy love, and with grace to pray to Thee constantly to help me even till death. I ask it all of Thee, I hope for it, through the merits of Thy Son Jesus, and the blessed Virgin Mary. O my chief advocate! help me with Thy prayers.[310]

O Mary, in spite of the impurity of my tongue, may I always invoke your name, which is the breath of my life. I will repeat again and again, "Mary, Mary," especially at the hour of death. Let me forget every other name except Jesus and Mary. May I be invoking your names at my last breath.[311]

---

[309] Saint Alphonsus Liguori, *The Way of Salvation and of Perfection*, 328. This prayer is written by St. Bonaventure to Jesus Christ, to obtain His Holy Love.

[310] Saint Alphonsus Liguori, *The Way of Salvation and of Perfection*, 228.

[311] Saint Alphonsus Liguori, *Glories of Mary*, 51.

Act of Reparation to the Sacred Heart of Jesus[312]

O sweet Jesus, whose overflowing charity for men is requited by so much forgetfulness, negligence, and contempt, behold us prostrate before Thee, eager to repair by a special act of homage the cruel indifference and injuries, to which Thy loving Heart is everywhere subject.

Mindful alas! that we ourselves have had a share in such great indignities, which we now deplore from the depths of our hearts, we humbly ask Thy pardon and declare our readiness to atone by voluntary expiation not only for our own personal offenses, but also for the sins of those, who, straying far from the path of salvation, refuse in their obstinate infidelity to follow Thee, their Shepherd and Leader or, renouncing the promises of their Baptism, have cast off the sweet yoke of Thy Law.

We are now resolved to expiate each and every deplorable outrage committed against Thee; we are now determined to make amends for the manifold offenses against Christian modesty in unbecoming dress and behavior, for all the foul seductions laid to ensnare the feet of the innocent, for the frequent violations of Sundays and Holy Days, and the shocking blasphemies uttered against Thee and Thy Saints. We wish also to make amends for the insults to which Thy Vicar on earth and Thy priests are subjected, for the profanation, by conscious neglect or terrible acts of sacrilege, of the very Sacrament of Thy Divine Love, and lastly for the public crimes of nations who resist the rights and teaching authority of the Church which Thou hast founded.

[312] Ripperger, *Holy Hour of Reparation*, 5–7.

Would that we were able to wash away such abominations with our blood. We now offer, in reparation for these violations of Thy divine honor, the satisfaction Thou once made to Thy eternal Father on the Cross and which Thou continuest to renewest daily on our Altars; we offer it in union with the acts of atonement of Thy Virgin Mother and all the Saints and of the pious faithful on earth; and we sincerely promise to make recompense, as far as we can with the help of Thy grace, for all neglect of Thy great love and for the sins we and others have committed in the past. Henceforth we will live a life of unswerving faith, of purity of conduct, of perfect observance of the precepts of the Gospel and especially that of charity. We promise to the best of our power to prevent others from offending Thee and to bring as many as possible to follow Thee.

O loving Jesus, through the intercession of the Blessed Virgin Mother, our model in reparation, deign to receive the voluntary offering we make of this act of expiation; and by the crowning gift of perseverance keep us faithful unto death in our duty and the allegiance we owe to Thee, so that we may all one day come to that happy home where, with the Father and the Holy Spirit, Thou livest and reignest, God, forever and ever. Amen.

VII.

FROM WHY TO HOW

This concept of inherited guilt is not an isolated theological matter and finds overlap in several key areas of theology. One primary way is bringing into light the importance of the authority structure—with its twofold ends of protection and provision—and the effect of abdication of authority as creating a vulnerability for those under one's authority. In addition, the concept also speaks to both the perfect mercy and perfect justice of God, while also deepening our understanding of sin and its effects, and the oft-forgotten temporal punishment due to sin.

The developed theology of the Church teaches that due to the nature of evil, there remains punishment for sin. As the *Catechism* states, moreover, due to the nature of evil and the offense against God's holiness, all sin requires satisfaction be made. Thus, "the temporal punishment due to sins" remains even for those "whose guilt has already been forgiven" (CCC 1471). Holy Mother Church offers a remedy of mercy through her sacraments, Jubilee Years, and the acquiring of indulgences.

The effects of sin and subsequent spiritual battle find their origins in the Fall. The initial effect of the "tragic consequences of this first disobedience" is the spiritual punishment of our first parents: "Adam and Eve immediately lose the grace of original holiness" (CCC 399). That is, they personally suffered a spiritual punishment: loss of the state of grace (life of God in the soul) and subsequent separation from God. A second effect is the compounding (notably, temporal) effects of sin and death now entering the human family, to include disordered relationships, hostility, etc. (see CCC 400). Not only do Adam and Eve suffer a spiritual consequence but also a temporal effect: "Death makes its entrance into human history" (CCC 400) and "the world is virtually inundated by sin" (CCC 401). Like the truck driver in chapter IV above, Adam and Eve alone are punished for their sin, but a compounding effect upon others due to the sin is introduced. The "contagion" of the original sin means essentially a privation of goods, as Saint Augustine argues. The human family now lacks the fullness of the preternatural state before the Fall with its provision and protection of blessing.

The *Catechism* further notes how the effects of Adam and Eve's sin, the privation of blessing, are both *familial* and *communal*. It states that the primary effects are first felt in their offspring: "Cain's murder of his brother Abel and the universal corruption . . . follows in the wake of sin." Similarly, the temporal effect of sin is also seen in the larger community: "Sin frequently manifests itself in the history of Israel, especially as infidelity to the God of the Covenant, and as transgressions of the law of Moses." These twofold effects upon family and community continue today, hence the *Catechism* asserts, "even after Christ's atonement, sin raises its head and countless ways among Christians" (CCC 401). This is why, for example, generational spirits work along the lines of authority, both familial and communal. If we recall that the family is the "domestic church" (CCC 2685), we see the effects of grave sins work in a parallel manner in both constructs.

Recall also the teaching of Saint Thomas that just as a child is something of the parents, so also "the people is something of the king's, and so the people is punished that in its punishment the king may be punished." That is, the punishment of the sins of a people and *avon avot* applies not just to families but to communities, where the iniquities of the king are visited upon the people. The same logic here applies to other structures of authority. Thus, he affirms that the inherited guilt of a temporal punishment of sins as familial can also be seen in other constructs, such as government. Saint Thomas states, building on Saint Gregory the Great:

> And this is especially the case, as Gregory says, when the people's sins deserve having a sinful king established over them or having a king who is permitted to fall into sin, as Job 34:30 says: *who makes a hypocrite to reign on account of the people's sins*. And so it is clear that the people is also punished for its own sin.[313]

Thus, as with children who offer no impediment of virtue and righteous living to the effects of their parents' sins, Saint Thomas affirms that God also punishes wicked rulers in the people. In addition, he states that the people are punished for their own wickedness by having wicked rulers placed over them. This implies that even beyond the constructs of families and government, there could also be a temporal effect of sins in other constructs such as religious orders, corporations, etc. That is, just as the effects of gravely sinful behavior of a father can be experienced by his children, so also the grave sins of a bishop can be experienced in his priests and flock. The life of David, moreover, highlights the familial and communal effects of sin quite clearly.

313 Saint Thomas Aquinas, *II Sent.*, d. 33, q. 2.

This leads us to a question: How did the sin of Adam become the sin of all his descendants? And does sin have effects beyond the individual who commits it? That is, as Julian of Eclanum argued, it does seem unjust, or at least inconsistent, that a merciful God would punish children for the sins of their parents. Julian repeatedly accused Saint Augustine of "the treachery of the traducianists" when he claimed that any guilt of a parent's sin can be inherited. In rejecting that God punishes sin and that the effect of the sins of the father can carry down to the children, however, Julian had to conclude that "it remained unshaken that there is no inheritance of sin. For it is agreed that the means by which the guilt of parents passed to their children and that of children to their parents was not generation."[314] All sin, Julian argued, is imitated, and a loving God would not let a child suffer.

To get there, Julian ignored the context of the biblical texts he cites and collapses divine law into human law. Specifically, he appealed to Moses's words in giving civil laws ("Father shall not be put to death for their children, nor children for their fathers; only for his own guilt, shall a man be put to death," Dt 24:16). This verse and an isolated verse from the prophet Ezekiel ("Only the one who sends shall die. The son shall not be charged with the guilt of his father, nor the father be charged with the guilt of his son. The virtuous man's virtue shall be his own, as a wicked man's wickedness shall be his own," Ez 18:20) seemingly gave to him his mic-drop moment against Saint Augustine, when he claimed that with this "lightning bolt the whole structure of inherited sin collapses."[315] Thus, Julian argued that any later decrees by Moses or the prophets supersede God's own words at Sinai. As cited earlier, however, the Council of Trent affirms as the unanimous consensus of

[314] Saint Augustine, *Answer to the Pelagians III*, 292.
[315] Saint Augustine, *Answer to the Pelagians III*, 293.

the Fathers "that the Lord will take vengeance on it, even to the third and fourth generation. That such was, at all times, the doctrine of the Fathers, a reference to their writings will place beyond the possibility of all doubt." Accordingly, Saint Augustine showed that God reveals Himself in stages, but He does not change.

According to the developed teachings of the Church, moreover, "in Adam's sin, all are implicated in Christ's justice." This is because, as the *Catechism* states:

> By yielding to the tempter, Adam and Eve committed a personal sin, but this sin affected the human nature that they would then transmit in a fallen state. It is a sin which will be transmitted by propagation to all mankind, that is, by the transmission of a human nature *deprived of original holiness and justice*. And that is why original sin is called "sin" only in an analogical sense: it is a sin "contracted" and not "committed"—a state and not an act. (CCC 404)

The effect of their disobedience brought about a "curse" upon the first couple (cf. Gn 2:19). Original sin, then, means a corruption of nature which results in a privation of original goods—holiness and justice. It is, moreover, a privation of a good just as a curse is a privation of blessing. The "good substance" of pre-Fall humanity now became corrupted to such a degree that only Baptism can reverse its effects.

There is always a danger, however, to place the blame of our "teeth on edge" (that is, our present suffering) upon someone else. Admittedly, most proponents of intergenerational sin and the healing of the family tree have not studied the works of Saints Augustine or Thomas or know the ancient debate which led up to the dogma of original sin (and the rejection of traducianism). In their defense, however, they have stumbled upon a phenomenon de facto and try in earnest to help people. A negative byproduct, however, is a tendency for people to blame their sins on their ancestors and not take personal responsibility for their own lives. As a result, many ask *Why is this happening to me?* But few ask *How can this make me holy?* If we focus on the devil, the physical, and the sins of the past, we lose sight of Christ, the spiritual, and the opportunity for grace in the present moment. This leads some to use the Mass as a means to break the "controlling force" of the sins of ancestors so that they no longer suffer in the present. This is oversimplistic and a misuse of the Sacred Liturgy in a way counter to its intrinsic, propitiatory nature. Healing is reconciliation with the Father, and this reality is what the Mass makes truly present.

This topic also brings to the surface the need for satisfaction for sin through redemptive suffering as a remedy for the family to grow in holiness. In cases of possession where there is a familial component, the individual is generally not an innocent victim. Like the people of God in the Old Testament who abandoned their religious patrimony for false gods, few who struggle under diabolic affliction are the "righteous grandson" of Ezekiel. Even rarer is found a child under the age of reason who is possessed, as the boy in Mark's Gospel who was possessed "since infancy." The latter are, to be clear, the rare exceptions, but it still happens today. Those rare exceptions do suggest that diabolic affliction can have a familial component (and, therefore, a familial solution).

Like the inhabitants of Jerusalem under siege, many today ask *why* they are suffering. The majority of people who fall under diabolic influence, however, have generally followed (or imitated) the sins of their parents, abandoned the Catholic faith (or have had no faith), and have fallen into grave sins themselves. These sins are commonly a combination of some form of idolatry/witchcraft and deviant sexual behavior. The main three false gods of the surrounding nations that kept resurfacing, recall, were Chemosh, Astarte, and Molech (cf. 2 Kgs 23:13), who were worshipped through sexual acts (including homosexual and bisexual) and appeased through child sacrifice. Are we any different today? Like the inhabitants of Jerusalem, many people will point to their ancestors and blame a "generational sin" as to why they are suffering but often fail to see where they themselves "hated" God, the divine Bridegroom, through their own sinful actions of idolatry, fornication/sexual deviancy, homosexuality, and abortion/contraception.

Those who highlight apparent contradictions in Scripture and assert that theology evolves often conclude that the words of Ezekiel and Jeremiah on individual responsibility indicate that the words of God Himself at Sinai are now nullified. As Jesus, however, stated: "Do not think that I have come to abolish the law or the prophets. I have not come to abolish, but to fulfill. Amen, I say to you, until heaven and earth passed away, not the smallest letter, or smallest part of a letter will pass from the law until all things have taken place" (Mt 5:17–18). Thus, if Jesus does not abolish the Law, neither do Moses or the prophets. To this end, both Saint Augustine and Saint Thomas are clear that the green grapes proverb does not mean that God has changed or that His words at Sinai are nullified. Rather, both note the "both/and" in distinguishing between personal responsibility for sins and also that God does sometimes punish the father's sins in his children. Both also emphasize that there are two systems of justice—divine and human—and what would be unjust at a human level cannot be applied to divine justice. As God spoke through Isaiah, "My ways are not your ways" (Is 55:8). God, in His divine providence, knows what is best for us.

Accordingly, the Fathers examined the effects of the sin of our first parents as having introduced into the human family an affliction and a struggle in which each person finds himself (see CCC 409). In arguing for the reality of an original sin, Saint Augustine used the concept of inherited guilt and *avon avot* as central to his explanation of how the twofold effects of the sin of our first parents carry into all of humanity. That is, to prove that there is an original sin, he used the concept of a generational curse as his main argument. Notably, he emphasized the words of God at Sinai that *God says* that He "inflicts punishment for their fathers' wickedness on the children of those who hate me down to the third and fourth generation" (Ex 20:5). This, he argued, was not only evidence for the concept of an inherited guilt but also proof of an original, or *archetypal,* sin which set the pattern for all subsequent sin. For both Saint Augustine and Saint Thomas, the truth of *avon avot* is a *sine qua non* for understanding original sin. Thus, the sin of our first parents introduced into the human family a negative effect which, in turn, meant a pathway for diabolic influence. All subsequent sin follows the same pattern of the original one in that there will be both a spiritual and a temporal effect.

Specifically, Saint Augustine helped to formulate our understanding of the effects of the Fall as twofold (the sin itself and the effect of the sin). He described the need for sanctifying grace to remedy the effects of the Fall, while acknowledging a continued, lingering, and negative effect of the postlapsarian (after the Fall) human condition. In simple terms, Baptism restores the life of grace to the soul, but the effects of the first sin of Adam and Eve still linger in the human condition. This post-baptismal, lingering effect of the Fall means a disordered tendency toward sin (which in the developed theological language of the Church came to be known as *concupiscence*).

The distinction between the sin and the effect of sin is the key to understanding the *how* of *avon avot* and also eases the tension between an apparent contradiction between the "God of the Old Testament" (as punishing and harsh) and the "God of the New Testament" (as loving and merciful). Saint Bonaventure's affirmation that demons are God's instruments of our purification and of punishment for sins means that, in His divine providence, the demons assist our *anabasis* by purifying us of all that separates us from union with God. In this movement, He allows us to make satisfaction, like the Jerusalem inhabitants, for our sins and those of our fathers. This means that at times, He invites someone within a family to be an *alter Christus*, another Christ, to make satisfaction for the sins.

Some ancient manuscripts of the Gospel of Saint Mark recount also that the father of the possessed boy cried out "with tears" to Jesus. When a father sees his children suffer as the result of his sins, he is brought to tears and repentance, as was David. The holy tears of compunction go a long way in the spiritual life. Jesus gives further insight on how to drive out "this type (Greek, *genos*) of demon"—namely, the generational spirit that plagues a person:

1. Jesus works within the authority structure and goes directly to the father, as he will be key to his son's liberation. Healing is reconciliation with the heavenly Father, and it generally begins with the earthly father.
2. When asked by His disciples why they could not drive the demon out that had been present "since childhood," Jesus nuances it differently in Saint Mark than in Saint Matthew. In the former, it is in the positive: "This kind can *only* come out through prayer and fasting" (Mk

9:29); in the latter, in the negative: "But this kind *never* comes out except by prayer and fasting" (Mt 17:21). Notably, "fasting" takes many forms, but always involves the mortification of the will and an offering to God in reparation for sins.

3. Jesus emphasizes the need for faith by both parents and the ministers of the Church. In Saint Mark, the father's faith was deficient while in Saint Matthew, Jesus tells the disciple that it was "because of your [the apostles'] little faith" that they could not drive out the demon (Mt 17:20). Faith and a penitential posture will be key in these matters, not only in parents but also in the ministers of the Church.
4. Deliverance is not a matter of finding the right formula or prayer, or the person with the special charism of deliverance. For liberation, faith and the ordering of the household must be supplemented through prayer and fasting (a penitential posture)—by those in the household and also the ministers of the Church and those who serve them. Holiness is the primary factor.
5. Faith in Jesus must be present and ongoing, particularly in the face of suffering—and especially in the seeming helplessness of witnessing a child suffer affliction.

We fight an ancient enemy, and the ancient weapons are best. The clarion call for today's Catholics, therefore, is to return to the ancient faith and devotions. In working with cases for many years now, I have discovered a certain maxim, or truism, from the field; namely, the enemy enters through sin, but he holds through heresy. The sin is often offering false worship of idolatry and grave sexual sins, but any mortal sin can be an entry point. Once inside, he whittles away at areas where we fail to conform ourselves to the revealed truths of the Roman Catholic faith. Sin, as the *Catechism* states, darkens the intellect and weakens the will (see CCC 402–6), and the enemy exploits both by leading us to false beliefs while habituating us into patterned, and self-destructive, sinful behaviors. We are a hylomorphic being—that is, a body-soul composite. The actions we do with our bodies—holy or unholy—have spiritual ramifications.

The saints are our exemplars. Saint Cyprian of Carthage was born in North Africa around AD 200 and converted to Christianity from paganism in a time of intense persecution. Ultimately, he was beheaded for refusing to renounce the Holy Name of Jesus Christ. In a letter written to encourage the church in times of persecution, he leaves a timely message for us today:

> Divine providence has now prepared us. God's merciful design has warned us that the day of our own struggle, our own contest, is at hand. By that shared love which binds us close together, we are doing all we can to exhort our congregation, to **give ourselves unceasingly to fastings, vigils and prayers in common. These are the heavenly weapons which give us the strength to stand firm and endure; they are the spiritual defences, the God-given armaments that protect us.** Let us then remember one another, united in mind and heart. **Let us pray without ceasing**, you for us, we for you; by the love we share we shall thus relieve the strain of these great trials.[316]

These are our weapons, our God-given armaments, for spiritual combat in an age of resurging paganism: bodily mortifications and other forms of fasting, private vigils before the Blessed Sacrament, and communal prayers together are the ancient weapons that shield us in battle. The opening prayer for Ash Wednesday echoes this:

[316] Saint Cyprian of Carthage, Epistle 56.5, in *The Writings of Cyprian*, vol 1, 192.

Grant us, O Lord, to begin our Christian warfare with holy fasts; that as we are about to do battle with the spirits of evil, we may be defended by the aid of self-denial. Through Christ our Lord. Amen.[317]

These are the ancient means by which we both make satisfaction for sin and also free the soul for her ascent to God.

I close with the advice of Saint Peter Damian, who was asked for words of comfort by a directee who was suffering many trials. Echoing the *synkatabasis* and *anabasis* of Saint Irenaeus, he writes:

You asked me to write you some words of consolation, my brother. Embittered by so many tribulations, you are seeking some comfort for your soul. You asked me to offer you some soothing suggestions. But there is no need for me to write. Consolation is already within your reach, if your good sense has not been dulled. My son, come to the service of God. Stand in justice and fear. Prepare your soul; it is about to be tested. These words of Scripture show that you are a son of God and, as such, should take possession of your inheritance. What could be clearer than this exhortation?

Where there is justice as well as fear, adversity will surely test the spirit. But it is not the torment of a slave. Rather it is the discipline of a child by its parent.

Even in the midst of his many sufferings, the holy man Job could say: Whip me, crush me, cut me in slices! And he would always add: This at least would bring me relief, yet my persecutor does not spare me.

But for God's chosen ones there is great comfort; the torment lasts but a short time. Then God bends down, cradles the fallen figure, whispers words of consolation. With hope in his heart, man picks himself up and walks again towards the glory of happiness in heaven. Craftsmen exemplify this same practice. By hammering gold, the smith beats

[317] Lefebvre, *St. Andrew Missal*, 272.

down the dross. The sculptor files metal to reveal a shining vein underneath. The potter's furnace puts vessels to the test. And the fire of suffering tests the mettle of just men. The apostle James echoes this thought: Think it a great joy, dear brothers and sisters, when you stumble onto the many kinds of trials and tribulations.

When men suffer pain for the evil they have perpetrated in life, they should take some reassurance. They also know that for their good deeds undying rewards await them in the life to come. Therefore, my brother, scorned as you are by men, lashed as it were by God, do not despair. Do not be depressed. Do not let your weakness make you impatient. Instead, let the serenity of your spirit shine through your face. Let the joy of your mind burst forth. Let words of thanks break from your lips.

The way that God deals with men can only be praised. He lashes them in this life to shield them from the eternal lash in the next. He pins people down now; at a later time he will raise them up. He cuts them before healing; he throws them down to raise them anew. The Scriptures reassure us: let your understanding strengthen your patience. In serenity look forward to the joy that follows sadness. Hope leads you to that joy and love enkindles your zeal. The well-prepared mind forgets the suffering inflicted from without and glides eagerly to what it has contemplated within itself.[318]

Prayer to Remove Generational Spirits

Lord Jesus Christ, Incarnate Son of God of the Father, Thou who hast chosen to enter into human history by being carried in the womb of Thy Blessed Mother Mary, grant, I beseech Thee, that any demons that may have been introduced into my generational line by anyone of my ancestors may be blocked

[318] Cited in *The Liturgy of the Hours III*, 1383–85.

from passing to the subsequent generations. I ask Thee that if the evil spirit entered the generational line by the sin of one or more of my ancestors, that Thou wouldst pardon the temporal punishment due to their sin and free us from the demon's involvement in our lives. Blessed Virgin, we ask thee to offer the Precious Body, Blood, Soul, and Divinity of thy Son to God, the Father, in reparation for the sins of those ancestors who may have introduced any evil spirits into my generational line, as well as any subsequent sins that may have resulted from the evil spirits affecting those of the generational line. If any evil spirit has been introduced into my generational line as a result of a curse or malefice done by someone outside my family, I ask thee to give me the grace to forgive them wholeheartedly, and I ask Thee, Jesus, to break the curse or malefice, if it is still in place. God the Father, I forgive them for any of the effects of their sin that they may have committed against my family line and for any damage it may have caused. Jesus, I ask Thee to forgive me of any sins that may be the result of any generational spirits in my family, and I ask Thee to block any power the evil spirits may have gained in my generational line as a result of my own sin. Heal any damage in the lives of the members of my family as a result of the generational spirit. I bind and completely and utterly reject, with a full force of my will, any sin or spiritual defect of mine, as well as any temptation, allurements, or power that any generational spirit may have over me as a result of my sin or the sin of any other person. I do this in the Holy Names of Jesus and Mary and in the Name of the Father and of the Son and of the Holy Spirit. Amen.

Epilogue: An Interview with Father Chad Ripperger

In this final section, I offer a brief explanation of how to identify and militate against familial curses in light of the above conclusions. The following is a discussion with exorcist Father Chad Ripperger on how to identify and root out familial spirits.

Q. The Gospel account of the exorcism of the boy with demon (Mk 9:14–29) suggests that even young children can be afflicted by demons. What is the youngest case of possession you have ever seen?
A. The youngest case that I have had was a ten-month-old blonde hair, blue-eyed baby girl.

Q. How could you tell she was possessed?
A. She exhibited the classic signs of possession.[319]

[319] An eyewitness to this case affirmed that specifically the infant showed an aversion to the sacred (which, in effect, is a sign of occult knowledge that an object is blessed, for example) and a preternatural strength. The latter is often seen in the display of physical attributes beyond one's strength, which includes what is called shapeshifting. In this case, when a sacred object was applied to the infant, her body would contort and change appearances in most remarkable ways. When a sacred object or priestly stole was applied to her as part of the Rite of Exorcism, her physical appearance changed beyond the human, to include her head expanding to the size of a basketball, her total appearance completely discolored, eyes bugging out,

Q. Was there a familial element to this case?
A. Yes. Generally, a familial curse comes in through someone committing a grave sin. In the case of the baby girl, it was eventually discovered that the maternal great-grandmother to the little girl practiced evil things, and it was through her that we think it got into the generational line before it started passing through. This was kind of a classical case. The baby cleans up very quickly because children usually do. So, basically once we discovered the entry point in the family line, did some severing prayers and two sessions of Chapter Three (of the Rite of Exorcism) and she was liberated. In this case, the mother had always been very virtuous her entire life. The father was also a very virtuous man, but he struggled with certain interior doubt. Once he shored that up, liberation came quickly.

Q. How does someone find out if there is a curse operant?
A. What I usually do when I'm trying to sort these things out is to remind people that it boils down to three things. The first is just observing basic patterns—moral, psychological, physical, or other kinds of behavior patterns in the family. By just watching the patterns, you can often discern the effects of sins present in the form of a curse. So, if you notice that everybody has a problem with fear, or everybody has a problem with lying or something like that. If you observe the right thing and then you do binding prayers against it, that is when you will start to notice things shift. So, once you see that pattern emerge by basic observation, you can do binding prayers against those specific things. The opposite may also be an indicator. If you are binding a bunch of stuff and

---

and her teeth became sharpened to a point, like those of an animal. Plus, she exhibited an animal-like diabolic ferocity at the presence of anything sacred, and even at the sight of the exorcist and the beginning of exorcistic prayers.

nothing is happening, that is an indicator that you have not hit the target yet.

Q. So you have to do some detective work, in a sense.
A. Right. Then sometimes you have to try to figure out what is the nature of the thing. So, I often recommend going to the various siblings and parents and try tracing it back to the cause. Was there an event that happened somewhere? For example, one person I know, the family all dealt with this low, generalized fear. It was very low grade and didn't block them from doing anything, but it was always there. Nobody had ever talked about it, but they all had it in some form. And then we traced it back through the generational line up to a very specific event that happened with one of their grandparents. So once we found out what that was, we could then start binding any demon that got in from that event. So, once you trace it back to a specific event, you can start binding anything associated with the event and that will often stop it.

Q. And the second step?
A. The second part is looking at the daughter sins in relationship to the vices or deadly sins so that you can be more specific in your work against it.

Q. That is from Saint Thomas Aquinas, correct?
A. Correct. Saint Thomas lists each of the seven deadly sins and the corresponding "daughter vices" which accompany each (see Appendix). So, for example, if you know that the family is highly introspective, that they are always ruminating about stuff, that can be an indicator of fear because fear drives rumination. Or, you know that they have pride issues, one of the things that you will see in the family very consistently is intemperance issues like gluttony, alcoholism, drug use, and sixth commandment violations/sexual sins. Or, a lot of times

when guys have problems with anger, the real issue is not the anger. The real issue is that they have a tender heart, but they do not process emotions well, and they do not suffer well. So, once you see the pattern emerge, then look for what various vices or sins or negative psychological issues are connected to other things, then you can now more directly militate against it with virtue.

Q. Can you expand on what you mean by militating against?
A. Basically you develop the virtues contrary to it or healing in relationship to it.

Q. By healing, you mean psychological healing?
A. Yes. By working on the psychological issues in relationship to it, you address the natural side of it because the demon drives that too. So, part of it is developing the natural virtues and the proper psychological (mental) habits vis-à-vis the thing.

Q. This is because the demon is driving the defect, correct?
A. Correct. And you should confess sins related to the vice while working on developing the counter-virtue.

Q. If not, you end up playing "whack-a-mole" and never getting to the root cause of the spiritual or psychological defect and, therefore, to the demon that is often driving the behavior?
A. Precisely. It is basically knowing which things cause which, and Saint Thomas is a helpful starting point, knowing which things cause which. A lot of times I tell people to start with the daughter vices of lust, anger, or avarice, etc. People will say they are concerned about XYZ, or this or that or the other thing, then I will just start asking him: What's underneath that? Is there something underneath that that's driving that

behavior and that is the root cause? Keep going until you get to the root cause. A lot of times the primary behavior we are seeing is not necessarily the thing that is driving it. So knowing how things are interconnected can get you to that stage.

Q. Can you give an example?
A. So, by going to the root causes, you can find out, for example, a person might think they are dealing with a demon of self-loathing, but behind it is a demon of abandonment, or something like that. That is really what is driving this person to a patterned, sinful behavior, or an unwillingness to have decent relationships.

Q. You said it was a three-step process. What is the third step?
A. The third step is that I always just tell people to pray to Our Lady of Sorrows to reveal to you what is blocking grace, or any spiritual defect, the nature of the thing that is afflicting you, or the nature of the demon you are dealing with and in the context of that.[320] Demons are master tacticians, so they drive behaviors in certain areas when their actual nature is something else. This is because they want you focusing all your energy in trying to clean up an issue that's not really the problem.

For example, Beelzebub, who, technically speaking, is the demon of fear but is also the demon of impurity. He only

---

[320] As Father Ripperger says elsewhere: "It is highly recommended that one prays to Our Lady of Sorrows to ask her to reveal what the nature of the generational spirit is and how they may have entered the generational line so that specific binding prayers may be said against them and virtues may be developed to combat them. It is also salutary to have Masses offered in reparation for any sin that may be the cause of the generational spirit as well as healing of the members who may still suffer the effects of the evil spirit and for the propose of any souls in purgatory that may still be there as a result of sins they committed at the behest of the evil spirit." Ripperger, *Laity*, 26.

drives the impurity via fear, generally speaking. So if you have an impurity problem, well, do you have a problem with fear? Or do you have a problem with these other things? By asking Our Lady of Sorrows what the nature of the thing is, then just watching for an ordinary grace, she will reveal it to you. Sometimes she will give someone else the grace to summon the grace, to say something so that you see it; they say something that will then unpack it.

Q. What else is involved in the militating against it?
A. There is doing specific binding prayers, for example, against any spirits that you have identified. Also, Marian consecration and praying to Our Lady, asking for those specific virtues, etc. The other thing is having Masses said and then doing spiritual warfare stuff against it like saying the Prayer Against Generational Spirits. Offering you Communions, Rosaries, penances, sacrifices. Sometimes having a priest pray over you and relationship to it.

Q. And then what happened after you got to the event in that case?
A. So then, basically from that point on, we just started severing it and they started working on courage and stuff like that and it cleaned it up pretty quick. Because, as you know, if you do not get the specificity, you can be praying until the cows come home, but you're not going to get anywhere.

Q. But this is something that people can generally do on their own without an exorcist?
A. Yes, without an exorcist, I mean sometimes. If they find out with the nature of it is, sometimes they are going to need an exorcist to get it cleaned up. But a lot of times once they find out what the nature of it is—so like it's fear—well, then you start working on fortitude and confidence, keeping your

focus on the good, joy, things like that. Work on the counter thing and then doing binding prayers that concentrate on it. Having Masses said for the dead. You just go all out. Sometimes if you can find a good exorcist who actually believes in the stuff and will actually do it, he can start doing severing prayers over the individuals that suffer from it. A lot of times that will clean it up.

Q. You have several good talks out here on Catholic courtship. What do you recommend for engaged couples in light of these types of familial/spiritual baggage?
A. I have not done weddings for a couple years now, but anytime I would do weddings, I would always tell them make a general confession—either to me or someone else—the day before, the night before the wedding. I tell them that I want to meet both of you to go over it and then give them that list of spirits in the back of the *Deliverance Prayers for the Laity* book.[321] And I tell them to go through and mark every single thing that you can possibly think that would pertain to your family. Then I just sit down and just sever any generational spirit and clean up the generational baggage before they even get married.

Q. Okay, it sounds simple.
A. Yeah, I don't think it's that complicated. I should say that it seems counterintuitive, but the more reliable way to get the specificity of the generational spirit is going to be through asking Our Lady of Sorrows to reveal it and getting the grace. Consistently, people end up coming across the stuff, and it is much more accurate that way. It is not going to be some mystical revelation. It will just be a grace to see it, and then all the sudden you know, enlightened in the mind. And then,

[321] See Ripperger, *Laity*, 101–10.

of course, once you see what it is, you can get to work. As I mentioned, the family that I was helping sort it out figured out that they got the grace to see that it was fear. But it was not until someone in the generational line had mentioned an event that had happened that we realized that was when the thing got in.

Q. Freemasonry seems to be on the rise these days. How do you identify Freemasonic curses and how do you sever them?

A. Like for the generational spirits, if you know the patterns for Freemasonry, then the Freemasonic ones are going to be fairly consistent. The first one is just watching for patterns, such as respiratory issues in the family, problems of infidelity, divorce, stuff like that. But there is also fear and things like that. I would just tell people to do an elementary investigation of their family history, make sure you know whether there was something in the line or not from Freemasonry.

Q. And to sever it?

A. Well, the pathway out in addition to things discussed above is just to say the Prayers to Break the Freemasonic Curse three times, but it is good to look at the protocol for that first.[322]

Q. Would you recommend that people not do the renunciations if they aren't sure of Freemasonry in the family?

A. I usually say it can't hurt. In fact, the reason I mention that is there was one priest that I know that was unaware that he had but he thought, you know, "maybe there was, so maybe I'll do it." And then he literally went bug-eyed during the first

[322] For an explanation of the prayers and protocol, see https://liberchristo.org/resources/printed-material/ and prayers in Ripperger, *Laity*, 122–35.

two times he did it (the renunciation prayers). And then after he completed it, his respiratory issues were gone.

Q. I want to end with this. You have elsewhere said that Our Lady has "perfect coercive power over demons."[323] I would like to repeat here what you have written on why you recommend we specifically go to Our Lady of Sorrows?

A. We ought also to petition her under the title of Our Lady of Sorrows in the spiritual combat for two reasons. The first is that when St. Joseph and Mary took Jesus to St. Simeon, he said to Our Lady that her heart would be pierced so that the thoughts of many would be revealed. Our Lady, by undergoing the passion with Christ, would merit an intimacy with God that no other creature had. As a result, He reveals things to her that He does not reveal to others. However, He will allow us to petition her so that she may reveal hidden things relating to the spiritual life. This is true in relation to our own defects, but especially in matters of spiritual combat. In spiritual warfare, precision is everything. In this respect, spiritual warfare is not any different than any other kind of warfare; the more accurate or specific the weapon, the more effective it will be. For this reason, if we pray to Our Lady of Sorrows, she will reveal to us the nature of the demon we are dealing with, whether that is in our own lives or in the lives of those to whom we have obligations. This provides us a specific target to combat.

The second reason to pray to Our Lady of Sorrows is because of the promises made by her to St. Bridgid of Sweden

[323] "Lastly, we cannot recommend the constant petition and perfect confidence in Our Lady enough. For She who has perfect coercive power over demons can protect us from any diabolic attack of any kind. In time, if we remain under Her mantle, no demons will dare approach us. Yet this only comes when we never offend Her Son and we have perfect confidence in Her." Ripperger, *Laity*, 9.

"I will defend them in their spiritual battles with the infernal enemy and I will protect them at every instant of their lives." Ultimately, we are powerless to protect ourselves and the spiritual warfare. Only Christ can protect us and those whom Christ has commissioned to protect us, among whom Our Lady stands above the rest. So it is in her that we placed our confidence.[324]

[324] See Ripperger, *Laity*, 9–10.

Appendix: Identifying Generational Spirits: The Seven Deadly Sins and "Daughter Vices"

1. **Lust** is "an inordinate desire for or enjoyment of sexual pleasure [which] does not conform to the divinely ordained purpose of sexual pleasure."[325] By its nature, it disorders reason and weakens the will. The vices or sins ("daughters") which rise from the deadly sin of **lust**:[326]

    a. Blindness of mind
    b. Thoughtlessness (inconsiderateness towards others)
    c. Inconstancy (inability to control emotions, etc. in relation to the events of life)
    d. Love of self
    e. Hatred of God
    f. Love of this world
    g. Despair of a future life (or despair of eternal life)
    h. Restlessness (or undue attachment to the present life)

2. **Pride** is "the inordinate esteem of oneself . . . contrary to truth." This includes "desiring to be considered better

[325] Hardon, *Modern Catholic Dictionary*, 326.
[326] Saint Thomas Aquinas, *ST* II–II, q. 153, art. 5.

than a person really is" and, therefore, the inordinate desire for one's own excellence, "holding oneself superior to others" which even leads to a rejection of God.[327] The vices or sins ("daughters") which rise from the deadly sin of **pride**:[328]

a. Vainglory (inordinate desire for praise)
b. Boasting (excessive talk of one's achievements)
c. Hypocrisy (claiming moral virtues one does not possess)
d. Disobedience (rebellion/refusal to obey rightful authority)
e. Arrogance (excessive sense of one's importance; disdain for others)
f. Presumption (overestimating one's abilities or merits; blindness to deficiencies)
g. Discord (causing disagreement, quarrelling, or division out of self-will)

3. **Greed**, or avarice/covetousness, is "a controlling passion for wealth or possessions" and the "excessive desire for money or material things" to include the use of "unlawful means to hold on to [one's] possessions."[329] Greed's insatiable desire for money thwarts the letting go of and the proper use of material goods. The vices or sins ("daughters") which rise from the deadly sin of **greed**:[330]

a. Treachery (treason, betrayal of confidence for personal gain)
b. Fraud (deceit or misrepresentation for financial gain)
c. Falsehood (dishonesty for material gain)
d. Perjury (lying under oaths for profit)

---

327 Hardon, *Modern Catholic Dictionary*, 437.
328 Saint Thomas Aquinas, *ST* II–II, q. 84, art. 2.
329 Hardon, *Modern Catholic Dictionary*, 238, 50.
330 Saint Thomas Aquinas, *ST* II–II, q. 118, art. 8.

e. Restlessness (inordinate anxiety, impatience, or agitation over wealth)
f. Violence (using force to seize others' possessions)
g. Hardness of heart (lack of mercy or charity, because of attachment to wealth)

4. **Envy** is "sadness or discontent at the excellence, good fortune, or success of another [which implies] that one is . . . somehow deprived of what one envies in another or even that an injustice has been done."[331] By its nature, it is a violation of charity and leads to behaviors and or attitudes which seek to diminish or harm the other person. The vices or sins ("daughters") which rise from the deadly sin of **envy**:[332]

   a. Tale-bearing (spreading rumors or gossip to harm another's reputation)
   b. Detraction (slandering or disparaging the reputation of another)
   c. Joy at another's misfortune (delight in problems or suffering of others)
   d. Sorrow at another's prosperity (saddened by the success or good fortune of others)
   e. Hatred (resentment or ill-will out of envy)

5. **Gluttony** is "the inordinate desire for the pleasure connected with food or drink," to include "eating far more than a person needs to maintain bodily strength; by glutting one's taste for certain kinds of food with known detriment to health; by indulging the appetite for exquisite food or drink; by consuming alcoholic beverages to the point of losing full control of one's reasoning powers."[333] Gluttony's lack moderation

---

[331] Hardon, *Modern Catholic Dictionary*, 189.
[332] Saint Thomas Aquinas, *ST* II–II, q. 36, art. 4.
[333] Hardon, *Modern Catholic Dictionary*, 189.

leads to moral and intellectual disorders. The vices or sins ("daughters") which rise from the deadly sin of **gluttony**:[334]

a. Unseemly joy (excessive happiness or pleasure in food and drink)
b. Overindulgence (foolishness, lack of restraint in behavior due)
c. Uncleanness (moral or physical impurity due to excess)
d. Loquaciousness (excessive talkativeness)
e. Mental dullness (clouding of the intellect, dizziness)

6. **Wrath**, or anger, is "an emotional sense of displeasure and usually antagonism [which] can be either passionate or nonpassionate, depending on the degree to which the emotions are excited."[335] When anger is not guided by reason, it leads to destructive and disordered effects. The vices or sins ("daughters") which rise from the deadly sin of **wrath**:[336]

a. Indignation (excessive or unjust anger against others)
b. Swelling of the mind (prideful anger, arrogance)
c. Clamor (loud or disorderly expressions of anger)
d. Injurious words (abusive speech aimed at harming others)
e. Quarrels (fighting, conflicts fueled by anger)
f. Violence (aggressive acts)

7. **Sloth** is "the sluggishness of soul or boredom because of the exertion necessary for the performance of a good work" which can be either a bodily or spiritual

[334] Saint Thomas Aquinas, *ST* II–II, q. 148, art. 6.
[335] Hardon, *Modern Catholic Dictionary*, 26.
[336] Saint Thomas Aquinas, *ST* II–II, q. 158, art. 7.

good. This is generally seen in "an unwillingness to exert oneself in the performance of duty because of the sacrifice and the effort required." Spiritual sloth can "also mean a repugnance to divine inspirations or the friendship of God due to the self-sacrifice and labor needed to cooperate with actual grace or to remain in the state of grace."[337] Sloth's aversion to spiritual goods leads some people to give up the pursuit of holiness and even abandoned God after a life of virtuous living, leading to neglect of duty and pursuit of lesser things The vices or sins ("daughters") which rise from the deadly sin of **sloth**:[338]

a. Despair (dread, loss of hope in spiritual goods due to laziness in pursuing them)
b. Pusillanimity (lack of courage in pursuit of virtue or in the arduous)
c. Sluggishness toward the commandments (neglect/indifference in observing divine precepts)
d. Spite (malefice arising from a rejection of spiritual effort)
e. Wandering of the mind after unlawful things (distraction or pursuit of sinful thoughts and desires)
f. Idleness (laziness or avoidance of work, especially in spiritual matters)

---

[337] Hardon, *Modern Catholic Dictionary*, 509.
[338] Saint Thomas Aquinas, *ST* II–II, q. 35, art. 4.

Bibliography

Alcántara-Mendoza, Rogelio. "La llamada oración de 'sanación del árbol genealógico.'" https://www.youtube.com/watch?v=O6fhePnS260. Accessed 2 January 2025.

Alphonsus Liguori. *The Way of Salvation and of Perfection*. In Eugene Grimm, trans. *The Complete Works: The Ascetical Works Volume II*. New York, NY: Benzinger Brothers, 1884.

———. *The Glories of Mary*. Liguori, MO: Liguori Publications, 2000.

———. *The Road to Bethlehem: Daily Mediations for Advent and Christmas*. Gastonia, NC: TAN Books, 2023.

Arendzen, John. "Manichaeism" in *The Catholic Encyclopedia*, vol. 9. New York: Robert Appleton Company, 1910.

Amorth, Gabriele. *An Exorcist Explains the Demonic: The Antics of Satan and His Army of Fallen Angels*. Manchester, NH: Sophia Institute, 2016.

———. *An Exorcist: More Stories*. San Francisco: Ignatius, 2002.

———. *An Exorcist Tells His Story*. San Francisco: Ignatius, 1999.

Apostolic Penitentiary. *The Gift of Indulgence* (29 January 2000). https://www.vatican.va/roman_curia/tribunals/apost_penit/documents/rc_trib_appen_pro_20000129_indulgence_en.html#:~:text=%E2%80%94%20have%20sacramentally%20confessed%20their%20sins,intentions%20of%20the%20Supreme%20Pontiff. Accessed 12 March 2025.

Aquinas, Thomas. *Catena Aurea: Commentary on the Four Gospels, Collected out of the Works of the Fathers, 4 vols*. Edited by John Henry Newman. Oxford, UK: John Henry Parker, 1841.

———. *Commentary on the Gospel of John Chapters 1–21*. Translated by Fabian R. Larcher. Vol. 2, Latin/English Edition of the Works of St. Thomas Aquinas. Steubenville, OH: Emmaus Academic, 2018.

———. *Commentary on the Sentences*. Edited by Beth Mortensen. Green Bay, WI: Aquinas Institute, 2017.

———. "Homily IV: The Sinful Soul." In John M. Ashley, trans. *Ninety-nine Homilies of S. Thomas Aquinas Upon the Epistles and Gospels for Forty-nine Sundays of the Christian Year*. London, UK: Church Press Company. 1867.

———. *Summa Theologica*. 5 vols. Translated by the Fathers of the English Dominican Province. Notre Dame, IN: Christian Classics, 1981.

Augustine of Hippo. *Against Julian*. In Matthew A. Schumacher, trans. *The Fathers of the Church*, vol. 35. Washington, DC: The Catholic University Press of America, 1957.

———. *Against Adimantus*. In John E. Rotelle, et al., eds. *The Manichean Debate*. Hyde Park, NY: New City Press, 2006.

———. *Answer to the Pelagians III*. In John E. Rotelle, ed. and Roland J. Teske, trans. *The Works of Saint Augustine: A Translation for the 21st Century*, vol. 25. Hyde Park, NY: New City Press, 1999.

———. *Confessions*. Translated by John K. Ryan. New York: Doubleday, 1960.

Benedict XVI. "Munus Regendi," General Audience (26 May 2010). https://www.vatican.va/content/benedict-xvi/en/audiences/2010/documents/hf_ben-xvi_aud_20100526.html.

Bird, T. E. "Psalms." In Bernard Orchard, et al, eds. *Catholic Commentary on Holy Scripture*. London, UK: Thomas Nelson and Sons, 1953.

Boersma, Hans. "Nuptial Reading: Hippolytus, Origen and Ambrose on the Bridal Couple of the Song of Songs." In *Calvin Theological Journal* 51 (2016), pp. 227–58.

Britannica Encyclopedia. "Pelagianism." https://www.britannica.com/topic/Pelagianism. Accessed 4 March 2025.

Boxall, Ian. "Matthew." In John J. Collins, Gina Hens-Piazza, Barbara Reid and Donald Senior, eds. *The Jerome Biblical Commentary for the Twenty-First Century, Third Fully Revised Edition*. London: Bloomsbury, 2022.

Calduch-Benages, Nuria. "Baruch." In John J. Collins, Gina Hens-Piazza, Barbara Reid and Donald Senior, eds. *The Jerome Biblical Commentary for the Twenty-First Century, Third Fully Revised Edition*. London: Bloomsbury, 2022.

Chrysostom, John. *Homilies on Genesis 1–17*. In Robert C. Hill, trans. *The Fathers of the Church*, vol. 74. Washington, D.C.: The Catholic University of America Press, 1986.

———. *Homilies on Matthew*. In Philip Schaff, ed. *Nicene and Post-Nicene Fathers, First Series*, vol 10. Translated by R. G. MacMullen. Buffalo, NY: Christian Literature, 1888.

———. *Homilies on John*. In Philip Schaff, ed. *Nicene and Post-Nicene Fathers, First Series*, vol 14. Translated by R. G. MacMullen. Buffalo, NY: Christian Literature, 1888.

Clement XII. *In Eminenti: Papal Bull Dealing with the Condemnation of Freemasonry*. https://www.papalencyclicals.net/clem12/c12inemengl.htm. Accessed 9 June 2022.

Conferencia Episcopal Española. *Su misericordia se extiende de generación en generación (Lc 1,50)*. 1 January 2024. https://www.conferenciaepiscopal.es/nota-doctrinal-sanacion-intergeneracional/ Accessed 12 March 2025.

Congregation for the Doctrine of the Faith. *Declaration on Masonic Associations* (November 26, 1983). https://www.vatican.va/roman_curia/congregations/cfaith/documents/rc_con_cfaith_doc_19831126_declaration-masonic_en.html . Accessed 21 February 2021.

Cyprian of Carthage. In Robert Ernest Wallace, trans. *The Writings of Cyprian*, vol. 1. Edinburgh: T&T Clark, 1868.

Danielou, Jean. *The Angels and their Mission According to the Fathers of the Church*. Allen, TX: Christian Classics, 1956.

De Caussade, Jean-Pierre. *Abandonment to Divine Providence*. Translated by E. J. Strickland. St. Louis: Herder, 1921.

DiFransico, Leslie. "Guilt." In John D. Barry et al., eds. *The Concise Lexham Bible Dictionary*. Bellingham, WA: Lexham Press, 2014.

DeGrandis, Robert and Linda Schubert. *Intergenerational Healing: A Journey to the Depth of Forgiveness*. San Francisco, CA: Praising God Catholic Association,1989.

Doyle, Charles Hugo. *The Sins of Parents*. Manchester, NH: Sophia Institute Press, 2022.

Fisher, John. "Cursing." *The Catholic Encyclopedia*, vol. 4. New York, NY: Robert Appleton Company, 1908.

Flannery, Austin, ed. *The Documents of Vatican Council II: The Conciliar and Post-Conciliar Documents*. Dublin: Dominican Publications, 1996.

Flavius Josephus. *Josephus: The Complete Works*. Grand Rapids, MI: Christian Classics Ethereal Library, 1985.

Freedman, David Noel, et.al, eds. *Anchor Bible Dictionary*, 6 vols. London: Doubleday, 1922.

General Council of Trent, 1545-63 A.D. https://www.papalencyclicals.net/councils/trent.htm. Accessed January 8, 2023.

George W. Bush Presidential Center: Freedom Collection. "Interviews with Han Nam-su."

https://www.bushcenter.org/freedom-collection/han-nam-su-three-generations-of-punishment#:~:text=Transcript,dismal%20future%20ahead%20of%20you. Accessed 28 August 2025.

Gesenius, Wilhelm. *Hebrew and Chaldee Lexicon*. Translated by Samual Prideaux Tregelles. New York, NY: John Wiley and Sons, 1894.

Giszczak, Mark. "The Canonical Status of Song of Songs in *m. Yadayim* 3.5." In *Journal for Study of the Old Testament* 41, 2 (2016).

Hahn, Scott, ed. *Catholic Bible Dictionary*. New York, NY: London: Doubleday, 2009.

Hampsch, John. *Healing Your Family Tree*. Goleta, CA: Queenship Publishing, 1989.

Hardon, John. *Modern Catholic Dictionary*. New York: Doubleday, 1980.

Harrington, Wilfred. *Mark,* New Testament Message, vol. 4. Wilmington, Delaware: Michael Glazier, Inc., 1979.

Hertz, J. H. *Pentateuch and Haftorahs*. London, UK: Concino Press, 1978.

Jerome. *Commentary on Jeremiah*. Translated by Michael Groves, et al., eds. Lisle, IL: IVP Academic, 2012.

Joseph, Peter. "False Religion: Generational Spirits, Curses, Healing the Family Tree." *Where Peter Is* (November 21, 2024). https://wherepeteris.com/false-religion-generational-spirits-curses-and-healing-the-family-tree/. Accessed May 12, 2025.

Joyce, Paul. "Ezekiel." In John J. Collins, Gina Hens-Piazza, Barbara Reid and Donald Senior, eds. *The Jerome Biblical Commentary for the Twenty-First Century, Third Fully Revised Edition*. London: Bloomsbury, 2022.

Kingsmill, Edmée. *The Song of Songs and the Eros of God: A Study in Biblical Intertextuality*. Oxford: Oxford University Press, 2009.

Lattey, C. "Jeremias" in Bernard Orchard, et al, eds. *Catholic Commentary on Holy Scripture*. London, UK: Thomas Nelson and Sons, 1953.

Leahy, Michael. "Ezechiel" in Bernard Orchard, et al, eds. *Catholic Commentary on Holy Scripture*. London, UK: Thomas Nelson and Sons, 1953.

Lefebvre, Gaspar. *Saint Andrew Daily Missal with Vespers for Sundays and Feasts.* St. Paul, MN: E.M. Lohmann, 1953.

Lefrois, Bernard J. "Semitic Totality Thinking." In *The Catholic Biblical Quarterly* 17, 2 (April 1995), 195–203.

Lewis, Charlton T. and Charles Short. *An Elementary Latin Dictionary.* Oxford: Oxford University Press, 1963.

Liberty in North Korea. "The North Korean People's Challenge: Life Inside the World's Most Authoritarian Country." https://libertyinnorthkorea.org/learn-nk-challenges. Accessed 7 May 2025.

Liddell, Henry George, Robert Scott, Henry Stuart Jones, and Roderick McKenzie, eds. *A Greek-English Lexicon.* Oxford: Clarendon Press, 1985.

Louw, Johannes P. and Eugene Albert Nida. *Greek-English Lexicon of the New Testament: Based on Semantic Domains.* New York: United Bible Societies, 1996.

McCall, Kenneth. *Healing the Family Tree.* Sewanee, TN: Sheldon, 1986.

———. *Healing the Haunted.* Goleta, CA: Queenship Publishing,1996.

McCallum, Nathaniel. "Inherited guilt in Ss. Augustine and Cyril." In Dylan Pahman, ed. *Treasures of Old and New: Themes in Orthodox Theology in Memory of Fr. Matthew Baker.* Jordanville, NY: Holy Trinity Seminary Press, forthcoming.

McHugh, John A. and Charles J. Callam. *Moral Theology: A Complete Course Based on St. Thomas Aquinas and the Best Modern Authorities.* New York, NY: Joseph F. Wagner, Inc. 1929.

Mills, Mary. "Isaiah." In John J. Collins, Gina Hens-Piazza, Barbara Reid and Donald Senior, eds. *The Jerome Biblical Commentary for the Twenty-First Century, Third Fully Revised Edition.* London: Bloomsbury, 2022.

Neudecker, Reinhard. "Does God visit the Iniquity of Fathers upon their Children?" In *Gregorianum* 81.1 (2001): 5–24.

Newman, John Henry. *An Essay on the Development of Christian Doctrine*. London: Aeterna Press, 2014.

Nowell, Irene. *101 Questions & Answers on Angels and Devils*. New York; Mahwah, NJ: Paulist Press, 2010.

Origen. *Homilies on Genesis and Exodus*. Translated by Ronald E. Heine. Washington, DC: Catholic University of America Press, 1982.

Ott, Ludwig. *Fundamentals of Catholic Dogma*. Rockford, IL: TAN Books, 2009.

Oxford Dictionary. https://www.oxfordlearnersdictionaries.com/definition/english/prototype. Accessed 1 March 2025.

Pascal, Blaise. *Pascal's Pensées*. New York: E.P. Dutton, 2016.

Patout Burns, J. "The Late Augustine Against Julian on Inherited Guilt." In Susanna Elm and Chistopher M. Blunda, eds. *Late (Wild) Augustine*. Leiden, Netherlands: Brill, 2021.

Paul VI. *Indulgentiarum doctrina* (January 1, 1967). https://www.vatican.va/content/paul-vi/en/apost_constitutions/documents/hf_p-vi_apc_01011967_indulgentiarum-doctrina.html. Accessed 15 February 2025.

Pius V. *The Catechism of the Council of Trent*. Translated by J. Donovan. Hawthorne, CA: Christian Book Club of America, 1975.

Pius IX. *The Syllabus of Errors: Condemning Current Errors*. December 8, 1864. https://www.papalencyclicals.net/pius09/p9syll.htm. Accessed 10 May 2025.

Pius X. *Ad Diem Illum Laetissimum: On the Jubilee of the Immaculate Conception* (2 February 1904). Kansas City, MO: Angelus Press, 1999.

———. *Pascendi Dominici Gregis: On the Doctrines of the Modernists* (8 September 1907). https://www.vatican.va/content/pius-x/en/encyclicals/documents/hf_p-x_enc_19070908_pascendi-dominici-gregis.html. Accessed 12 March 2025.

Pius XII. *Mystici Corporis: On the Mystical Body of Christ and Our Union in it with Christ.* St. Paul, MN: Pauline Books, 1943.

Ripperger, Chad. *Deliverance Prayers for Use by the Laity*. Denver, CO: Sensus Traditionis, 2020.

———. *Dominion: The Nature of Diabolic Warfare*. Keensburg, CO: Sensus Traditiones, 2022.

———. *Holy Hour of Reparation to the Sacred Heart of Jesus: For Neglect of and Negligence in Priestly and Religious Vocations.* Denver, CO: Sensus Traditionis, 2004.

———. *Introduction to the Science of Mental Health*. Denton, NE: Sensus Traditionis, 2013.

———. "The Sixth Generation." In *Latin Mass* (Summer 2012), 34–39.

Rosales Acosta, Dempsey. "Lord of Hosts." In John D. Barry et al. eds. *The Concise Lexham Bible Dictionary*. Bellingham, WA: Lexham Press, 2021.

Rossi, Benedetta. "Jeremiah." In John J. Collins, Gina Hens-Piazza, Barbara Reid and Donald Senior, eds. *The Jerome Biblical Commentary for the Twenty-First Century, Third Fully Revised Edition*. London: Bloomsbury, 2022.

Rumble, L. *Catholics and Freemasonry*. St. Paul, MN: Radio Replies Press, 1964.

Santamaria, Luis. "Can we 'heal our family tree' and wipe out 'ancestral sin'?" In Aleteia (12/02/18). https://aleteia.org/2018/12/02/can-we-heal-our-family-tree-and-wipe-out-ancestral-sin.

Schneider, Daniel. *Eve Was Named an Apostle*. Eugene, OR: Wifp and Stock, 2023.

———. *The Liber Christo Method: A Field Manual for Spiritual Combat*. Gastonia, NC: TAN Books 2023.

Siegfried, F. "Creationism." *The Catholic Encyclopedia*. New York: Robert Appleton Company, 1908. http://www.newadvent.org/cathen/04475a.htm. Accessed 12 December 2024.

Slavin, Robert. "St. Thomas and His Teaching on the Family." In *Dominicana* 18.3 (September 1933), 135–41.

Smit, Johannes. *De Daemoniacis in Historia Evangelica*. Roma: Sumptibus Pontificii Instituti Biblici, 1913.

Ssemanula, Yozefu. *The Healing of Families: How to Pray Effectively for Those Stubborn Personal and Familial Problems*. Self-Published, 2011.

Tanner, J. Paul. "The History of Interpretation of the Song of Songs." In *Bibliotheca Sacra* 154, 613 (1997), 23–46.

Teresa Benedicta of the Cross. In L. Gelber. and Michael Linssen, eds, and Waltraut Stein, trans. *The Hidden Life: Essays, Meditations. Spiritual Texts*. Washington, DC: ICS Publication, 1992.

Tertullian. *Against Marcion*. In Alexander Roberts, James Donaldson, and A. Cleveland Coxe, eds. *Ante-Nicene Fathers: The Writings of the Fathers down to A.D. 325*, vol. 3. Peabody, MA: Hendrickson, 1995.

Tomson, Peter J. "The Song of Songs in the Teachings of Jesus and the Development of the Exposition of the Song," in NTS 61 (2015), 429–47.

Van der Toorn, Karel, Bob Beckling and Pieter W. van der Horst, eds, *Dictionary of Deities and Demons in the Bible*. Grand Rapids, MI: William B. Eerdsman, 1999.

Villeneuve, André. *Nuptial Symbolism in Second Temple Writings, the New Testament, and Rabbinic Literature: Divine Marriage at Key Moments of Salvation History*. Boston: Brill, 2016.

Weiss, Dov. "Sins of the Parents in Rabbinic and Early Christian Literature." In *The Journal of Religion*, 97.1 (January 2017).

Weller, Philip. *Roman Ritual,* vol. 1: *Sacraments and Processions.* Boonville, NY: Preserving Christian Publications, 1952.

———. *Roman Ritual,* vol. 2: *Christian Burial, Exorcism, Reserved Blessings, Etc.* Boonville, NY: Preserving Christian Publications, 1952.

United States Conference of Catholic Bishops. *The Roman Ritual: Book of Blessings.* New York: Catholic Book, 1989.

———. *Jubilee 2025 – Pilgrims of Hope.* https://www.usccb.org/jubilee2025. Accessed 21 January 2025.

———. *The Liturgy of the Hours III.* New York, NY: Catholic Publishing, 1975.

Zerwick, Maximilian and Mary Grosvenor. *A Grammatical Analysis of the Greek New Testament* (Roma: Editrice Pontificio Istituto Biblico, 2007).